AUSTRALIAN ARMY CAMPAIGNS SERIES - 14

TO KOKODA

NICHOLAS ANDERSON

ARMY·HISTORY·UNIT

PROTECTING ARMY HERITAGE
PROMOTING ARMY HISTORY

©Copyright Army History Unit

CP2-5-169

Campbell Park Offices

PO Box 7911

CANBERRA BC ACT 2610

(02) 6266 2239

(02) 6266 4044 – fax

First published 2014

See National Library of Australia for Cataloguing-in-Publication entry.

ISBN: 978-1-922132-95-6

Published by Big Sky Publishing, Sydney

Cover and typesetting by Think Productions, Melbourne

Printed in China through Asia Pacific Offset Limited

Front cover and title page: AWM027058. Its description is: *A happy group of four bearded soldiers of the 2/31st Battalion on the Kokoda Trail between Nauro and Menari.*
Back cover background: AWM 026855
Back cover top right: ART23615
Back cover bottom right: (NAA030) Bomana Cemetery

CONTENTS

SERIES INTRODUCTION

In 2004, the then Chief of Army's Strategic Advisory Group, the Australian Army's senior generals, established a scheme to promote the study and understanding of military history within the Army. The focus was the Army's future generation of leaders and, from this, the Campaigns Series was created. The series is intended to complement the Army's other history publications which are major analytical works of high quality, academically rigorous and referenced.

The Campaigns Series focuses on leadership, command, strategy, tactics, lessons and personal experiences of war. Each title within the series includes extensive visual sources of information — maps, including specifically prepared maps in colour and 3D, specifically commissioned artwork, photographs and computer graphics.

Covering major campaigns and battles, as well as those less known, the Australian Army History Unit and its Campaigns Series provide a significant contribution to the history of the Australian Army and an excellent introduction to its campaigns and battles.

Roger Lee
Army Historian

ACKNOWLEDGEMENTS

This book is dedicated to my grandmother, Brenda Williamson whose indomitable spirit I so admire. This is a trait she shares with the men of her generation whose deeds are told in this book.

A number of people have helped me throughout the process of writing this book and to them I warmly extend my thanks.

My parents, Kim and Steve Anderson, offered unceasing encouragement as I grappled with my task and could not have been more accommodating.

My colleague and friend, Andrew Richardson, was extremely helpful and assisted at all stages of the project. In particular, he read an early draft of the manuscript and provided extensive comments to assist in its improvement.

Gary Traynor and Karl James from the Australian War Memorial provided invaluable help with my research and writing. GT spent many hours poring over maps with me and reading through the manuscript to help correct any errors. His passion for the Kokoda Trail and the campaign is unmatched. Karl answered many phone calls and never complained as I discussed points with him that to the casual observer would have seemed pedantic.

Peter Williams' Kokoda book was published as I was researching my own. Much correspondence passed between us as we discussed different aspects of the campaign. We did not always agree — in fact it was more common for us to disagree. However he never shied away from offering assistance and I enjoyed our robust debates.

I must also thank the queen of the librarians, Karyn Hall. Karyn has a wicked sense of humour and went above and beyond to help provide me with research material at the click of a finger. More importantly, she saved me from imprisonment after being labelled a 'delinquent borrower' by the library's computer system when the 50 plus books I loaned from her passed the 13 months overdue limit.

I couldn't have asked to walk the Kokoda Trail for the first time with a better crew. Mo Rifat, Rob Nelson, Clint Palmer, and especially Dan Crosbie, are four fine soldiers, and even better blokes.

Thank you to Cathy McCullagh for editing the manuscript into its final form. Cathy is very experienced and was a pleasure to work with. Credit is due to Mark Wahlert, who drew the organisational charts and produced the images of weapons for the sidebars. Thank you also to Denny Neave and Big Sky Publishing for producing such a high-quality book and for supporting Australian military history.

Few have done as much to safeguard and promote the history of the Australian Army as Roger Lee. I thank him for giving me the opportunity to study this engrossing campaign.

This book would never have been finished without the loyal support of Tiny. The thought of finishing this book for her drove me on and I will never forget her valuable support.

Overwhelmingly, the one quality displayed by those mentioned above and others I haven't been able to name is patience and for this I extend my heartfelt thanks. Researching, writing and preparing this book for publication consumed my life. It fostered a near-obsession with the campaign and the Kokoda Trail. The Trail is etched in the Australian spirit and the opportunity to research and work on this project was a privilege for which I will be forever grateful.

ABBREVIATIONS

2IC	second-in-command
ADC	aide-de-camp
AIF	Australian Imperial Force
AMF	Australian Military Forces
ANGAU	Australian New Guinea Administrative Unit
BHQ	battalion headquarters
Bn	battalion
C-in-C	Commander-in-Chief
CO	Commanding Officer
Comd	commander
Coy	company
DCM	Distinguished Conduct Medal
DGMS	Director General Medical Services
GHQ	General Headquarters
GOC	General Officer Commanding
GSO1	General Staff Officer 1
GSO2	General Staff Officer 2
HMG	heavy machine-gun
IJA	Imperial Japanese Army
IJN	Imperial Japanese Navy
IO	Intelligence Officer
LO	Liaison Officer
LMG	light machine-gun
LOB	left out of battle
LTCOL	lieutenant colonel
MC	Military Cross
MDS	medical dressing station
MIA	missing in action

MMG	medium machine-gun
NCO	non-commissioned officer
NGF	New Guinea Force
NGVR	New Guinea Volunteer Rifles
OC	Officer Commanding
OR	other ranks
PIB	Papuan Infantry Battalion
PNG	Papua New Guinea
POW	prisoner of war
RAP	Regimental Aid Post
RMO	Regimental Medical Officer
RSM	Regimental Sergeant Major
SNCO	senior non-commissioned officer
SWPA	South-West Pacific Area
US	United States
USAAF	United States of America Air Force
VADM	Vice Admiral
VC	Victoria Cross

INTRODUCTION

The campaign along the Kokoda Trail in 1942 sits prominently in the Australian national psyche, second to only one other campaign — Gallipoli. Gallipoli captures the popular imagination because it was on the sands and craggy rock faces of Anzac Cove on the Turkish peninsula that the nation was born. It was along the Kokoda Trail, however, that the nation came of age.

With Japanese forces entrenched in New Guinea, Australia was forced to confront the possibility of invasion. However, while the Japanese had certainly considered an invasion of the Australian mainland, it was ruled out as unviable since the number of soldiers required to garrison the vast continent would have stretched the *Imperial Japanese Army* to breaking point. Yet the sense of threat that pervaded Australia at that time cannot be overstated. Once the nature and potency of that threat is fully appreciated, it is easy to understand why Kokoda is held in such reverence.

The popularity of the Kokoda Trail lies in the heroics of the story. It contains the essential ingredients of the epics of yore: Australian soldiers, outnumbered and unprepared, pushed to the brink of defeat, only to rise at the eleventh hour to vanquish a bitter enemy. Of course, the reality is nowhere near as dramatic.

Recent critical publications have shed new light on the Kokoda campaign. Access to previously untapped Japanese records has provided a new perspective, indicating that certain aspects of our understanding of the campaign may be inaccurate. In some cases, these publications have proven that incidents have been exaggerated or accounts have been embellished. Other aspects of the campaign appear to have no stronger foundation than myth.

That certain elements of the story did not occur exactly as we have come to accept is not surprising. The imprecision of reports from the front is a natural consequence of the claustrophobic nature of jungle warfare with its limited lines of sight, the 'fog of war' and the difficulty of conducting complex operations with only the most basic of communications equipment. Historians and authors with a wont to colour the gaps have been equally guilty of mythologising the campaign. Australian war correspondent Osmar White disparaged this tendency in 1945, writing that 'The Australian soldier needs no fictions nor propaganda to justify him as a fighting man.'

That said, it is important to emphasise that, even if the historical record requires minor adjustment, this does not diminish the bravery and exploits of the men who fought on the Trail. The Owen Stanley Ranges constitute one of the harshest battlefields that man has ever encountered. The Australian soldiers who bore arms in such terrain can be forever proud of their exemplary service to their country.

The Kokoda campaign can be split into two distinctive phases. The first phase comprises the Japanese landings on the beaches near Giruwa (the preferred Japanese name for the

Buna-Gona area), followed by their capture of Kokoda and southern advance along the Kokoda Trail towards Port Moresby. The second phase involves the Australian counter-attack launched from Imita Ridge which pushed the Japanese back across the Owen Stanleys.

This study of the Kokoda campaign concludes with the Australian recapture of Kokoda on 2 November 1942. There is much to justify the inclusion of the Battle of Oivi-Gorari and the Battle of the Beachheads under the banner of the Kokoda campaign as the units that fought these battles were the same that fought on the Kokoda Trail, and these battles were all part of the larger overall operation designed to destroy the Japanese presence in Papua. However, those operations are of sufficient magnitude to warrant their own extended telling in other books within this series.

Fighting along the Kokoda Trail occurred because both the Allies and the Japanese sought to occupy the land surrounding Buna to establish an airfield. Why Buna was so important, and how and why the Pacific War began in the first place requires some recounting of history.

For hundreds of years the Japanese maintained an isolationist approach to the world. That changed in 1865 when US Navy Captain Matthew Perry sailed into Yokohama Harbour. The Japanese had two options: they could resist militarily and inevitably lose to a technologically advanced adversary, or they could submit and emulate the mass industrialisation that had changed the face of Europe and North America. Choosing the latter option would enable Japan to build its own great empire. This was the course of action that the Japanese decided to take and thus began the Meiji Restoration, essentially a sustained period of westernisation and modernisation. This process was incredibly successful. Within three decades the Japanese economy had been transformed.

The final years of the nineteenth century saw frenetic manoeuvring among the nations of Europe as they each sought to expand their territorial assets. Japan was no different, although its rapid growth exposed its inherent weaknesses: lack of space and a dearth of natural resources. To continue to expand and rival the leading states of Europe, Japan needed new territory. The obvious and easiest place to expand was to the west. Manchuria in the north-east of China, the Korean peninsula and the Pacific ports of Russia became hotbeds of military ambition as East Asian nations tussled for regional supremacy.

Victory in the First Sino-Japanese War won Japan territory, including Formosa (now known as Taiwan). However, it was victory in the Russo-Japanese War of 1904–05 that alarmed the 'old world' and signalled the rising power of Japan. For the first time in history an Asian nation had defeated one of the traditional European empires.

During the First World War, the Japanese fought on the side of the Allies. Japan's role was small and generally limited to naval escort duties and the seizure of German territories in the Pacific. This minor role did not reflect Japan's desire for military action and, if anything, was at least partially a result of Allied Command's belief that the Japanese made inferior soldiers. Relations between the West and Japan deteriorated when the signatories to the Treaty of Versailles failed to incorporate a promised clause recognising the equality of races. Relations were damaged further still by the restrictions imposed by the Washington Naval

Treaty of 1922 which set limits on the size and number of warships that the victorious Allied powers could build during the inter-war period. The Japanese opposed the terms vigorously, denouncing them as unfair.

By 1931 the Japanese military, supported by the rise of ultranationalists, had gained the ascendancy within the country's domestic political sphere. As a consequence, Japan became increasingly belligerent in its dealings with China and the two nations fought intermittently throughout the 1930s. Japan further isolated itself from the world when it withdrew from the League of Nations (predecessor to the United Nations), ostensibly because it rejected the League's criticisms of Japanese actions in China.

A League of Nations General Assembly. The League was founded as a result of the Paris Peace Conference held in 1919 at the conclusion of the First World War. The League's goals included disarmament, preventing war through collective security, settling disputes between countries through negotiation, and improving global welfare. However, diplomacy failed and the League proved powerless to rein in the militarist actions of Japan (among others) throughout the 1930s (AWMP03757.004).

By 1937, the Japanese military had fabricated two events (the Mukden and Marco Polo Bridge Incidents) in order to justify the escalation of their dispute with China into a fully fledged war. Despite quickly overrunning Manchuria and major Chinese ports, the war dragged on into the 1940s, exacerbating Japan's shortage of raw resources.

Japan then turned its gaze to the north. This led to a series of border clashes with Russia, each resulting in resounding defeats. Discouraged by this, Japanese attention reverted southwards, and when France was conquered by Nazi Germany, Japan saw its opportunity. The French colony of Indochina (modern Vietnam, Cambodia and Laos) was rich in resources and occupying this area would allow the Japanese to tighten the blockade they had imposed on China. In a perfidious move, Japan occupied Indochina. This action provoked immediate condemnation from the United States which swiftly imposed an oil embargo on Japan and demanded the withdrawal of all Japanese forces. This prompted a year-long round of diplomatic jostling as the two countries attempted to negotiate an agreement to end the impasse. As Japan's resource crisis intensified, limiting its ability to wage war in China, the United States refused to budge from its demand that Japan withdraw from Indochina. Japan prepared for war with the West.

Japan's preparations culminated in simultaneous strikes on Pearl Harbor, Wake Island, the Philippines, Malaya and Hong Kong on 7 December 1941. In order to inflict maximum damage, Japan launched the attacks prior to a formal declaration of war while maintaining the pretence of continuing to negotiate a peaceful solution. The attack on Pearl Harbor was designed to destroy the US Pacific Fleet and inflict such massive damage that the United States would lose the will to fight. The plan backfired spectacularly. Instead of intimidating the United States, the surprise attack infuriated the American public and provided the stimulus for US entry into the Second World War.

The USS West Virginia burns following the surprise attack on Pearl Harbor which triggered the Pacific War (official US Navy photograph # C-5904).

In fighting this war, the Japanese aim was to seize the natural resources required to supply its military: oil, gas and rubber. Having achieved this aim, the Japanese planned to establish a defensive perimeter to protect their newly acquired territories from the inevitable Allied counter-attacks. In the initial six months following the outbreak of the Pacific War, Japan was significantly assisted by the Allied decision to concentrate on defeating Nazi Germany first. Facing a disorganised opposition, the Japanese conquered Allied territories in quick succession and dominated the seas that lay in between. The Japanese advance appeared unstoppable.

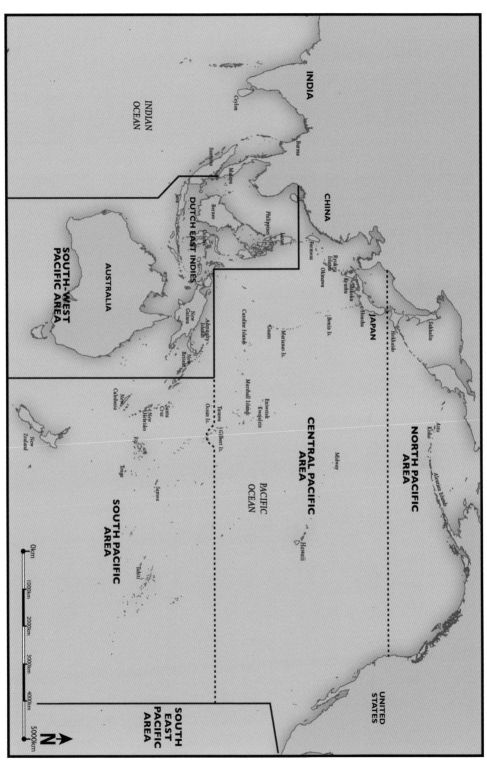

The Pacific Theatre.

The Japanese were far from naïve. They did not believe that they could definitively defeat the United States, or indeed any of the other Allies for that matter. Instead, they hoped that the Allies would be deterred once they realised the enormous cost of reclaiming their captured colonial possessions. In this way, the Japanese hoped that rapid success would translate to a stronger hand at the negotiating table, enabling them to retain their newly acquired territories.

In implementing this strategy, the Japanese constructed a major naval and air base on the island of Truk in the South Pacific. But the protection of Truk required the capture of another major air and sea base further to the south-east. Thus they subdued the Australian garrison protecting Rabaul on the Papua New Guinean island of New Britain and established a major base of operations there. In order to protect Rabaul, the defensive arc had to be pushed even further outwards, to encompass the southern islands of the Solomons and Port Moresby. Advancing into these areas would also allow the Japanese to sever the lines of communication between Australia and the United States, and would prevent the Allies using Australia as a base to launch counter-attacks.

The initial Japanese plan for the capture of Port Moresby involved a seaborne attack. An invasion force en route to Port Moresby was intercepted by the US Navy and Royal Australian Navy resulting in the Battle of the Coral Sea. Although both sides suffered similar casualties, the battle was a strategic victory for the Allies because the invasion was thwarted and the Japanese fleet returned to Rabaul having failed to achieve its objective.

Port Moresby — the objective of the Japanese assault across the Kokoda Trail in 1942. The shipping facilities and a portion of the township are visible in this photo (AWM025876).

This setback prompted the Japanese to activate their secondary plan. This entailed an overland march on Port Moresby, a concept that had been investigated prior to Coral Sea. Reconnaissance had been conducted across the northern coastline of New Guinea and, in a region pockmarked with coastal swamps and swathes of kunai grass, the area around Buna was identified as the most suitable location to construct an airfield. This airfield would have several advantages. First, it would reduce the extensive return travel time for aircraft flying from Rabaul to attack Port Moresby. Second, aircraft based at the airfield could provide air cover for the soldiers who would press southwards across the Owen Stanleys towards Port Moresby.

It was this chain of events that led directly to the Kokoda campaign, fought from the Japanese landings at Giruwa on 21 July 1942 until the recapture of Kokoda by Australian forces on 2 November 1942.

In any analysis of the Kokoda campaign, it is important to understand that the events did not occur in a vacuum. Throughout the campaign, actions on Guadalcanal directly influenced events on the Kokoda Trail, particularly in relation to Japanese plans and the movement of their troops. The turning tide of the battle on Guadalcanal caused much anxiety within the Japanese high command and, as a result, they never fully committed all the resources landed in Papua to the Kokoda campaign. The Japanese always expected that, at some stage in the future, they might need to redirect resources from Papua to Guadalcanal, which they considered the more important strategic objective.

The Battle of Milne Bay, fought on the eastern tip of Papua, also had direct implications for the Kokoda campaign, which at the time was at a critical juncture. Indeed, the victory of the Australians at Milne Bay represented the first time the Japanese had been defeated in a land battle. It shattered the aura of invincibility that surrounded the Japanese military and boosted the confidence of Allied armies across the Pacific. It also significantly reduced the threat to Port Moresby and released resources, held back for a possible defence of the city, for use in the Kokoda campaign.

Finally, in Australia, a power struggle and clash of personalities at the top of the Allied command structure was triggered in reaction to events occurring along the Kokoda Trail. In turn, this so-called 'crisis of command' had a direct impact on the conduct of the Kokoda campaign.

The Allied victories in the Kokoda, Guadalcanal and Milne Bay campaigns and the Allied naval victories in the Coral Sea and at the Battle of Midway signalled the turning point in the Pacific War. Although it was to continue for another two and a half years, the Japanese were thereafter firmly on the defensive, consigned to fighting a static war that saw their territorial acquisitions dwindle as the Allies advanced closer and closer to the Japanese home islands.

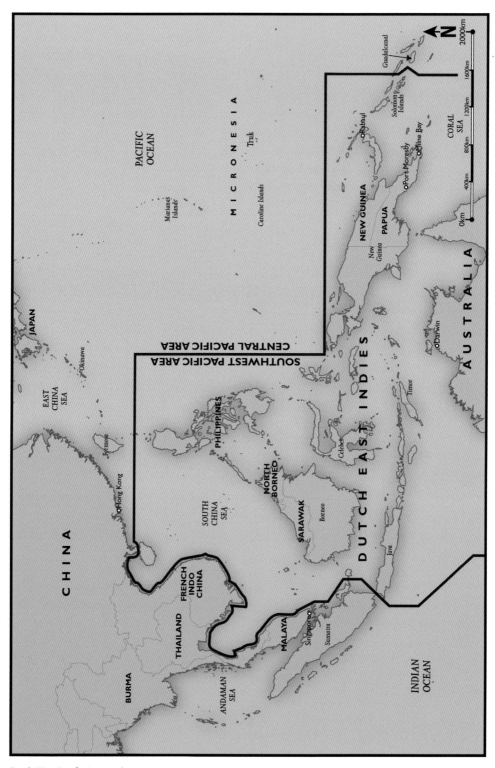

South-West Pacific Area, 1942.

TRAIL OR TRACK?

Whether to call the route from Kokoda to Owers' Corner the 'Kokoda Trail' or the 'Kokoda Track' has long provoked heated debate. It was and remains a point of contention. In short, the answer to whether the name 'Kokoda Trail' or 'Kokoda Track' should be used is that both are correct and either can be used.

Prior to the Second World War the route had no formal name, as the tendency was to name routes after the destination to which one was travelling. In this case, Kokoda was the destination of European travellers heading to the goldfields in northern Papua and thus Kokoda was the village name sometimes attached to the route.

When the Kokoda campaign began, the route still lacked a uniform name. Some Australians referred to it as the 'Kokoda Track', but more commonly it was referred to simply as the 'Track'. The naming issue is further complicated by the fact that the route from Owers' Corner to Kokoda is not a linear or permanent entity and has changed over time. For example, if a tree fell and blocked the path or a landslide washed away a portion, the natives would cut a new track around the obstruction rather than clear or repair the damage. Approximately 60% of the current Kokoda Trail follows the original route, while the villages of Deniki, Isurava, Kagi, Efogi, Nauro and Ioribaiwa have all moved from their wartime locations.

There are also many segments of the Trail where paths diverge and then reconnect. When Lieutenant Bert Kienzle cut a new track from Templeton's Crossing to the Myola Lakes, this became the preferred route during the campaign and to this day. To the west, the original route that connected Kagi to Templeton's Crossing directly over the summit of Mount Bellamy diminished in importance. Disuse saw it swallowed by the jungle.

Proponents of both names have advanced a number of reasons in support of their favoured term.

Those who favour 'Track' maintain it is a colloquial Australian bush term. The diggers favoured it, as have the writers of the battalion histories. Many Kokoda veterans dislike the name 'Kokoda Trail' because they regard the word 'Trail' as an Americanism and its usage as popularised by Americans.

This belief may be incorrect, particularly as the Australian correspondent Geoff Reading claimed responsibility for this designation. His first use of the title was in a story for Sydney's *Daily Mirror* newspaper, filed from Port Moresby on 26 October 1942, which carried the bold headline: 'Kokoda Trail … a Diary of Death'. Reading's motivation was entirely practical: 'I did it because along with the other correspondents at the time, I didn't know what to call it … I got sick of typing descriptions such as Imita–Ioribaiwa–Nauro track. I called it Kokoda Trail to save typing.'

Those who prefer 'Trail' cite the label used on the Australian Army's Battle Honours. The Papua New Guinea Place Names Committee, part of the PNG government's Department of Lands, has formalised the name of the route from Owers' Corner to Kokoda as the 'Kokoda Trail'. And, finally, Kienzle (who lived in the Kokoda region as a rubber planter before the war) wrote that he always thought of the route as a 'Trail'. His rationale was that a trail was already established whereas one could cut a new 'track' through the jungle at any time.

There is no correct answer to the question of which term should be used — it is simply a matter of preference. For consistency, the name Kokoda Trail will be used throughout this book. When referring to the two routes between Efogi and Templeton's Crossing, Kokoda Trail will be used for the current route that Kienzle cut, while Mount Bellamy Trail will be used when referring to the route between Kagi and Templeton's Crossing.

Members of the 16th Brigade moving north along the Kokoda Trail towards the front line in October 1942 (AWM027054).

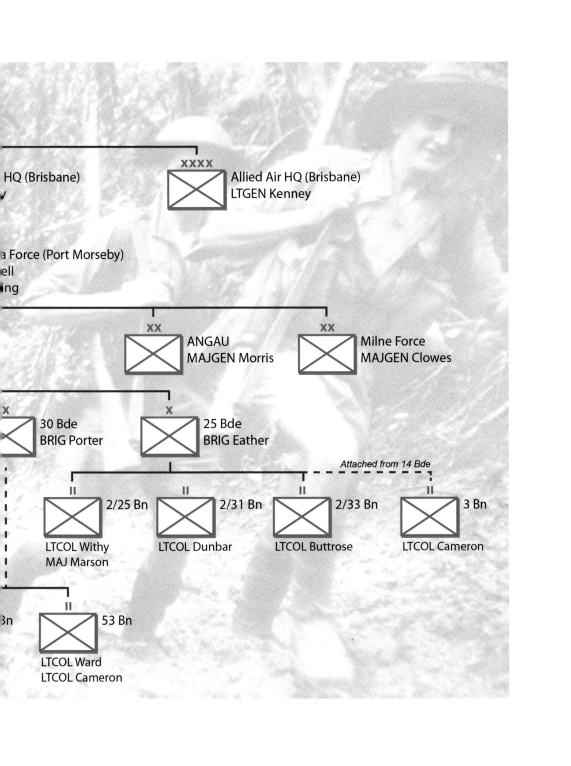

HQ (Brisbane)

xxxx
Allied Air HQ (Brisbane)
LTGEN Kenney

a Force (Port Morseby)
ell
ing

xx
ANGAU
MAJGEN Morris

xx
Milne Force
MAJGEN Clowes

x
30 Bde
BRIG Porter

x
25 Bde
BRIG Eather

Attached from 14 Bde

II
2/25 Bn
LTCOL Withy
MAJ Marson

II
2/31 Bn
LTCOL Dunbar

II
2/33 Bn
LTCOL Buttrose

II
3 Bn
LTCOL Cameron

3n

II
53 Bn
LTCOL Ward
LTCOL Cameron

Owers' Corner to Kokoda

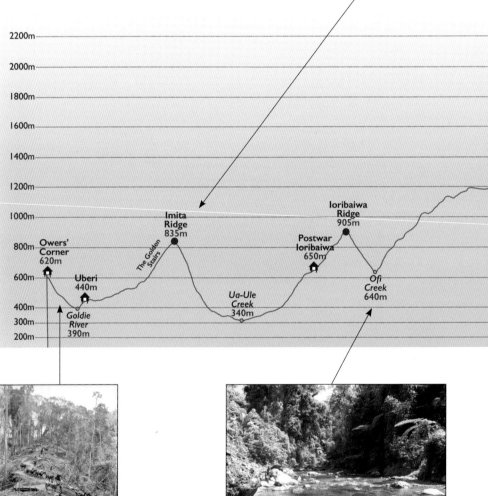

2200m

2000m

1800m

1600m

1400m

1200m

1000m

800m

600m

400m

300m

200m

Owers' Corner 620m

Uberi 440m

Goldie River 390m

The Golden Stairs

Imita Ridge 835m

Ua-Ule Creek 340m

Postwar Ioribaiwa 650m

Ioribaiwa Ridge 905m

Ofi Creek 640m

M.. Ra 13

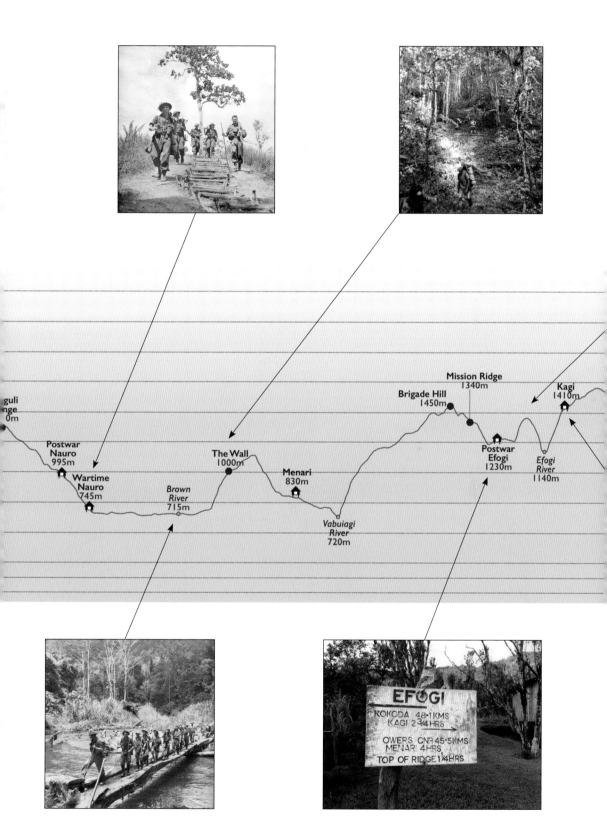

guli
nge
0m

Postwar
Nauro
995m

Wartime
Nauro
745m

Brown
River
715m

The Wall
1000m

Menari
830m

Vabuiagi
River
720m

Brigade Hill
1450m

Mission Ridge
1340m

Postwar
Efogi
1230m

Efogi
River
1140m

Kagi
1410m

EFOGI

KOKODA 48·1KMS
KAGI 2¾HRS

OWERS CNR 45·5KMS
MENARI 4HRS
TOP OF RIDGE 1¼HRS

ALLIED CHAIN OF COMMAND
1942

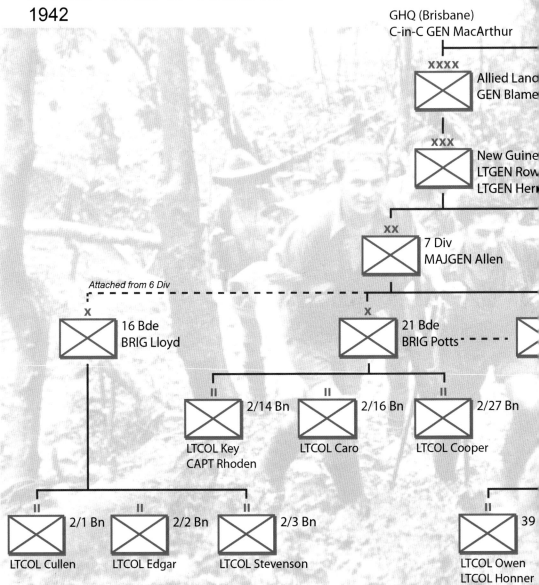

GHQ (Brisbane)
C-in-C GEN MacArthur

xxxx
Allied Land
GEN Blame

xxx
New Guine
LTGEN Row
LTGEN Her

xx
7 Div
MAJGEN Allen

Attached from 6 Div

x
16 Bde
BRIG Lloyd

x
21 Bde
BRIG Potts

|| 2/14 Bn
LTCOL Key
CAPT Rhoden

|| 2/16 Bn
LTCOL Caro

|| 2/27 Bn
LTCOL Cooper

|| 2/1 Bn
LTCOL Cullen

|| 2/2 Bn
LTCOL Edgar

|| 2/3 Bn
LTCOL Stevenson

|| 39
LTCOL Owen
LTCOL Honner

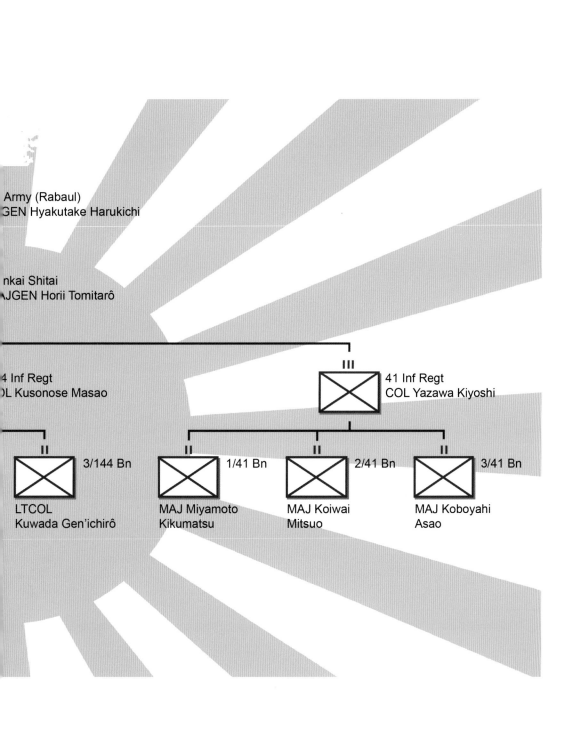

Army (Rabaul)
GEN Hyakutake Harukichi

nkai Shitai
JGEN Horii Tomitarô

4 Inf Regt
OL Kusonose Masao

III
41 Inf Regt
COL Yazawa Kiyoshi

II
3/144 Bn
LTCOL
Kuwada Gen'ichirô

II
1/41 Bn
MAJ Miyamoto
Kikumatsu

II
2/41 Bn
MAJ Koiwai
Mitsuo

II
3/41 Bn
MAJ Koboyahi
Asao

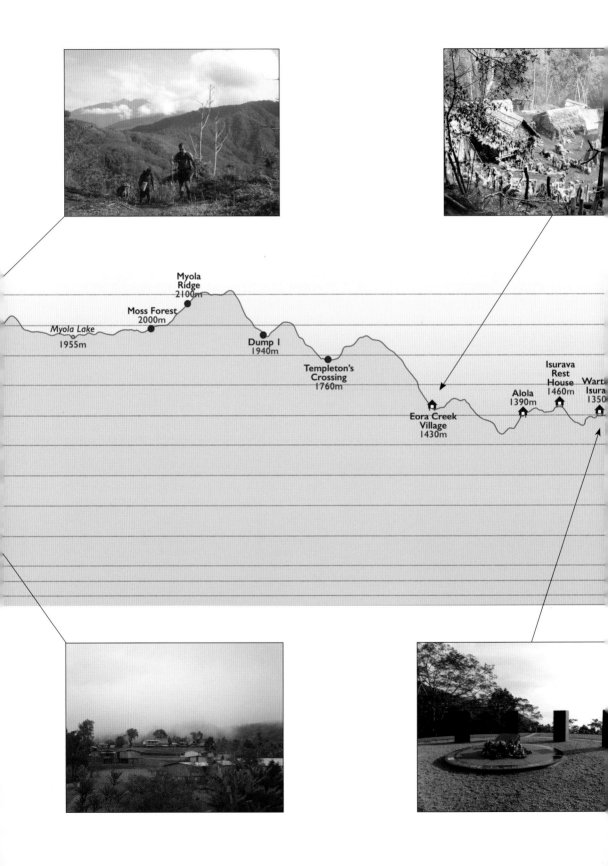

Myola Ridge
2100m

Moss Forest
2000m

Myola Lake
1955m

Dump I
1940m

Templeton's
Crossing
1760m

Eora Creek
Village
1430m

Alola
1390m

Isurava
Rest
House
1460m

Warti
Isura
1350

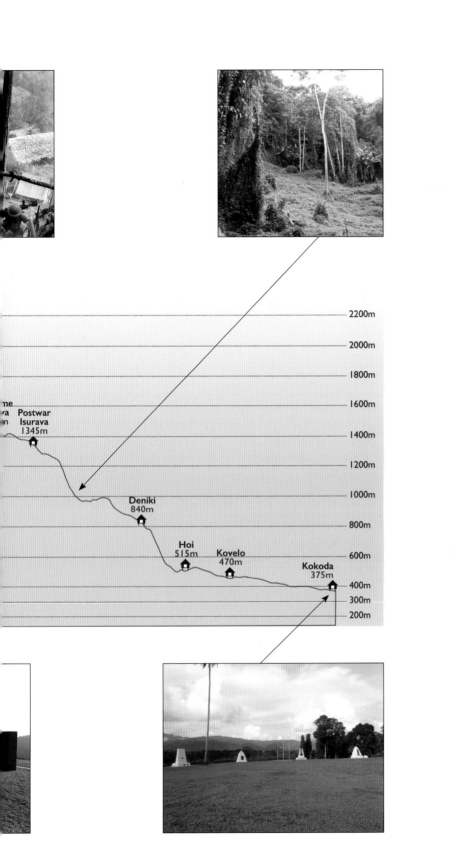

Postwar
Isurava
1345m

Deniki
840m

Hoi
515m

Kovelo
470m

Kokoda
375m

2200m
2000m
1800m
1600m
1400m
1200m
1000m
800m
600m
400m
300m
200m

JAPANESE CHAIN OF COMMAND
1942

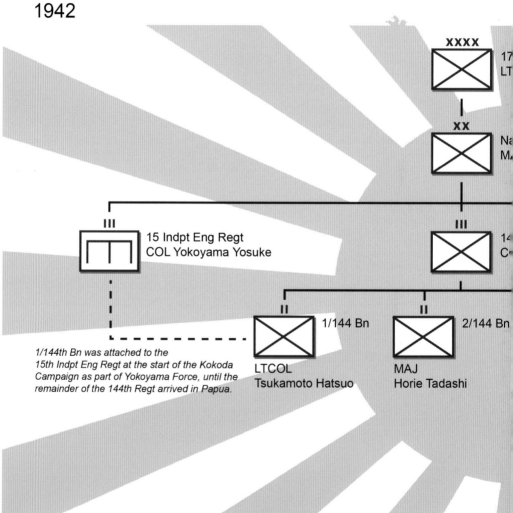

xxxx

17
LT

xx

Na
M.

III

15 Indpt Eng Regt
COL Yokoyama Yosuke

III

14
C

II

1/144 Bn

LTCOL
Tsukamoto Hatsuo

II

2/144 Bn

MAJ
Horie Tadashi

*1/144th Bn was attached to the
15th Indpt Eng Regt at the start of the Kokoda
Campaign as part of Yokoyama Force, until the
remainder of the 144th Regt arrived in Papua.*

STAGES OF THE KOKODA TRAIL

The Kokoda Trail is a functional route. Long before Europeans arrived in Papua it was used by the native people to commute from village to village. To this day, it remains in operation and is used regularly by the Papuans whose villages dot its length.

Europeans first used the Kokoda Trail to reach the goldfields in the north of Papua and afterwards for the transportation of mail. They noted that the natives who had created the Trail had made little effort to follow the normal method employed when creating a walking track. For example, it did not follow contour lines. Instead, it would often scale the highest part of a peak and then descend directly down the other side. When the Trail met a creek or a river, it would cross the water repeatedly, rather than follow one bank.

The start of the Kokoda Trail at the northern (Kokoda) end (N. Anderson, NAA001).

The vertical gain of the Kokoda Trail exceeds 5000 metres as does the vertical descent. From Owers' Corner to Kokoda, the length of the Trail is 96 kilometres; however distances along the Trail are difficult to gauge, and the amount of time taken to travel between two points is often used rather than an actual measure of the distance travelled.

At the time the Kokoda campaign began, the Trail was physically longer. This was because the southern end was anchored at a location called McDonald's Corner, named after the

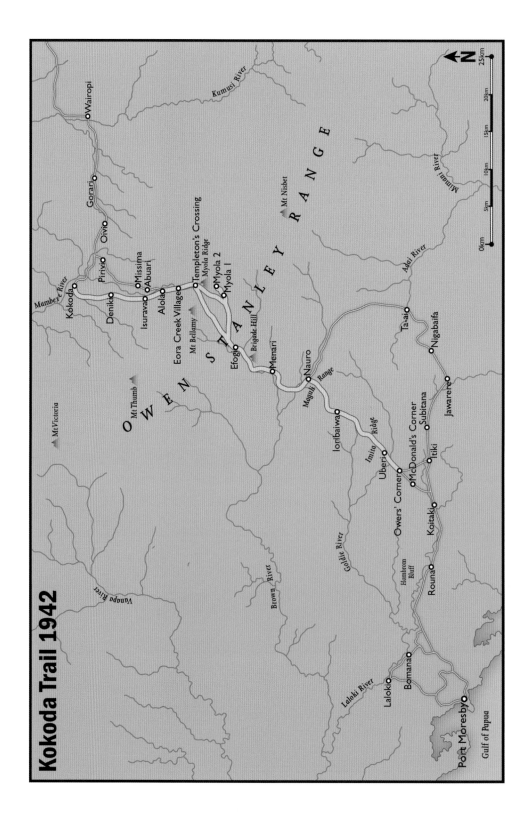

nearby homestead of Percy McDonald. Army surveyor Lieutenant Noel Owers was able to extend the jeep-head further north to the eponymously named Owers' Corner which shortened the distance. The original plan called for the road to be extended even further towards Kokoda; however the rapid enemy advance and the ruggedness of the country saw the idea discarded.

A fundamental misconception of the Kokoda Trail, held by both sides prior to the campaign, was the belief that it passed through a great opening in the Owen Stanleys known as the 'Kokoda Gap'. The Japanese were convinced this 'Gap' allowed an easy passage across the mountains, while some of the senior officers at Allied General Headquarters (GHQ) in Brisbane believed it to be a narrow fissure in the mountains. American Engineer-in-Chief, Major General Hugh (Pat) Casey, suggested that the Australians demolish the 'Gap' with dynamite. In reality, the 'Gap' was nothing more than an 11-kilometre depression in the mountains that was marginally lower than the surrounding peaks. It was far from impregnable, and is the reason the Kokoda Trail was the favoured route of the many crossings that traversed the Owen Stanleys.

The terrain and weather that characterises the breadth of Papua is extraordinarily varied. It is a land of extremes. From the beachheads on the north coast to the foothills of the Owen Stanleys at Kokoda, the weather is humid and the land is marked by swampy bogs and flats of kunai grass. Along the Trail itself, the weather changes constantly. At some locations, particularly sections of the Trail that are exposed to the sun such as the northern face of Brigade Hill, it is exceptionally hot. In comparison, the higher sections of the Trail, between Myola and Eora Creek, are very cold because of the altitude and frequent precipitation.

The topography of the Trail is generally steep. A notable exception is the area around the two dry lakebeds at Myola which provide rare flat land. Everywhere, the jungle is extremely dense. At Eora Creek and Templeton's Crossing, the sun is obscured by thick foliage which ensures these areas remain perpetually damp.

Warrant Officer Class 2 John Corbett of the 2/16th Battalion wrote that the most difficult part of the Kokoda Trail was 'The going up and down ... Looking up there and seeing the thousands of steps there and thinking — gee, I've got to get to the top of that. And then getting up the top and looking down and seeing a thousand down the other side — thinking — gee, I've got to go down there ... the progress you made was negligible. You know, you'd walk so hard for so long and you got nowhere. As the crow flies — in some cases all that hours and hours that you'd taken — you might have only made four hundred yards. That ... used to dampen your spirits a little — you felt you were getting nowhere.'

Major battles of the Kokoda Campaign

First Battle for Kokoda	28–29 July 1942
Second Battle for Kokoda	8–10 August 1942
Battle of Deniki	13–14 August
Battle of Isurava–Abuari	26–30 August 1942
The Fighting Withdrawal	31 August–5 September 1942
Battle of Brigade Hill	6–8 September 1942
Battle of Ioribaiwa	13–16 September 1942
Battle of Myola Ridge	11–14 October 1942
Battle of Templeton's Crossing	16–20 October 1942
Battle of Eora Creek	22–28 October 1942

Main Australian Units and Commanders of the Kokoda Campaign

(Note: names in brackets indicate replacements in chronological order. Information relates solely to the campaign in the Owen Stanleys.)

New Guinea Force (NGF)	Major General Basil Morris (Lieutenant General Sydney Rowell) (Lieutenant General Edmund Herring)
7th Division Headquarters	Major General Arthur Allen (Major General George Vasey)
16th Brigade	Brigadier John Lloyd
2/1st Battalion	Lieutenant Colonel Paul Cullen
2/2nd Battalion	Lieutenant Colonel Cedric Edgar
2/3rd Battalion	Lieutenant Colonel John Stevenson
21st Brigade	Brigadier Arnold Potts (Brigadier Ivan Dougherty)
2/14th Battalion	Lieutenant Colonel Arthur Key (Lieutenant Colonel Hugh Challen)
2/16th Battalion	Lieutenant Colonel Albert Caro
2/27th Battalion	Lieutenant Colonel Geoffrey Cooper
25th Brigade	Brigadier Kenneth Eather
2/25th Battalion	Lieutenant Colonel Charles Withy (Lieutenant Colonel Richard Marson)
2/31st Battalion	Lieutenant Colonel Colin Dunbar (Lieutenant Colonel James Miller)
2/33rd Battalion	Lieutenant Colonel Alfred Buttrose
30th Brigade	Brigadier Selwyn Porter
39th Battalion	Lieutenant Colonel William Owen (temporarily Major Allan Cameron) (Lieutenant Colonel Ralph Honner)
53rd Battalion	Lieutenant Colonel Kenneth Ward (temporarily Major Allan Cameron)

3rd Battalion	Lieutenant Colonel Albert Paul (Lieutenant Colonel Allan Cameron)
2/1st Pioneer	Lieutenant Colonel Arnold Brown
2/6th Independent Company	Major Harry Harcourt
14th Field Regiment	Lieutenant Colonel Herbert Byrne (Lieutenant Colonel Walter Hiscock)
Papuan Infantry Battalion (PIB)	Major William Watson
2/5th Field Company	Major Bruce Buddle
2/6th Field Company	Major Douglas Thomson
2/14th Field Company	Major Ronald Tompson
2/4th Field Ambulance	Lieutenant Colonel Arthur Hobson
2/6th Field Ambulance	Lieutenant Colonel Frederick Chenhall
14th Field Ambulance	Lieutenant Colonel Malcolm Earlam
Australian New Guinea Administrative Unit (ANGAU)	Major General Basil Morris

Main Japanese Units and their Commanders Of The Kokoda Campaign

(Note: names in brackets indicate replacements in chronological order. Information relates solely to the campaign in the Owen Stanleys.)

17th Army Headquarters	Lieutenant General Hyakutake Harukichi
South Seas Force (Nankai Shitai)	Major General Horii Tomitarô
55th Infantry Group Headquarters	Major General Oda Kensaku
144th Infantry Regiment	Colonel Kusunose Masao (temporarily Tsukamoto Hatsuo)
1/144th Battalion	Colonel Tsukamoto Hatsuo
2/144th Battalion	Major Horie Tadashi (Major Katô Kôkichi)
3/144th Battalion	Lieutenant Colonel Kuwada Gen'ichirô
41st Infantry Regiment	Colonel Yazawa Kiyoshi
1/41st Battalion	Major Miyamoto Kikumatsu
2/41st Battalion	Major Koiwai Mitsuo
3/41st Battalion	Major Kobayahi Asao (Major Murase Gohei)
55th Cavalry Regiment 3rd Company (less one platoon) plus 55th Cavalry Regiment Pom-pom Gun Squad	Lieutenant Kawashima Seiki
55th Engineer Regiment 1st Company plus Materials Platoon (part-strength)	Captain Takamori Hachirô
55th Supply Regiment 2nd Company	Lieutenant Sakigawa Toshiharu
55th Division Disease Prevention and Water Supply Unit (part-strength)	Captain Yamamoto Susumu
55th Division Medical Unit (one-third strength)	Captain Akao Hamakichi
55th Division 1st Field Hospital	Captain Bandô Jôbu
5th Mountain Artillery Regiment 1st Battalion	Lieutenant Colonel Hozumi Shizuo
15th Independent Engineer Regiment	Colonel Yokoyama Yosuke

Chapter 1

THE PRELUDE

Papua New Guinea did not feature prominently in the Australian mindset prior to the Second World War. This mindset changed rapidly once Japan's aggressive posturing provided a strong indication that armed conflict with the West was inevitable. In Australia's case, this would pose a threat to its northern borders.

The region known as Papua — the southern and south-eastern portion of the New Guinea mainland — had been an Australian territory since 1906, having earlier been a protectorate of Britain. The northern part of New Guinea, including the islands of the Bismarck Archipelago, had been captured from the Germans in the early stages of the First World War. At the 1919 Paris Peace Conference, Australian Prime Minister Billy Hughes demanded that Australia maintain control of these possessions to keep them from 'the hands of an actual or potential enemy'. His argument was persuasive, and a mandate was awarded in 1920, with civil authority established in 1921.

Australia never realised the full economic potential of New Guinea, its economic output limited to rubber and copra exports and to gold mines, primarily worked in the Bulolo Valley near Wau. Australian efforts to establish complete control of the two territories were limited by numerous factors including the scant investment of resources, the terrain, and the ethnic divisions of the native tribes that constituted the vast bulk of the population.

Strangely, despite its potential as a bulwark against aggressive action from the north, the fortification of New Guinea generally, and Port Moresby specifically, occurred only in piecemeal fashion prior to 1941. The senior military officer in Port Moresby was Major General Basil Morris, Commander of the 8th Military District.

Major General Basil Morris, Commander of the 8th Military District and later GOC ANGAU (AWM025597).

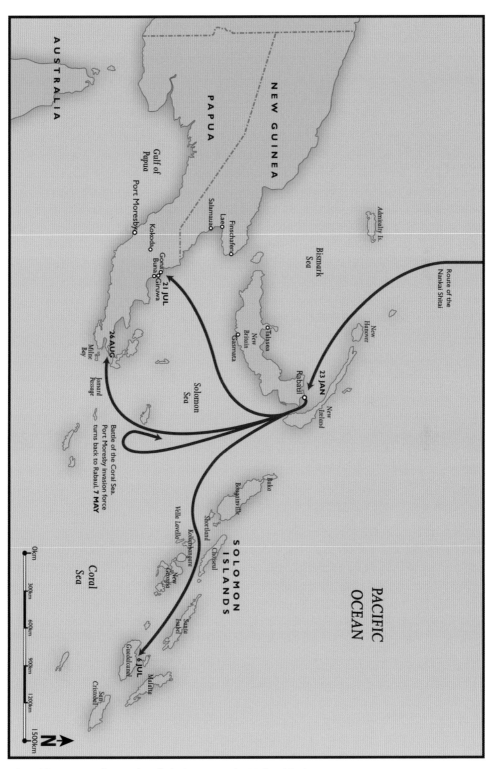

Adapted from Peter Williams, *The Kokoda Campaign 1942: Myth and Reality*, p. 12.

The soldiers under Morris' command were organised into three primary groups: the 30th Brigade (militia), of which at that time only the 49th Battalion was in Port Moresby; the Papuan Infantry Battalion (PIB), raised in 1940 for the defence of Papua and comprising natives led by European officers and non-commissioned officers (NCOs); and the New Guinea Volunteer Rifles (NGVR). This latter group consisted of local Europeans who felt obliged to take the defence of their land and homes into their own hands.

When the Pacific War erupted, the rapidity of Japanese conquests across South-East Asia and the Pacific Ocean sent a clear signal that war would eventually reach mainland New Guinea. The threat crystallised when Rabaul was captured on 23 January 1942. By 3 February the Japanese were bombing Port Moresby and reconnoitring the New Guinea mainland from the air. Bombing raids on Port Moresby provoked mass panic and the civil administration began to unravel. With the populace in disarray, civil authority could not maintain control and martial law was announced. On 15 February Morris assumed control of New Guinea from the island's administrator and, on 21 February, the Australian New Guinea Administrative Unit (ANGAU) was formed to function as a military administrative unit. ANGAU's primary responsibilities involved the maintenance of law and order, the supervision of labour and the duty of care for native welfare.

Morris' problems were countless. First and foremost, there were insufficient naval and air assets to adequately defend Port Moresby and the troops garrisoning the city were regarded as low quality. On 3 January 1942 the 30th Brigade had been reinforced with the arrival of its remaining two battalions, the 39th and the 53rd. While the 39th, originally from Victoria, had been pieced together from various other units, the men were eager to learn and trained vigorously. The 53rd's genesis was entirely different and provided the catalyst for the woes that would plague it throughout the Kokoda campaign. First, unlike the 39th whose members had generally volunteered for service with that unit, the 53rd was cobbled together from a myriad of New South Wales detachments, with local commanders taking the opportunity to offload their most troublesome characters.

As the 53rd was scheduled to leave Sydney for active service on Christmas Day 1941, many of its members resented the fact that they had been denied Christmas leave. The lack of opportunity to farewell their families significantly eroded morale. As the battalion was under strength, approximately 100 men were effectively co-opted into service and told they were deploying forthwith. To compound matters, the troops were not informed of their final destination, told only that they were sailing to Townsville. The battalion's *esprit de corps* plummeted when the ship diverted towards Port Moresby mid-voyage.

On arrival in Port Moresby, further malady ensued. The careless manner in which the ship had been loaded meant that mosquito netting, a necessity in a country rife with malaria, had been packed at the bottom of the ship. All stores thus had to be unloaded before this critical item could be unpacked and used to ward off the tiny carriers of the disease. Further, Port Moresby's development as a major Allied base was in its infancy. It lacked adequate port facilities and sufficient labour to work the wharf. The soldiers of the 53rd were thus put to work unloading their own ship. This became the pattern in the following months as the men were directed to manual labour tasks. This severely diminished their ability to train and prepare for the looming fight against the Japanese. In fact, some members of the 53rd lacked even the most basic skills of soldiering. When the battalion was eventually ordered forward, some troops were unfamiliar with their weapons and had no idea how to operate them.

Leadership was the other compelling difference between the 39th and 53rd battalions. In April 1942, the militia battalions were offered experienced AIF officers to steel their ranks. The lion's share of those allocated to the 30th Brigade was transferred to the 39th Battalion. The 53rd was not as fortunate, and the quality of its leadership was markedly inferior to that of its sister battalion. The Commanding Officer (CO) of the 53rd, Lieutenant Colonel Kenneth Ward, was an amiable and confident man, but he lacked the experience of the COs of the 39th, Lieutenant Colonels William (Bill) Owen and Ralph Honner.

On 17 March US General Douglas MacArthur arrived in Australia. He had been ordered to leave the Philippines to assume the position of Commander-in-Chief South West Pacific Area (SWPA), the region that encompassed Australia and all the islands to the immediate north and north-west. News of his appointment was communicated to the Australian people the following day. MacArthur's command subsumed all land, naval and air assets of the Allied countries within the SWPA. Changes were also afoot within the Australian leadership structure. In 1942, General Thomas Blamey had been appointed to two senior positions, Commander-in-Chief Australian Military Forces and Commander of Allied Land Forces, SWPA.

General Thomas Blamey. Australia's foremost soldier during the Kokoda campaign (Australian Army Engineers Museum, ECMP3302).

Doubts existed over the leadership in Port Moresby, particularly over whether Morris was the right man to organise the defence of a post that was growing in importance. While these doubts were first aired at a meeting of the War Cabinet in early January 1942, they were not addressed until 9 April when Blamey issued orders that reorganised the 8th Military District from a peacetime administrative structure into New Guinea Force (NGF), an operational headquarters with responsibility for conducting all military operations in New Guinea. Blamey's former Chief of Staff, Lieutenant General Sydney Rowell, was appointed General Officer Commanding (GOC) NGF and subsequently replaced Morris in August.

Lieutenant General Sydney Rowell, GOC New Guinea Force. During the Kokoda campaign his feud with General Blamey would cost him his job and create long-lasting controversy. By the 1950s he had returned to favour and would serve as Chief of the General Staff (modern-day Chief of Army) (AWM026582).

On 12 May MacArthur told Australian Prime Minister John Curtin, 'We have … in this theatre at the present time all the elements that have produced disaster in the Western Pacific since the beginning of the war.' Despite this grim assessment, several puzzling decisions were made that suggest the threat to Port Moresby had been underestimated. It was not until April 1942 that AIF units, primarily anti-aircraft gunners, were committed to the defence of the city. In May Blamey sent the untested 14th Brigade (militia, including the 3rd Battalion which would feature in the Kokoda campaign) to Port Moresby, reasoning that the main threat to Port Moresby was a seaborne invasion which the militia could successfully oppose. He wanted the AIF brigades of the 7th Division — the 21st and 25th — held back and trained in Australia for MacArthur's grand overall offensive strategy. Historian David Horner concludes, '[It is] clear that both MacArthur and Blamey made vital strategic miscalculations, at the expense of the lives of many soldiers and the careers of subordinate commanders, but neither would admit it.'

By 15 June 1942 the volatile situation called for stern measures. Morris enforced regulations which allowed him to terminate existing native labour contracts and made all New Guinea natives liable for conscription for any labour required by the military. Rates of pay and conditions of service were described in detail, including the provision of food and other necessities. Care was taken to prevent too many men being conscripted from the same village although, as the war situation worsened, this directive was less rigorously applied. Lieutenant Bert Kienzle, who had lived in Papua for many years and was able to speak the native language of Motu, was drafted to ANGAU and directed to organise native labour. This was a mammoth task and he quickly realised that his charges were very despondent, their morale low. He immediately took steps to reverse this by ensuring that their sub-standard living conditions were improved, and by explaining the enormity of the danger posed by the Japanese.

On 20 June Blamey ordered Morris to prepare for the possibility of a Japanese invasion of Papua. Allied Command anticipated that a Japanese force would land on the north coast, march across the Owen Stanley Range and assault Port Moresby. In response, an Australian force would concentrate in the Kokoda area where it would delay any Japanese advance, hold and protect Kokoda, and arrest any movement of enemy troops through the 'Kokoda Gap'. The force was codenamed 'Maroubra' and comprised the 39th Battalion and the PIB, which was already actively patrolling the region.

On 24 June Morris relayed these instructions to the 39th Battalion. This battalion was not selected for any particular reason other than its position in a reserve area within the Port Moresby defences. The Commander of the 30th Brigade, Brigadier Selwyn Porter, believed that, even once the battalion moved north of the Owen Stanleys, its prime responsibility would involve little more than guarding airfields. Porter's own assessment is telling; he later wrote: 'In my opinion, NO unit in this BDE was capable of carrying out operations in the field, at this time.'

B Company, led by Captain Sam Templeton, was the first sent across the Kokoda Trail to implement the battalion's orders. The men left a staging post at Uberi on 8 July with Kienzle guiding them, and arrived in Kokoda on 14 July.

The Allies realised well prior to the start of the Kokoda campaign that it was critically important to establish a base at Buna. Under Operation Providence, the Buna area was to be occupied for the construction of an airfield. But their lack of urgency cost the Allies dearly, as the Japanese had their own designs on Buna and took the initiative.

The Japanese MO Operation, the original plan for a seaborne invasion of Port Moresby, had been thwarted by a combined US and Australian naval fleet at the Battle of the Coral Sea. A more crushing defeat followed at the Battle of Midway, in which four Japanese aircraft carriers were sunk. The defeat at Midway prompted the cancellation on 11 July of the ambitious FS Operation (the capture of Fiji, New Caledonia and Samoa) and refocused Japanese attention on Port Moresby, this time to be captured in an overland invasion. The Japanese knew this would be difficult. In the years preceding the Pacific War they had gathered intelligence on New Guinea through the work of *Imperial Japanese Navy* (*IJN*) and *Imperial Japanese Army* (*IJA*) operatives disguised as scientific researchers and businessmen. Their intelligence formed the basis for Japanese plans, and they were aware that the Owen Stanleys represented a formidable natural barrier.

The attack across the Owen Stanleys would be spearheaded by Major General Horii Tomitarô and his *Nankai Shitai* (South Seas Force).

Major General Horii Tomitarô, Commander of the *Nankai Shitai*. Source: Wikipedia

The major elements of this force were two infantry regiments, the *41st* and *144th*. These two regiments contained battle-hardened regular solders, fresh from the fighting in Malaya and China. They had already captured Guam and Rabaul prior to their planned venture into Papua. Success had bred confidence and, while in Rabaul, the troops spent the time between missions honing their fitness for the march on Port Moresby. Carrying packs laden with volcanic sand, they repeatedly climbed and descended the volcanoes that rimmed the outskirts of Rabaul. By the afternoon of 20 July, men and material had been loaded into two transport ships, *Ryoyo Maru* and *Ayatosan Maru*, moored in Rabaul Harbour. This was *Yokoyama Force*, the advance party of the *Nankai Shitai*, comprising mostly engineers, native labourers and the *1/144th Battalion*. They departed for Buna at 8.00 pm, a small convoy flanked by two destroyers and two cruisers. While the voyage was uncomfortable the passage was uncontested. Within 24 hours the first Japanese soldiers were spilling onto the beaches of northern Papua.

Chapter 2
THE LANDINGS

Gona Beach on the north coast of Papua, typical of the beaches utilised by the Japanese for their landings (N. Anderson, NAA003).

With the landing of *Yokoyama Force* and the establishment of a beachhead, Captain Ogawa Tetsuo's company of the *1/144th* began the advance towards Kokoda. The troops travelled as far as Sambo by truck and then continued on foot and by bicycle. For the Australians, the first 24 hours following the landings were characterised by confusion and disorganisation. The solidly built Major William Watson, a former captain of the Australian rugby union team and a decorated soldier, was in command of the PIB, the 105 Papuans and six Australians under his command scattered across a number of posts along the north coast of Papua. Initially they patrolled the area between Kokoda and the beachheads seeking some clarity on Japanese intentions. They felled trees and laid obstacles across the roads to hinder Japanese movement.

Papua's European population was alarmed by the landings as the Japanese were notorious for their brutal treatment of captured civilians. Many civilians heeded advice and fled the area. Others waited, confident that they would still have time to escape before the arrival of the invading Japanese. Many of those who decided on this latter course of action were either captured or betrayed to the Japanese and then murdered.

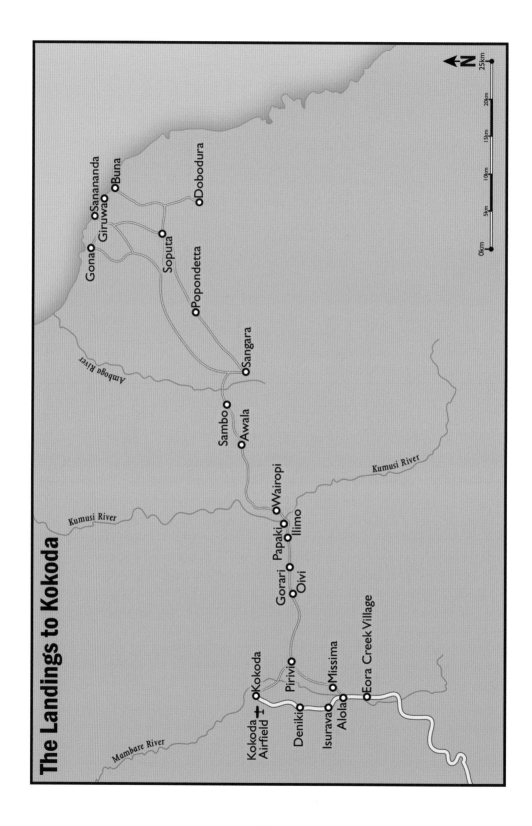

The Landings to Kokoda

Captain Sam Templeton worked frenetically. He travelled to Buna on the morning of the landings and unwittingly passed close to Japanese forces as he raced to meet a transport sailing around New Guinea carrying supplies for his B Company. On the return leg to Kokoda he received news of the Japanese landings, immediately ordering Lieutenant Arthur Seekamp's 11 Platoon to move to Awala, Lieutenant Harold Mortimore's 12 Platoon to march to Gorari, and Lieutenant Gough Garland's 10 Platoon to remain in Kokoda to protect the aerodrome.

When Templeton arrived back at Kokoda he was informed of the imminent arrival of the 39th's new CO, Lieutenant Colonel Bill Owen. Templeton decided to wait for him, but Owen's flight was delayed and he did not reach the village until 24 July. The two veteran soldiers then set off to inspect the forward elements of B Company.

Ogawa's men moved with the rapidity that typified Japanese conquests during the early stages of the Pacific War. On several occasions the Japanese narrowly avoided contact with Australian forces as they pushed inland. The first contact finally occurred close to Awala on 23 July. A PIB group led by Lieutenant John Chalk had been anticipating the arrival of enemy forces after discovering a Japanese campsite at nearby Sangara the day before. At around 4.00 pm the Japanese approached, using a group of natives to screen their movement. Chalk and his men opened fire and the Japanese quickly retaliated, using machine-guns, mortars and a field gun. The overwhelming disparity in firepower ensured that the contact was brief and, as the Japanese moved to flank the PIB, their resistance evaporated. The majority of the Papuans fled into the jungle.

The PIB was the first unit to confront the Japanese following their landing in Papua and push towards Kokoda (AWM044358).

Seekamp's 11 Platoon arrived at Awala just as this contact was playing out. Watson ordered Seekamp to hold the village for at least half an hour to enable the PIB soldiers who had not absconded to pull back and establish themselves in Ongahambo, the next village further back towards Kokoda. However, Seekamp instead led his platoon back to Wairopi on the banks of the Kumusi River, followed soon after by Watson and several of his men once they had destroyed all the useful stores in Ongahambo. The Papuan natives in Watson's force continued to desert until only a handful remained alongside the small contingent of loyal European officers and NCOs. They crossed the wire bridge which spanned the powerful Kumusi and then destroyed the bridge in the hope of delaying the Japanese.

By 9.00 am on the morning of 24 July, the picture was becoming clearer and Templeton was forming some idea of the magnitude of the incursion his company faced. He sent Seekamp a message instructing: '1,500-2,000 Japs landed at Gona Mission Station. I recommend that your action be contact and rearguard only — no do-or-die stunts. Close back on Kokoda.' B Company's second-in-command, Captain Cathcart Stevenson, arrived at Wairopi an hour and a half later and confirmed the orders, telling Seekamp that the fallback position was 12 Platoon's site at Gorari. Around midday the indefatigable Lieutenant Harold Jesser from the PIB swam the Kumusi and reported that the Japanese had camped in Awala the previous evening and were still there at 7.00 am that morning. At 2.30 pm the Japanese appeared on the eastern shoreline of the Kumusi. A brief firefight ensued before Seekamp, his men and the remaining members of the PIB withdrew and joined 12 Platoon in Gorari.

By now, Owen and Templeton had arrived in Gorari to inspect the Australian defences. Ambush positions were set approximately 700 metres east of the village. Seekamp and Mortimore's platoons were positioned to cover the road with a Bren gun on the left and a Lewis gun on the right, while the remaining PIB soldiers were tasked with covering the flanks. By now fatigue was setting in and the Australians manning the machine-guns were rotated every hour to ensure they remained vigilant. Satisfied with the arrangements, Owen left for Kokoda the next morning, hoping that further reinforcements would arrive by air during the day.

Just before noon on 25 July as the men on the Lewis gun were rotating through, the first of the Japanese came into sight, wheeling a bicycle. He was a scout and was followed by several others also pushing bicycles. The attentive Japanese soldier noticed the foliage moving close to where the Lewis gun was hidden and dived for cover in the bush on the side of the road. The Australians held their nerve and their triggers. Not long after, the scouts returned to their bicycles and once again pushed forward along the track. Mortimore allowed the leading enemy troops to pass the flanking positions hoping to ensnare as many as possible in the trap.

However the Japanese remained suspicious, and one soldier raised his rifle and pointed it directly at the Lewis gun team. Mortimore could wait no longer and gave the order to fire. The Australians opened up with a strong volley and killed an estimated 15 enemy before being forced to withdraw the 700 metres back towards Gorari. The short withdrawal gave the Australians some breathing space as further enemy entered the fray. Not long after, however, Japanese machine-guns and mortars arrived and were brought to bear on the pressed defenders. Outnumbered and outgunned, they withdrew to the Oivi Pass.

By the time the Australians staggered into Oivi at 7.30 pm they were utterly exhausted. Stevenson left the group and returned to Kokoda to inform Owen of the latest developments. Owen ordered that Oivi be held at all costs — unless the force was surrounded. He still hoped to reinforce the small number of B Company troops at Oivi with men from his battalion as they arrived forward. He had earlier signalled Major General Morris and informed him bluntly, 'Must have more troops, otherwise there is nobody between Oivi and Dean.' Owen was referring to Captain Arthur Dean, Officer Commanding (OC) C Company, 39th Battalion, who at that moment was leading his company across the Kokoda Trail, but was still several days' walk away. Owen's signal continued, 'Will have drome open for landing. Must have two fresh companies to avoid being outflanked at Oivi. Advise before 3 am if airborne troops not available.'

The lack of serviceable aircraft in Port Moresby hampered Morris' ability to meet Owen's request. Instead of two companies, the best that he could do was to send Lieutenant Doug McClean's 16 Platoon from D Company. Even then, the platoon had to be divided in half and flown to Kokoda by a single aircraft in two separate flights. The first flight carrying McClean arrived at 10.00 am on 26 July. He disembarked and led his half platoon directly to Oivi. The plane then returned to Port Moresby and picked up the remainder of the platoon led by Sergeant Ted Morrison. The troops spent the 20 minutes of flying time removing their new Bren guns from their crates and cleaning the packing grease from them. At 11.30 am the second flight touched down at Kokoda, and the moment the troops' feet hit the ground they too were ordered to march straight to Oivi.

The Japanese reached Oivi at 3.00 pm. McClean's arrival had bolstered the defenders' numbers, although Morrison's party had yet to arrive. The two and a half platoons prepared to confront the attacking force of over 200 men. At first the Australians were able to parry the Japanese, resisting their initial forays. But soon they were surrounded, and the strength of the Japanese attacks forced them to their secondary position on the plateau behind them. Once on the plateau they formed a tight perimeter as the Japanese continued to press.

Tropical rain fell persistently throughout the murky evening. The Japanese were wary following the earlier ambush at Gorari. Rather than rushing, they were prudent and employed guile in their attempt to probe and penetrate the Australian perimeter. The firing between the two forces was sporadic, with occasional bursts of excitement. The Japanese called to the Australians in English, hoping to lure them out from their cover. Templeton was worried that Morrison, approaching with his half-platoon, might run into the enemy who were trying to encircle the position. He decided to set off towards Kokoda to warn them. Shortly after he left, a shot punctured the silence. Templeton was never seen again.

The loss of Templeton, the 39th Battalion's paternal figurehead, was a huge blow to the morale of the tiny force. The remaining troops could only assume that he had stumbled across some of the Japanese attempting to encircle the position. Major Watson once again took command of the defence.

The situation remained grim. The Australian troops were so weary that, in some cases, they were literally falling asleep across their weapons. Recognising the growing Japanese threat to their rear, McClean and Corporal Charles Pyke crawled towards the blockade and scattered some of the enemy troops with hand grenades, easing the pressure. The screams of wounded enemy soldiers signalled their success.

Watson conferred with one of his trusted natives, Corporal Sanopa. Sanopa knew the country well and suggested that the best way to escape the enemy stranglehold was to head south where the Japanese presence was most thinly spread. Sanopa led the troops as they broke out in this direction, planning to swing around and rejoin the road to Kokoda, having travelled closer to the village. After ploughing through heavy jungle and making little progress, Sanopa turned the party directly towards the Australian supply dump at Deniki, which he reasoned might be easier to reach.

In evading the clutches of the Japanese, six Australian troops were inadvertently left behind at Oivi. Realising they were alone, these men also made a break from the plateau and headed towards Kokoda. They travelled parallel to the road and were fortunate to avoid detection by the Japanese.

The track to Deniki from Kokoda climbs sharply once it reaches the northern edge of the Owen Stanleys (M. Rifat, NAA004).

As the morning of 27 July dawned, Owen had lost contact with his men in Oivi and now feared the worst. As a consequence, he decided to abandon Kokoda. He ordered the supplies in the village — the same supplies that had earlier been shipped around New Guinea in very arduous circumstances — be destroyed to prevent their use by the Japanese. They were moved into several buildings and torched. Owen and his men then left for Deniki, from where they would have a clear view of Kokoda and its airstrip in the Yodda Valley below.

Later that afternoon, the six soldiers who had been left behind in Oivi entered Kokoda, astonished to find the village unoccupied. The men were hungry and picked through the smouldering fires searching for any of the burnt supplies that might still be edible. They scavenged enough for a basic meal and bedded down for the night, their exhaustion overriding their concern that the Japanese would arrive at the village at any moment.

When Owen reached Deniki he discovered that Watson and the soldiers he had presumed lost at Oivi had arrived at the supply dump before him. When the six men who had spent the night in Kokoda also arrived in Deniki the following morning and informed him that Kokoda remained free of Japanese, Owen realised his mistake. Not only had vital supplies been destroyed, but the opportunity to fly in further reinforcements had been lost because the village had been abandoned. Owen immediately prepared to reoccupy Kokoda.

Chapter 3

THE FIRST BATTLE FOR KOKODA

The village from which the eponymous Kokoda Trail takes its name was the site of two separate battles during the early stages of the campaign. Although relatively small in terms of the total numbers engaged and the casualties sustained, the village of Kokoda itself was of vital importance. It had the only operational airstrip between Port Moresby and Buna-Gona, providing the sole rapid means of resupply and reinforcement.

Nestled in a cleft in the mountains, Kokoda and its rubber plantation are sited on an elongated escarpment that juts from the northern side of the Owen Stanleys. The escarpment is dwarfed by the surrounding mountains, but its tip provides a commanding panoramic view of the surrounding countryside. During the campaign, the most important building in the village was a Papuan Administration post at the northern end of the escarpment.

On 28 July, Lieutenant Colonel Owen, having realised the folly of evacuating Kokoda prematurely, organised his men in Deniki and marched them to reoccupy the village. According to different sources, he had with him anywhere between 81 and 130 men. Accompanying the group was medical officer Captain Geoffrey Vernon, a veteran of the First World War. He was a well-known figure in Papua during the inter-war years, almost 60 years old and partially deaf. However, his physical limitations were balanced by his courage and devotion to his men.

If Kokoda and its airstrip could be held, then the force retained the ability to be reinforced by air. By 11.30 am the Australians had reached the village and Owen sent an urgent signal to Port Moresby: 'Re-Occupied Kokoda. Fly in reinforcements including 2 Platoon and four detachments of mortars. Drome opened.'

As luck would have it, at that very moment two Douglas transports loaded with reinforcements were airborne. The two aircraft circled the airstrip as the Australians on board watched their fellow soldiers on the ground busily clearing the airstrip of obstacles. However, the American pilots were reluctant to risk a landing and, despite the forceful insistence of their passengers, returned to Port Moresby without landing their troops. The 39th Battalion's sole opportunity to boost its numbers had been lost.

Without hope of reinforcement, Owen began arranging a defensive perimeter on the tip of the escarpment. The Papuan Administration post lay at its core, the troops forming a semi-circle around the building. The steep slope of the escarpment would make the task of rushing up the sides difficult for the attackers and provided the defenders clear lines of sight. From this vantage point the surrounding approaches could be observed, in particular the road that ran east to Oivi, which was the likely avenue of the Japanese advance. A trench was dug along the line of the rubber plantation to protect the rear of the position.

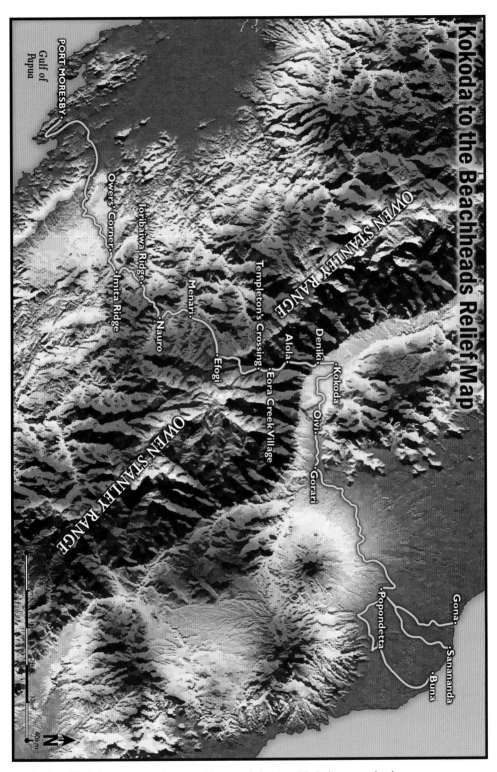

Kokoda to the Beachheads Relief Map

Based on http://kokoda.commemoration.gov.au/about-the-kokoda-track/kokoda-topography.php

View from the Kokoda escarpment looking east along the Kokoda-Oivi road. The Japanese approached from this direction (M. Rifat, NAA005).

At 1.30 pm Japanese troops were spotted approaching along the Kokoda-Oivi road. As they neared the escarpment they darted off the road and the Australians realised that they were sneaking towards their flanks. B Company remained alert, anxiously waiting throughout the afternoon for the inevitable Japanese attack. Their unease was heightened at dusk as the Japanese attempted to unsettle them with bizarre catcalls followed by the occasional volley of rifle fire or the random explosion of a mortar round. The attack proper finally came during the early hours of 29 July. At 2.30 am, Captain Ogawa's *1st Company* of the *1/144th* stormed the escarpment.

In fighting typical of what was to follow throughout the campaign, Ogawa attacked head on while probing the flanks searching for a weak spot. Owen had requested mortars and received none, whereas Ogawa was equipped with knee mortars and one Type 92 battalion gun. This 70mm artillery piece required immense physical effort to carry but was used to great effect and gave the Japanese a distinct advantage. It invariably allowed them to outgun the Australians in every battle.

While the Australians withstood Ogawa's frontal attacks, responding with a hail of rifle fire and a flurry of grenades, the battalion gun proved deadly. While the defenders held firm on the escarpment, casualties began to mount.

Sensing the fragility of the situation, Owen moved brazenly among his men, opting for courageous leadership over caution. The men considered him fearless. Lieutenant Garland commented later that Owen, 'wanted to show his leadership, and he walked around the

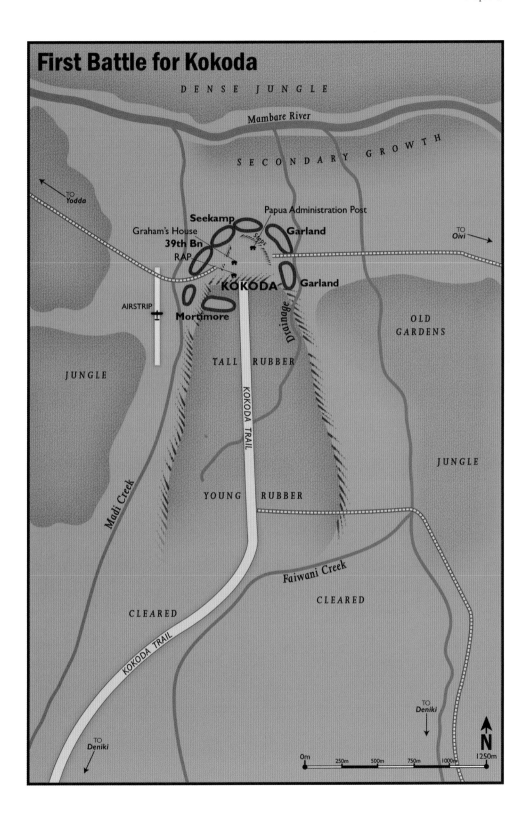

First Battle for Kokoda

DENSE JUNGLE

Mambare River

SECONDARY GROWTH

TO
Yodda

Seekamp

Papua Administration Post

Graham's House

39th Bn

Steps

Garland

RAP

TO
Oivi

KOKODA

Garland

AIRSTRIP

Mortimore

Drainage

OLD
GARDENS

JUNGLE

TALL RUBBER

JUNGLE

Madi Creek

KOKODA TRAIL

YOUNG RUBBER

Faiwani Creek

CLEARED

CLEARED

KOKODA TRAIL

TO
Deniki

TO
Deniki

N

0m   250m   500m   750m   1000m   1250m

perimeter where we were all lying down … I said to him, "Sir, I think you're taking an unnecessary risk walking around the troops like that." "Well," he said, "I've got to do it.'"

Less than an hour after the battle had erupted, Owen was at the forefront of the Australian defence in a fighting pit, side by side with his troops. He peered down his rifle sight, preparing for another shot at the attacking Japanese, when he was spotted by an enemy sniper who shot him in the head. Owen slumped into the fighting pit. Vernon and Lieutenant Peter Brewer struggled to move their semi-conscious commander to a stretcher they had positioned on the lip of the escarpment. From there they rushed him to a native hut being used as the Regimental Aid Post (RAP) where Warrant Officer John Wilkinson was waiting. In the light of a lantern, the severity of Owen's wound was apparent. The bullet had struck above the right eye. His skull and brain had been punctured and the bullet had failed to exit. A sense of dejection engulfed the room.

Owen suffered several violent convulsions. The medics did all they could to stop the bleeding and make their dying commander as comfortable as possible. In quick succession, several more wounded soldiers were brought into the RAP. Each time Wilkinson lifted the lantern to inspect new patients, the illumination acted as a beacon and the makeshift hospital was sprayed with bullets from a Japanese machine-gun. The steepness of the escarpment's sides provided the medics the merest protection as the rounds whizzed over their heads and through the building's grass roof.

Lieutenant Colonel William (Bill) Owen, CO of the 39th Battalion. Owen had previously served with the AIF, escaping capture by the Japanese at the fall of Rabaul. He was killed leading his inexperienced militia battalion from the front in the First Battle for Kokoda (P05414.001).

Owen's wounding dealt a critical blow to the Australians' tenuous hold on Kokoda. Shortly after the loss of their commander, the Japanese infiltrated their lines. Along the escarpment, Australian soldiers were finding it difficult to differentiate between friend and foe. With the perimeter compromised, Major Watson — now in command — gave the order to retreat.

Vernon agreed with the decision: '[B]y withdrawing, we took the wisest course … Besides the advantage in numbers, they had others. Particularly in that our line of retreat was practically undefended, and open to them had they worked around to our rear. In that case, the entire force would have been surrounded, and capture or death the fate of every individual.'

Fortunately for those defenders, a thick mist enveloped Kokoda in the early hours of the morning which enabled them to retreat through the rubber plantation without detection. The dying Owen was left in the RAP. In the final moments of the battle the Japanese suffered a serious setback of their own with the death of Captain Ogawa. This soured their victory and possibly contributed to their decision not to pursue the retreating Australians.

Most of the Australians reached Deniki at dawn on 29 July. Captain Cathcart Stevenson signalled Port Moresby: 'Kokoda lost this morning. Blow the drome and road east of Oivi.' The loss of the airstrip meant that resupply and reinforcement would now have to traverse the length of the Owen Stanleys. It was a depleted and downcast force that paused in Deniki awaiting the appointment of a new leader.

Chapter 4

THE SECOND BATTLE FOR KOKODA

The Second Battle for Kokoda was an unusual affair, encompassing fighting in Kokoda, Deniki and Pirivi and along the numerous tracks that linked these three villages.

Following the death of Lieutenant Colonel Owen, Allan Cameron, the Brigade Major of the 30th Brigade, was appointed to take provisional command of the 39th Battalion and Maroubra Force. Opposing the Australians was the Japanese *1/144th Battalion*, commanded by Lieutenant Colonel Tsukamoto Hatsuo.

Cameron arrived at Deniki on 4 August, by which time the bulk of the 39th Battalion had also arrived, having marched across the Kokoda Trail. Cameron was a proactive officer and eager to dictate terms to the enemy. He immediately set his sights on the recapture of Kokoda. His plan to accomplish this goal comprised three elements and utilised the three recently arrived companies of the 39th Battalion. C Company would enter Kokoda via the Kokoda Trail, A Company would approach Kokoda along a middle track that was little known and seldom used, while D Company would move along a third track to a blocking position close to the village of Pirivi, much further to the east, where the Australians could intercept any Japanese reinforcements moving towards Kokoda along the Kokoda-Oivi road.

Cameron's arrival, coupled with the completion of a telephone line that provided more reliable communications with Port Moresby, reinvigorated the Australians. On assuming command, Cameron immediately called the officers and senior NCOs before him. They were left with no illusions concerning their new commander's opinion of their performance thus far. If the men had expected praise for their efforts in delaying the enemy they were to be disappointed; Cameron instead delivered a sharp rebuke.

He chastised B Company for its actions at the First Battle for Kokoda, reproaching them for wilting under fire and being too hasty to withdraw. Special criticism was reserved for the men he had encountered on the Kokoda Trail moving southwards during his march forward to Deniki. He accused these men of cowardice and of having fled the battlefield. They had been apprehended and brought forward to rejoin the battalion. Cameron declared that B Company was finished as a fighting force and would be disbanded. Its members were to be allocated to the battalion's other companies. Once his initial anger dissipated, several of the officers persuaded Cameron that disbanding the maligned company would be counter-productive. Nevertheless, it was reduced to a non-combat ancillary role and moved rearwards to Eora Creek Village.

On 5 August Cameron sent reconnaissance parties along the three intended routes of advance. Each party was reasonably successful in reconnoitring its objectives. The patrol that

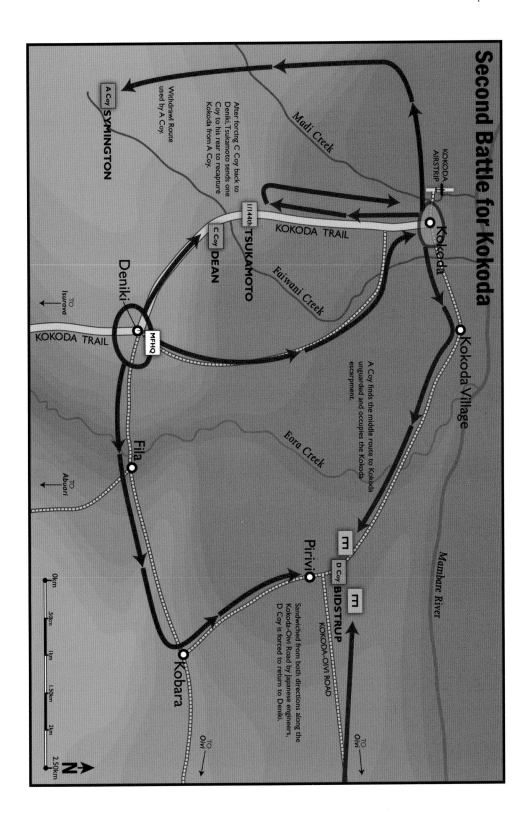

Second Battle for Kokoda

explored the middle track was able to approach the outskirts of Kokoda without any Japanese interference, confirming the Australians' suspicions that the Japanese were unaware of the existence of this track. The patrols were not completely successful however, as they were unable to ascertain the size of the Japanese force owing to its wide dispersal. But Cameron was satisfied and set 8 August as the date for the attack. Final instructions were issued to his company commanders on the afternoon of 7 August.

Japanese commander Tsukamoto was also hatching plans for a Japanese offensive. By 7 August the entire *1/144th* Battalion had consolidated in Kokoda and Tsukamoto planned to march against Deniki the next day. Thus, 8 August found both forces moving towards their objectives — Tsukamoto leading the *1/144th* south from Kokoda towards Deniki, and Cameron and Captain Dean's C Company marching north from Deniki towards Kokoda.

C Company had advanced just 180 metres from Deniki when it came under fire from the dense scrub on the right-hand side of the Trail. The Australians returned fire and silenced the enemy hidden there before continuing on. Not long after, they met one of their own patrols which had been scouting ahead since the day before. The patrol leader, Lieutenant Stewart Johnston, reported that they had observed the Japanese preparing defensive positions on the Kokoda escarpment. He also said they had skirmished with a Japanese patrol. Johnston guessed that the failed ambush of C Company was probably conducted by that same Japanese patrol in an effort to prevent his group returning to Deniki.

C Company pressed on until the men were halted by machine-gun fire at Faiwani Creek near the modern-day village of Hoi. Dean ordered a pincer movement to annihilate the post, but the Japanese quickly withdrew. This allowed C Company to cross the creek unmolested, although their formations were broken and the company dispersed. Not long after, Dean was shot in the stomach by a sniper, having moved just 50 metres from the creek. He died almost immediately and Lieutenant Richard McNamara assumed command.

C Company was well behind schedule. The attack on Kokoda was to occur at noon, but the appointed time came and passed, and the Australians were still nowhere near their target. Some 370 metres beyond Faiwani Creek they again came under fire. McNamara ordered four sections — two on either flank — to neutralise the opposition or locate an alternative route into Kokoda. As the day lengthened, these efforts failed, mainly because C Company had collided with Tsukamoto and the majority of the *1/144th*. McNamara did not believe he could reach Kokoda before dark so he ordered C Company to return to Deniki.

A Company's progress along the middle track to Kokoda was vastly different. Captain Noel Symington and his men were able to move directly to the eastern side of the Kokoda escarpment where they formed up without any opposition. In fact, no Japanese were even sighted until the company marched into Kokoda, where they chanced upon a group of approximately 50 Japanese engineers strengthening the defences in the village and rubber plantation. At first the Japanese were unfazed by the approaching Australians until one Japanese soldier realised what was happening and frantically alerted his complacent colleagues. Some minor fighting occurred before the engineers fled the village in disarray. In their haste to retreat towards Oivi, they left behind a plethora of items including weapons, ammunition, medical supplies and, most importantly, intelligence: a Japanese notebook and topographical map. Corporal Sanopa was immediately sent back to Deniki with the crucial material.

Once the immediate area surrounding Kokoda had been cleared and secured, Symington ordered his men to dig in, occupying the same positions as B Company during the First Battle for Kokoda 10 days earlier. A flare was set off to indicate that Kokoda had been captured, but the signal was missed, probably because Cameron was not overlooking Kokoda from Deniki, but was with C Company down at Faiwani Creek. Symington's men heard the gunfire from C Company's confrontation across the valley, but remained ignorant of what had transpired.

Further to the east, Captain Maxwell Bidstrup's D Company had been the first company to depart Deniki that morning. While the men had moved quickly, opposition was soon encountered in Pirivi, where a group of Japanese troops was scavenging in native gardens for food. Several casualties were suffered before the village was secured and the company moved on towards its designated objective — the junction of the Pirivi track and the Kokoda-Oivi road. When D Company reached the intersection later that afternoon, they startled a group of Japanese engineers improving the road.

The two sides fought bitterly. Bidstrup found it difficult to maintain contact between his platoons because of the thick jungle foliage that separated them. Several men acting as communication runners between the platoons disappeared and were never seen again. Further complicating D Company's tenuous position was the arrival during the fighting of another group of Japanese engineers. This was the same group that had earlier fled Kokoda when A Company captured the village.

D Company was now hemmed in at the track junction, attacked from both directions of the Kokoda-Oivi road. At 2.30 pm Bidstrup sought to withdraw to Pirivi to regroup, but was unable to because 17 Platoon was completely cut off and impossible to contact. He therefore remained in position and tried to re-establish contact with his isolated platoon. By 5.50 pm, determined efforts to restore contact had failed. No sound of fighting could be heard from Kokoda and Bidstrup assumed that the attack there had failed. He made the decision to withdraw, hopeful that the missing platoon would recall its earlier orders which specified a return to Deniki in the event of being separated. The withdrawal was successfully completed and, with great physical effort, the majority of D Company reached Deniki the next day, followed a day later by the bedraggled lost platoon.

By the morning of 9 August, Symington, who was in Kokoda, had not heard from Major Cameron and was uncertain of the fate of the rest of Maroubra Force. Dean's C Company had failed to arrive as planned. A Company had travelled light in the belief that securing the airfield at Kokoda would allow it to receive reinforcements and resupply from the air. Food and ammunition were low, but no supply aircraft appeared. Several patrols were sent to scout the surrounding area, one of which discovered the body of Lieutenant Colonel Owen. The fallen commander was buried with due dignity.

By this time Sanopa had reached Deniki. The intelligence bounty was delivered and news of A Company's exploits was relayed to Cameron with a request for urgent replenishment. Tsukamoto had also received reports that the Australians had snuck into Kokoda behind him. In response, he sent a company of the *1/144th* back along the Kokoda Trail to reclaim the village. The company reached the village at 11.30 am and crept closer and closer to the Australian positions preparing to attack.

A Company's sentries spotted the approaching enemy wearing camouflage uniforms and caked in mud. They held their fire until the Japanese were virtually standing on them and then unleashed with rifles and grenades. The defenders took casualties but were able to withstand the tenacious assault. When no breakthrough was forthcoming, the Japanese occupied positions in close proximity to the Australians. Throughout the day and into the evening, they sniped and fired intermittent shots, punctuating the lulls between more concerted attempts at forcing a breakthrough. The repeated failures to crack A Company caused angst within the Japanese ranks. Platoon commander Second Lieutenant Hirano wrote, 'Every day I am losing my men, and I could not restrain tears of bitterness.'

The next day, 10 August, the Japanese again harassed A Company but remained unable to force the Australians off the Kokoda escarpment. The fighting intensified as each successive thrust increased in intensity. A Company continued to resist, watching anxiously for the resupply that never materialised. Early morning patrols launched from Maroubra Force Headquarters in Deniki had been unable to reach Symington and air reconnaissance could not verify with certainty that A Company still occupied Kokoda. As a result aircraft did not drop supplies and refrained from strafing the attacking Japanese.

Symington was beginning to doubt that his men could hold their ground much longer. Without resupply and reinforcement the position was untenable. At 5.30 pm the Japanese launched a massive assault, throwing everything they had at the exhausted Australians. But still A Company remained anchored to the escarpment, a testament to the discipline and resolve exhibited by these men. Soldiers with gunshot wounds remained at their post, aware that there was no-one to replace them if they left the line. Private William Troeth passed out after being shot three times through the shoulder, jaw and hand. Having regained consciousness, Troeth required a blood transfusion to survive the severe shock and blood loss. He responded to the treatment and rejoined the defence, winning the admiration of the men around him.

The perimeter held firm until 7.00 pm when Symington decided he could no longer hold Kokoda. One by one, A Company's platoons began withdrawing down the western edge of the escarpment. Negotiating the dangerous wire bridge that spanned Madi Creek to the west of the escarpment, they crossed the airstrip and managed to reach the relative safety of the jungle on the far side. The weary Australians rested there for the night, thankful that the Japanese did not pursue and contest their withdrawal.

Criticism has been levelled at Tsukamoto's command, suggesting he should have sent more than one company to recapture Kokoda. Some Japanese veterans implied that their commander was drunk which may have affected his judgement. In Tsukamoto's defence, he may have been reluctant to detach too large a force to move back and recapture Kokoda when he knew there was still a sizeable Australian force towards his front in Deniki.

The major consequence of the Second Battle for Kokoda was that the Australian offensive — the first during the Kokoda campaign — prompted the Japanese to overestimate the number of Australians opposing them. A Company's daring capture of Kokoda, coupled with its stout resistance once the village was occupied, was particularly effective in delaying the Japanese attack on Deniki. In turn this stalled the overall Japanese advance to Port Moresby, the success of which was predicated on speed. The timing of this setback, which coincided with the landing of American Marines on Guadalcanal, caused ripples that reverberated across the south-west Pacific all the way back to Lieutenant General Hyakutake Harukichi at *17th Army Headquarters* in Rabaul. Despite criticism that Cameron's bold manoeuvre was unnecessary, it surprised the Japanese and led to a rethink of Japanese strategy in the entire theatre.

The Kokoda Trail between the Kokoda escarpment and Deniki (M. Rifat).

Chapter 5
DENIKI

The Battle of Deniki was relatively short, lasting little more than 24 hours. It was notable for the fact that this was the first time during the Kokoda campaign that the Australians were able to concentrate more than a single company in the same battlespace.

On 11 August, as the Second Battle for Kokoda petered out, Major Cameron was in Deniki still trying to contact Captain Symington's A Company. Presuming A Company still held Kokoda, NGF sent a message to Cameron telling him that supplies would be air-dropped the following morning, barring inclement weather or confirmation that the village had been lost. Not long after this, A Company's fate was revealed. A native runner arrived in Deniki bearing a message for Cameron from Symington. The message stated that A Company was in the hills to the west of Deniki, struggling on a circuitous route to rejoin Maroubra Force. Symington reported that the Japanese were active and estimated their strength in the Yodda Valley at somewhere between 1000 and 2000 troops.

Cameron was alarmed by Symington's grim assessment. While it was considerably inflated, the result of the difficulty in determining enemy numbers in the dense foliage of the jungle, it appeared to corroborate what Maroubra Force could already observe. From its vantage point overlooking the Yodda Valley, large groups of Japanese soldiers were seen marching out of Kokoda in the direction of Deniki. Cameron realised that an attack was impending.

The Yodda Valley from Deniki. The Kokoda airstrip is clearly visible in the centre of the photo (M. Rifat, NAA006).

Cameron relayed an urgent signal through NGF to the Allied Air Force requesting close air support. But heavy cloud cover and the time required to arm the bombers saw the Air Force refuse Cameron's request. Worse still, the telephone line to Port Moresby worked erratically. As a consequence, the message that Kokoda had been abandoned was not received in Port Moresby until the afternoon of 12 August, after aircraft had already dropped the supplies that Symington had so desperately sought several days earlier straight into the hands of the grateful Japanese.

While events were stirring near Deniki, early August saw an increase in momentum in Port Moresby as the Australians reacted to the burgeoning threat posed by the *Nankai Shitai*. The 53rd Battalion (militia) was ordered to cross the Kokoda Trail to augment Maroubra Force and set out one company at a time from 12 August. Maroubra Force's first batch of AIF units was also being marshalled. In early August Brigadier Arnold Potts had arrived in New Guinea ahead of his 21st Brigade and, by 14 August, the brigade was camped at Itiki in the southern foothills of the Owen Stanleys. These experienced soldiers were veterans of the Syrian campaign. Combat-hardened and fit, they busied themselves with final battle preparations before the 2/14th and 2/16th battalions received orders to march to Kokoda on 16 August. Potts' final battalion, the 2/27th Battalion, would be held back to protect Port Moresby in case the city was directly attacked.

Early August also saw the arrival of senior Australian commanders in Port Moresby. On 11 August Lieutenant General Rowell flew in from Australia, having been appointed GOC NGF. He replaced Major General Morris who remained in Port Moresby as GOC ANGAU. Also arriving was Major General Arthur 'Tubby' Allen, GOC 7th Division.

Major General Arthur 'Tubby' Allen, GOC 7th Division, seated next to a portrait painted by Official War Artist William Dargie. Allen had been decorated for service during the Great War and had remained active in the Australian militia during the inter-war years (AWM023271).

As the Divisional Commander of the 21st Brigade, Allen had the opportunity to speak to its members before they began crossing the Kokoda Trail. In a sign that the terrain of the Trail was not yet understood, Allen told the company commanders to '… rush forward and sit on "The Gap" … The Owen Stanleys are impassable.' Allen was wrong. The Owen Stanleys were decidedly passable, and Lieutenant Colonel Tsukamoto was ready to prove this now that his rear was secure with Kokoda safely back in Japanese hands. He consolidated the *1/144th Battalion* in front of Deniki where it was poised to strike.

Major Cameron had reorganised his companies to meet the imminent attack. With A Company having moved to Eora Creek Village for recuperation, E Company was ordered forward to Deniki to replace its sister company. The Australian dispositions for the battle were, from left to right: E Company, C Company and then D Company. E Company arrived from Isurava at 5.00 pm and was forced to occupy its position in darkness, the men denied the opportunity to properly scope the ground. This would prove pivotal, as E Company's position — on a prominent blunt-nosed spur with the high ground of the battlefield to the left — would attract the bulk of Japanese attention. As the rain pelted down, the nervous Australians were ordered to stand to.

Tsukamoto waited until 9.50 am on the morning of 13 August before launching his attack along the breadth of the Australian line. C Company in the centre was tested, but it was the unblooded E Company on the left flank that absorbed the heaviest fighting. Captain William Merritt, OC E Company, later wrote that the Japanese came at his company 'up the hill, four or five abreast, in shorts and helmets.' Having not had the opportunity to reconnoitre the position, an entire section at the forefront of the company fell wounded within the first hour. Thompson sub machine-guns (Tommy guns) and grenades were used to stymie this initial onslaught.

The Japanese tactic involved shooting randomly in the direction of the Australians, hoping this would provoke a response which would betray their location. The Australians countered this ploy with fire discipline, holding their triggers until they were able to visually identify targets. Private Norm Downey recalled: 'One lesson we learned very quickly was that firing of automatic weapons could prove to be a one-way ticket to the "Pearly Gates" unless we shifted position very smartly after firing.'

At midday, during a brief interlude in the fighting, the unmistakeable sound of rattling mess tins was heard by Lieutenant Don Simonson, OC 20 Platoon in E Company. Crawling forward of his platoon, Simonson was astonished to discover that two groups of Japanese soldiers had taken a break from the battle to have lunch. The meal was short-lived. Simonson broke up the party with grenades and decommissioned two machine-guns. This action saw him awarded the Military Cross (MC) and win the respect of his men; said Downey, 'although at the time we reckoned he was a bloody twit for taking the risks he did, we all admired him.'

Fighting continued into the afternoon as heavy rain fell and a thick fog engulfed the mountainside. The men were tired and uncomfortable in the miserable conditions and

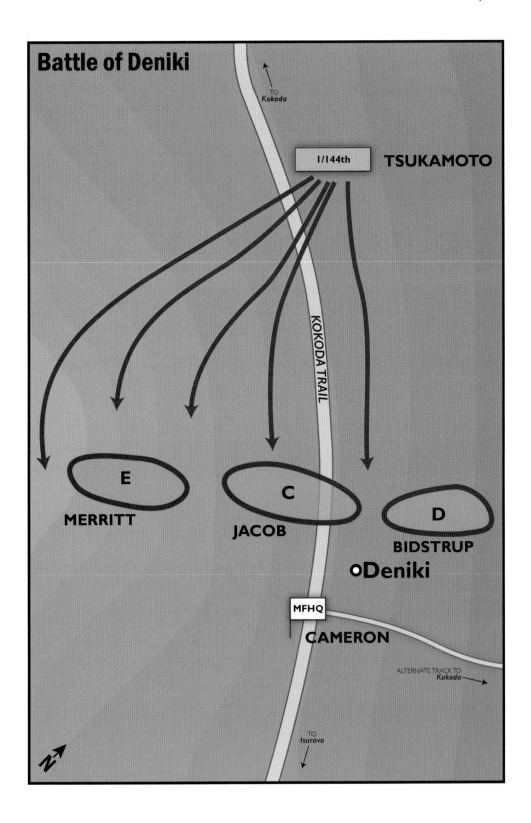

sporadic gunfire kept them occupied until 1.00 am. Adding further to the discomfort was the discovery of Japanese troops on the Trail behind their position. While the small number of enemy in this location suggested it was a scouting party, the fact they were there at all was unsettling.

Members of the 39th Battalion making their way south along the Kokoda Trail, each with gunshot wounds sustained at the Battle of Deniki. Each man had to walk for almost six days to reach the hospital and receive treatment (AWM026320).

Early on the morning of 14 August, the Japanese attacked with fresh gusto. Again it was the Australian left flank that bore the brunt. The Japanese moved above and behind E Company, encircling its position and isolating one of Merritt's platoons. Maroubra Force was now under attack from multiple directions and in grave danger. Casualties in E Company had already forced a tightening of perimeters, and C Company was sustaining blistering fire from enemy mortars. Cameron made the decision to withdraw higher into the mountains to Isurava. He signalled Port Moresby stating, 'We have done our best.'

The retreat to Isurava, the first retreat of many in the mountains, was completed with mixed results. Although it was conducted skilfully and in stages with one platoon moving backwards and holding a position before the remainder of the force moved through that platoon and so on, a large cache of supplies and the personal belongings of the men were left behind. Nonetheless, the Australians were confident that, despite giving ground, they were still close enough to the Yodda Valley to use Isurava as a launching pad to reclaim Kokoda and its precious airstrip.

Chapter 6
THE BATTLE OF ISURAVA-ABUARI – THE FIRST PHASE

Having retreated from Deniki, Maroubra Force pushed on to Isurava which became the site of the Kokoda campaign's first major battle. Allied Command had believed that reinforcing Maroubra Force with the 21st Brigade and the 53rd Battalion would reverse the succession of local defeats. What they did not count on was the fact that the Japanese had also been significantly reinforced. Major General Horii was now in Papua personally directing the *Nankai Shitai*. His force had been enlarged first by the arrival of the remaining battalions of Colonel Kusonose Masao's *144th Regiment*, the *2/144th* and *3/144th*, and then by the appearance of two battalions from Colonel Yazawa Kiyoshi's *41st Regiment*, the *2/41st* and *3/41st*.

In the lead-up to the Battle of Isurava-Abuari, the command of Maroubra Force changed three times. First, Lieutenant Colonel Ralph Honner replaced Major Cameron as CO of the 39th Battalion and of Maroubra Force. Honner, a veteran of the North African, Middle Eastern and Greek campaigns, was exactly the type of highly qualified and unflappable leader the 39th Battalion needed. His orders were to hold the Japanese on the northern side of the Owen Stanleys until relieved by the experienced AIF battalions which were on their way. A former schoolteacher, Honner made an immediate positive impression on his men and they felt confident that he had their welfare at heart. Among his inspired moves on assuming command was his decision to retain B Company. While Cameron still advocated the company's disbandment, Honner felt that this would be 'the final lethal act of contempt, destroying where I should be building.' To motivate the company, he allocated it the most dangerous sector of the Isurava defence — the 'post of honour' as he termed it — guarding the high ground on the left where the enemy was expected to attack.

Lieutenant Colonel Ralph Honner, CO of the 39th Battalion. A schoolteacher in civilian life, Honner was the calm and experienced leader the 39th Battalion needed during the Battle of Isurava-Abuari (AWM005638).

Brigadier Porter, commander of the 30th Brigade, then took temporary command of Maroubra Force until responsibility passed to Brigadier Potts who arrived forward on 23 August. Potts brought with him the 2/14th and the 2/16th battalions, and had orders to conduct aggressive operations to recapture Kokoda. It did not take Potts long to realise the impossibility of these orders, as Maroubra Force was beset with problems, the most glaring of which was the acute shortage of supplies.

Brigadier Arnold Potts, commander of the 21st Brigade. The Kokoda campaign was Potts' first assignment as a brigade commander. It would prove a stern test of his leadership and mettle (AWM099103).

Before the 21st Brigade had set out along the Kokoda Trail, NGF had promised Potts that 40,000 rations would be positioned at Myola awaiting his brigade's arrival. However, on reaching Myola, Potts was aghast to find that a paltry 8000 rations had been delivered. Instead of being greeted by a 25-day reserve for his 2000 troops — including stocks of small arms ammunition — only five days' rations awaited him, one-fifth of what was required. The shortage of supplies prevented any force larger than a company being based at the staging camps forward of Myola. This hamstrung Potts as he was forced to hold his AIF battalions in Myola until sufficient reserves could be stockpiled.

MYOLA

Myola is the name given to two dry lake beds situated high in the Owen Stanley Ranges. The lake beds are visually spectacular and stand out starkly against the dense jungle that surrounds them. During the Kokoda campaign, Myola was a location of great strategic importance because the flat, treeless ground allowed the Allies to use the area for air drops and later as a rudimentary airfield.

Following the loss of Kokoda Village, the problem of supplying a large army in the mountains assumed major proportions. There were never sufficient native porters to meet demand. Supply by land thus had to be supplemented from the air. Air drops were conducted at Nauro, Efogi and Kagi. However, when the Australians reached the northern end of the Kokoda Trail, an air-drop site north of Kagi had to be established to facilitate the continued movement of supplies to the front line.

ANGAU's Lieutenant Bert Kienzle recalled having seen the two dry lake beds while flying over the Owen Stanleys prior to the war. The lake beds were known to the local tribes, although they were frightened to approach the area, believing it to be a place of evil spirits. Kienzle received permission from his superiors to investigate the lake beds. Acting on local knowledge, he explored the headwaters of the Eora Creek and discovered the dry lakes. He named them 'Myola' after the wife of his friend and CO, Sydney Elliot Smith. The name Myola, an aboriginal word meaning 'break of day', proved a fitting choice, with Kienzle hopeful that using the Myola lake beds as an airfield would signify the beginning of a new opportunity for Maroubra Force. For many years after, his wife Meryl continued to ask him in jest why the lakes had not been named after her!

A surgical team in front of the tents of the main dressing station of the 2/4th Field Ambulance at Myola 1. The bare lake beds are surrounded by hills crowned with jungle growth as can be seen in the background. Myola's bareness is an anomaly, occurring nowhere else along the length of the Kokoda Trail (AWMP02424.107).

The shortage of supplies led to recriminations. Lieutenant General Rowell wrote that 'the closest scrutiny [had] established' that the supplies had been despatched from Port Moresby, and if they were not at Myola, it was the result of misdirected air drops. Historian Stuart Braga concurs, writing that Potts himself noted the unprofessional and unenthusiastic attitude of logistics staff along the Trail. Braga concludes, 'It is hard to see such uncooperative people making much effort to recover supplies dropped anywhere that was inconvenient.' The Official Historian Dudley McCarthy disagrees, blaming faulty staff work at NGF Headquarters for the missing supplies. McCarthy considered that it defied belief that such a large quantity of supplies could have simply vanished. He reasoned that the Myola lake beds stand out so obviously from the surrounding jungle that it would have been near impossible for so many of the air drops to have deviated from their target.

In an effort to address the flawed supply system, Potts replaced the inefficient logistics staff with his own staff. Further, Major General Allen repeatedly emphasised to Potts the necessity of withdrawing the 39th Battalion from Isurava, reasoning it was the only option to alleviate the supply shortage. Allen also stressed that stockpiling reserves of supplies was essential to sustain an offensive. Indeed, as late as 25 August, Potts still planned to march the 2/14th directly along the Trail to attack and secure Kokoda. As it happened, that plan was rapidly overtaken by events.

The Battle of Isurava-Abuari was fought on two battlefields separated by the striking gorge carved by the powerful Eora Creek through the northern end of the Owen Stanleys. On either side of the gorge are two prominent north-south running ridgelines. West of the gorge on the Isurava ridgeline was wartime Isurava (the village was re-established further to the north following the Kokoda campaign). The wartime village was situated between two small creeks, Front and Rear, which both feed down the slope into the much larger Eora Creek. Moving south through Isurava, the Kokoda Trail heads to the next village which is Alola. While the Trail continues south from Alola, a separate track branches off at the village, descending to Eora Creek which it crosses, before rising on the eastern side of the gorge. This track then skirts the Abuari ridgeline in a northerly direction, roughly parallel to the Kokoda Trail, passing through the villages of Abuari and Missima.

The 39th Battalion was entrenched in Isurava, while Maroubra Force Headquarters and the 53rd Battalion were concentrated in Alola. Horii's strategy was based on a two-pronged assault. He would use the *1/144th* to pin the Australians in Isurava and draw in all their available reserves, before sending the *3/144th* in a wide flanking westerly move to encircle the position. On the Abuari ridgeline, the *2/144th Battalion*, commanded by Major Horie Tadashi, had orders to encircle and annihilate the Australians in Alola.

In the days preceding the battle, a number of patrols from both sides pushed forward seeking information on the other's movements. Potts instructed his patrols to avoid becoming overly committed in an effort to hide the strength of his force. The tempo of contacts escalated until 26 August when wholesale fighting broke out and, around midday, the Japanese artillery began shelling Isurava. The battle had begun.

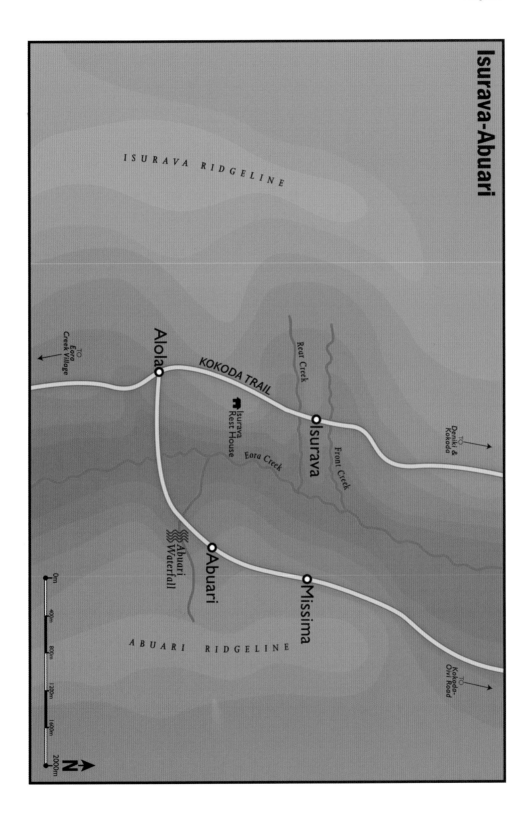

Isurava-Abuari

Eora Creek cuts a deep gorge through the northern end of the Owen Stanleys, as seen in this photograph looking north from Alola. Isurava ridgeline is on the left of the picture, Abuari ridgeline is on the right (N. Anderson, NAA007).

The first significant actions comprised attacks on Australian forward observation posts on either side of the gorge. On the Isurava ridgeline, approximately three-quarters of an hour's walk north of Isurava, a forward observation post manned by Lieutenant Robert Sword and two platoons from the 39th Battalion was subjected to an attack that lasted five hours. Sword's men fought with great vigour, withstanding the relentless assault.

Events on the Abuari ridgeline where Horie's men attacked a forward observation post in Missima were more ominous. The post was destroyed, largely because of poor patrolling by the 53rd Battalion. Potts was incensed and believed his earlier instructions to avoid over-commitment during contacts had been interpreted 'liberally' as, in some cases, the patrols had failed to even carry weapons. He spoke to the CO of the 53rd Battalion, Lieutenant Colonel Ward, and ordered him to take immediate action to rectify the damage. With Missima lost, he told Ward to move a company forward to occupy Abuari. Ward gave this task to Captain Thomas Cairns' B Company, which moved out at 5.50 pm.

Abuari ridgeline, as seen from Alola. Eora Creek rushes through the gorge that separates the parallel ridgelines (M. Rifat, NAA008).

In response to the 53rd's perceived failings, Potts signalled Allen and requested that the 2/27th Battalion be sent forward from Port Moresby as a fighting reserve since the 53rd's training and discipline was 'below the standard necessary for action'. Allen could not agree to the request as a large Japanese invasion force had just landed at Milne Bay. While the outcome of the Battle of Milne Bay remained uncertain, the 2/27th was needed to defend Port Moresby. Should the Japanese succeed in breaking through at Milne Bay, the approach to Port Moresby would be open.

The next morning, 27 August, the perilous position on the Abuari ridgeline deteriorated further as problems with the 53rd Battalion reached a head. Brigade Headquarters did not know whether Cairns had occupied Abuari the night before, and Potts was troubled by the lack of information from the battalion as a whole. Potts ordered Ward to secure the Abuari ridgeline by retaking Missima. Ward delegated this task to Captain Cuthbert King, who was ordered to move his D Company through Cairns to recapture Missima. The sense of urgency at Maroubra Force Headquarters was evidently not registering however, as King procrastinated and his company's move forward was delayed.

It was not until late in the afternoon that Potts was notified that Cairns and King had succeeded in clearing Abuari and were pushing on to Missima. But this information was erroneous, and the consequences were devastating. Ward, in possession of the same positive report that Potts had received, marched towards Missima with his adjutant, Lieutenant Rowland Logan, to take personal command. Close to Abuari they walked straight into a Japanese ambush and were killed. Worse still, Japanese troops were now reportedly beyond Abuari and making for the Eora Creek crossing. The difference between the glowing report of success and the reality of a Japanese advance on Alola sent Maroubra Force Headquarters into a spin.

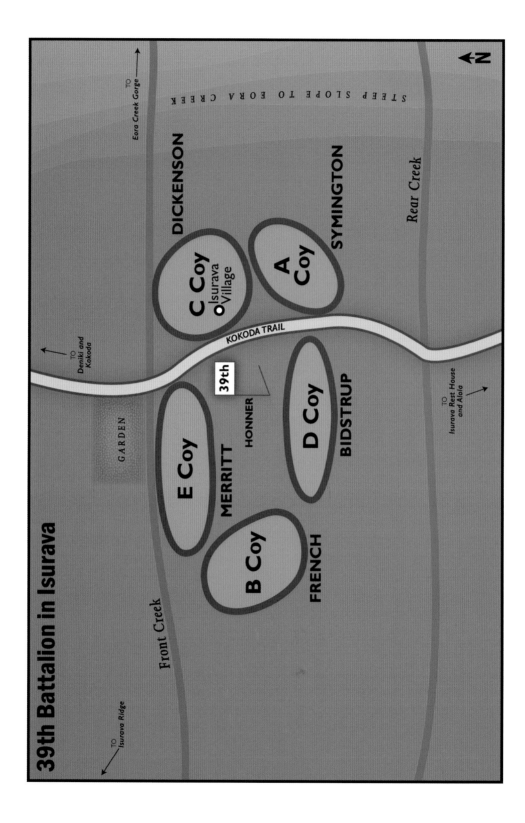

Potts was taking no chances. Major Charles Hawkins, second-in-command of the 53rd Battalion, was elevated to battalion commander to replace Ward and Potts ordered him to immediately secure the creek crossing and Abuari. He then instructed the company commanders of the 2/16th, with whom he had conferred in Alola, to return to their companies further south along the Kokoda Trail and march them forward with the greatest urgency the next morning to bolster the brittle right flank.

Who reported that Abuari had been cleared when it obviously remained a hive of Japanese activity? And what had happened to Cairns and King? The records do not specify who had reported Abuari as clear, but it appears most likely that the source was the 53rd Battalion's Intelligence Officer. On the morning of 27 August Potts, irritated that repeated requests for situation reports from the 53rd Battalion had elicited none, demanded that the required information be sent to his headquarters immediately. To this end, the battalion's Intelligence Officer was ordered forward at 11.30 am to investigate the situation near Abuari. There is no further reference in the records to this mission until an entry appears reporting Abuari clear. It is possible that, under pressure to satisfy Potts' forceful and time-critical demand, the Intelligence Officer may have erred — with tragic results.

As for Cairns and King, obtaining a clear picture of what had happened to these companies during the day is difficult. Rumours suggest that they disintegrated on first contact with the enemy, the men fleeing into the bush. This appears the most likely outcome as, by nightfall, almost 70 men from these companies remained missing. Forty filtered back to Australian lines during the night, however their accounts were sketchy and mired in confusion. It appears that Cairns and King were simply given orders beyond their capabilities. Lacking offensive spirit and with troops in poor physical condition, they crumbled against a much stronger foe.

With the track along the Abuari ridgeline left virtually open, Potts feared that the Japanese would make a decisive move on Alola. Strangely, that never occurred. Major Horie's failure to exploit the 53rd Battalion's capitulation gave Maroubra Force a crucial reprieve. Horie's inactivity remains a mystery. Historian Peter Williams suggests that the 53rd's fighting performance was sufficient to engender a degree of caution, stalling the *2/144th*'s advance. This theory seems unlikely, because Williams has mistaken the date of Cairns and King's defeat as having occurred two days later, on 29 August, by which time the 2/16th Battalion had already moved forward and replaced the militia. The most plausible explanation for the *2/144th*'s inaction was fatigue. When the battalion landed in Papua on 19 August it was immediately marched 130 kilometres in just seven days to join the *Nankai Shitai*'s offensive — an urgency driven by a need to prevent the Australians retreating deeper into the Owen Stanleys. This strenuous trek saw a large number of men fall behind. Many were still catching up as the battle commenced. Thus it seems likely that Horie was waiting for these men to catch up before committing his battalion to an attack on Alola.

The fighting on the Isurava ridgeline throughout 27 August was no less intense and Lieutenant Sword's forward post came under renewed attack. Sword remained upbeat, reporting that his men were in 'good heart'. Potts told him to hold the post as long as possible, but as the day progressed, Sword realised that this was pointless. An increasing number of Japanese were simply bypassing his position and filling the void between his post and Isurava. He ordered his men back to Isurava, but with the direct route along the Kokoda Trail blocked, the only possible escape route was westwards and upwards. Reaching the apex of the Isurava ridgeline, he then swung his men south where they met Lieutenant William Pentland, who had earlier been ordered to patrol along the ridgeline to monitor Japanese movements. Pentland's patrol merged with Sword's two platoons and moved south along the ridgeline towards the Australian lines.

With Sword's forward observation post abandoned, Japanese troops began to assault the 39th's main position in Isurava. After initially probing Captain Merritt's position in the centre, the Japanese troops attacked en masse across the ravine on which his defence was based. Attacking in waves, they rushed through his porous line. Even during this heavy fighting there were remarkable tales of humour. Merritt recalled: 'I was shaving in the river behind the perimeter when the attack came in. The CO, also washing there, grinned and said, "Captain Merritt, would you go up to your Company when you've finished your shave? The Japs have just broken through your perimeter." Honner was the coolest man I've ever seen.' Merritt was suitably shocked into action and ran to take charge of his company, his face still half-shaven.

On the high ground to Merritt's left, B Company was also being pummelled. The bodies of Japanese littered the ground in front of B Company's position, but still the attacks persisted. B Company's second-in-command, Lieutenant Garland, warned 39th Battalion Headquarters that the situation was dire and, unless reinforcement came swiftly, they would be unable to hold much longer. Honner told Garland that they must hold on at all costs, as nothing stood between B Company and Battalion Headquarters.

The desperately needed reinforcements soon arrived in the form of the 2/14th Battalion. One by one, companies from this battalion arrived at Isurava and replaced companies of the 39th in the front line. Captain Harold (Gerry) Dickenson's C Company was the first to arrive, having taken responsibility for the front right position at Isurava at dusk on 26 August. Then, on 27 August, shortly after Garland's request for help, Captain Claude Nye's B Company arrived. Nye's timely arrival enabled Honner to reinforce his own B Company. The appearance of the AIF troops provided a much-needed tonic for the embattled militia. Honner recalled: 'I do not remember anything more heartening than the sight of their confident deployment. Their splendid physique and bearing, and their cool, automatic efficiency ... made a lasting impression on me.'

By sundown on 27 August, Captain Rod Cameron's D Company of the 2/14th had arrived and replaced Merritt at the centre of the Isurava defence. This allowed the exhausted troops of the 39th to form a reserve and occupy the rear positions in the village. With the majority of the 2/14th now holding the front line in Isurava, plus A Company of the 2/14th in Alola as a reserve, Honner noted positively that there were now '... four times as many men holding our front and flanks as there had been the previous day.'

By contrast, Horii was displeased with the execution of the battle and, in particular, by the performance of the *1/144th*. Tsukamoto's battalion had been in Papua longer than any other from the *Nankai Shitai*. Continuous action and rising casualties had battered the battalion's morale. As a captured diary belonging to a Japanese soldier revealed, 'I don't know whether it's because the No.1 Battalion [*1/144th*] have had so many casualties but all ranks of commanders seem to have lost some of their offensive spirit.' A company from the *3/144th* was attached to the *1/44th* to boost its zeal for battle.

Despite the disappointing results, Horii was ready to activate the next part of his battle plan. He ordered Lieutenant Colonel Kuwada Gen'ichirô, CO of the *3/144th Battalion*, to commence an expansive movement around the western periphery of Isurava with his remaining companies. It was the first offensive move of the campaign for the *3/144th*, and would prove one of the critical factors that loosened Maroubra Force's grip on Isurava.

Chapter 7

THE BATTLE OF ISURAVA-ABUARI – THE SECOND PHASE

The second phase of the Battle of Isurava-Abuari began as both Maroubra Force and the *Nankai Shitai* brought fresh units into the fighting.

Brigadier Potts remained hopeful of holding the Japanese as the remaining elements of the 21st Brigade reached the front and replaced the militia. On 28 August both his battalion commanders reached the front — Lieutenant Colonel Albert Caro, CO of the 2/16th and Lieutenant Colonel Arthur Key, CO of the 2/14th. Caro's battalion would cement the Australians' right flank on the Abuari ridgeline, while at noon Key took responsibility for the left flank and the defence of Isurava from Lieutenant Colonel Honner. With its relief by the 2/14th, the 39th Battalion was to leave Isurava and return to Port Moresby in accordance with Major General Allen's earlier instructions. But Honner was having none of that. Certain that a single battalion alone could not hold Isurava, he said as much to Key and the two then persuaded Potts to allow the 39th to remain in Isurava in reserve behind the 2/14th.

On the Japanese side, Major General Horii initiated the next step in his plan to defeat the Australians. With the *1/144th* holding the 2/14th at Front Creek, Lieutenant Colonel Kuwada's *3/144th Battalion* swung high around the Isurava ridgeline during the night of 27/28 August. This proved difficult, as manoeuvring through the thick jungle in darkness saw Kuwada's companies become separated and, ultimately, fail in their attempt to move in behind the Australians. As Kokoda veteran Corporal Gilbert Simmons of the 2/25th Battalion would later attest, 'You can't move in jungle at night, it's only jet ink black … you lose complete orientation, you don't know where you are going.'

With Kuwada making little progress, Horii maintained his harassment of the Australians defending Front Creek. At dawn the Japanese mountain guns opened fire and blasted away for several hours. It was a massive bombardment, the heaviest of the campaign thus far. At 8.00 am the Japanese troops rushed forward, initially targeting Captain Dickenson's position, yelling madly as they attacked. Toshiya Akizawa later recalled, 'All we could do was leave the place we were in and attack up the hill. And we were being told from behind, "Attack! Attack!" So there was no courage. Only without thinking we attacked and attacked.'

Captain Nye's company, defending the high ground, was also being pressured, the brunt of the attack absorbed by Lieutenant George Moore's 11 Platoon. He and his men fought with great determination and prevented the Japanese from breaching the line, but not before Moore was killed. The Japanese attacks continued throughout the day, constantly chipping

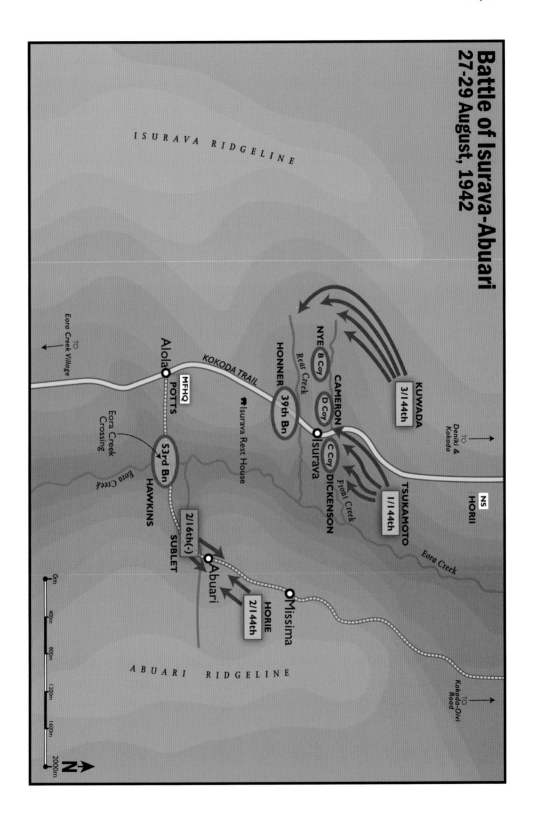

Battle of Isurava-Abuari
27-29 August, 1942

ISURAVA RIDGELINE

TO
Eora Creek Village

Alola

KOKODA TRAIL

MFHQ
POTTS

Eora Creek
Crossing

53rd Bn

Eora Creek

HAWKINS

SUBLET

2/16th(-)

Abuari

2/14th

HONNER
39th Bn

Rear Creek

NYE B Coy

D Coy

CAMERON

Isurava

C Coy DICKENSON

Front Creek

KUWADA
3/144th

TSUKAMOTO
1/144th

TO
Deniki &
Kokoda

NS
HORII

Eora Creek

Isurava Rest House

HORIE
2/144th

Missima

ABUARI RIDGELINE

TO
Kokoda-Oivi
Road

0m
400m
800m
1200m
1600m
2000m

N

away at the 2/14th's perimeter. At 3.30 pm a major surge was launched at Captain Rod Cameron's D Company in the centre. The line came close to being penetrated in several places and the position was in danger of being overrun until Lieutenant George Pearce's platoon from A Company in Alola dashed forward to counter-attack, preventing a breakthrough.

By nightfall, Key felt that the situation was in hand. His battalion optimistically estimated they had inflicted some 350 casualties on the enemy against their own confirmed casualties of four dead and 13 wounded. Almost all the members of the 2/14th Battalion had now arrived at the battlefield. With the arrival of Captain Phil Rhoden and Headquarters Company the next day, 542 of the 544 men who had set out from Itiki on 16 August had reached Isurava. This was a remarkable feat and speaks volumes for the physical condition of the AIF soldiers. However, Key's confidence was not to last.

On the dull, cloudy morning of 29 August, the battle escalated in intensity. The most vulnerable Australian sector remained Nye's position on the far left edge. The *3/144th* had once again navigated through the night in an attempt to move around and behind the Australians. From first light, Kuwada's *7th Company* launched more attacks against this position and each of Nye's platoons was sorely tested.

Lieutenant Lindsay Mason's platoon, guarding the westernmost border of the 2/14th's line, was having a torrid time. Throughout the day, the platoon fought a running battle with the Japanese, the ground to their front exchanged four times. When the balance of the *3/144th* in the shape of its *8th Company* joined the attack during the afternoon, the weight of Japanese numbers became impossible to counter. As the few surviving members of the platoon began to withdraw, Corporal Charlie McCallum provided a rearguard. McCallum, already wounded three times, used brute strength to fire a Bren gun with one arm and a Tommy gun with the other. He engaged the attackers, shooting them down as his comrades reached safety. When McCallum rejoined them, an estimated 40 enemy dead lay in his wake.

At the centre of B Company to Mason's right, Lieutenant Herbert (Butch) Bissett's platoon was also under siege. Despite withstanding 11 successive attacks throughout the day, casualties increased steadily, including Bissett, who was wounded in the torso by machine-gun fire. Members of his platoon carried him to safety, but the popular leader succumbed to his wounds during the night.

Further to the east down Isurava ridgeline, Captain Cameron's D Company was also subjected to continuous attack throughout the morning. Ably assisted by a platoon from A Company, the Australians expended an enormous quantity of ammunition and grenades in holding the Japanese at bay. When enemy soldiers managed to infiltrate the lines, bayonets were used to force them back. Captain Sydney Buckler, OC A Company, sensed the gravity of the situation and personally led a platoon from his company forward, fortifying the battalion's centre.

Below the Kokoda Trail, waves of assaults also targeted Dickenson's C Company. With the company's line dissolving, two groups of reinforcements rushed forward to galvanise the position. Lieutenant William Cox led a platoon from A Company, and Sergeant Ralph

Thompson moved forward with a group from Headquarters Company. Cox was quickly killed, forcing Corporal Lindsay Bear to take command. Bear's courage was obvious for all to see as he shot up to 15 enemy soldiers at point-blank range with a Bren gun, despite three bullet wounds to his legs.

Private Bruce Kingsbury, recipient of the first Victoria Cross awarded for an action on Australian territory (AWM100112).

Even with this reinforcement, the onslaught against C Company continued. The entire Isurava defence was under threat. Desperate to restore the position, Lieutenant Jack Clements led a counter-attack cobbled together from the remnants of his own C Company platoon and the survivors of Bear and Thompson's platoons. It was during this counter-attack that Private Bruce Kingsbury displayed outstanding gallantry. Kingsbury charged out from cover alone, racing towards the attacking Japanese firing a Bren gun from his hip. His bold action caused the attackers to run off in terror, many shot down by his accurate fire. As he paused to reload next to a large, distinctive rock, a Japanese sniper took aim and killed him with a single shot. The fearlessness of Kingsbury's move enabled the Australians to regroup and lock down Dickenson's perimeter. The Victoria Cross (VC) posthumously awarded to Kingsbury was the first for an action on Australian territory.

The memorial to Private Bruce Kingsbury, VC, at Isurava. Kingsbury was probably killed on the lower side of the large, distinctive rock in the background. Some eyewitness accounts claim that the Japanese soldier who shot Kingsbury was actually on top of the rock (D. Crosbie, NAA009).

By this stage, virtually every available man had been sent forward. Key's reserve (A Company) had moved up one platoon at a time to act as a tourniquet whenever the line ruptured. The 39th Battalion was dead on its feet. Such desperate circumstances produced many supreme acts of selflessness. Lieutenant Stewart Johnston, who was escorting a group of badly wounded 39th men south along the Kokoda Trail to Myola for treatment, received word of the dire situation in Isurava. Without hesitation, he wheeled the group around and led them back to Isurava, telling Honner, 'We heard the battalion was in trouble so we came back.' Similar grit was displayed by Lieutenant Sword leading the platoons that had been cut off from Maroubra Force when their forward observation post was overwhelmed on the first day of the battle. Having trekked for three days south along Isurava ridgeline without rations, Sword and his band emerged from the jungle at Maroubra Force Headquarters in Alola. 'Reporting patrol back in, Sir,' said Sword laconically, as his men gratefully accepted offers of warm food and coffee. The men enjoyed a brief respite before Sword marched them back to Isurava to rejoin the battle.

Despite this fortitude, mounting casualties and the incessant Japanese attacks on his every sector forced Key to reduce the length of his front line. This saw the high ground — Captain Nye's position — ceded to the Japanese. Kuwada took full advantage and drove forward his attack. Key now considered his battalion in grave danger. Potts assured him that relief would be provided by C and D companies of the 2/16th which he had ordered to attack across the high ground at Isurava the next morning. Key's fears were temporarily assuaged but, by 8.45 pm, he realised the Isurava position was unsustainable. He told Potts that the 2/14th line would not hold and sought permission to withdraw to the Isurava Rest House (the site of several native dwellings and a government rest house) approximately halfway along the Kokoda Trail between Isurava and Alola. Potts agreed, and a general order for withdrawal was given at 9.00 pm.

The withdrawal to the Rest House was remarkably successful given the extreme hazards involved. The Trail was in a terrible condition as tropical downpours had made the ground treacherous underfoot. With the Papuan carriers prohibited from being too close to the fighting, the wounded were stretchered out by the troops themselves. By 2.00 am Maroubra Force had completed its relocation to the Rest House.

Unaware of this dramatic chain of events were two companies from the 2/16th Battalion who were engaged in their own battle with Major Horie's *2/144th Battalion* on the Abuari ridgeline. At Isurava, the action had played out quickly once the AIF had assumed responsibility for the defence on 28 August. The same could not be said for the Abuari ridgeline, which was surprisingly quiet once the AIF took over from the militia. This ridgeline had been the source of greatest concern to Brigadier Potts, particularly following the 53rd Battalion's implosion on 27 August. As a consequence, Potts had ordered the company commanders from the 2/16th to bring their men forward as quickly as possible. Captains Grear McGee and Frank Sublet complied, arriving at Alola on 28 August with their A and B companies respectively. McGee and Sublet were ordered to secure Abuari before pressing as far forward along the Abuari ridgeline as possible. The two companies pushed forward and reached Abuari, finding no sign of the Japanese, and the Australians spent an unexpectedly quiet night in the village.

The next day, 29 August, McGee discovered why Abuari was empty — Horie had moved higher up the Abuari ridgeline, east of the track and Abuari Village. From this position, the *2/144th* was able to observe the Australian line of approach. McGee's A Company assaulted the position without success, taking several casualties. Sublet, who by then had orders from Caro to take command of both companies, moved around McGee in support. Even in partnership, the two companies could make no further inroads, leading Sublet to conclude that the Japanese could only be dislodged by a two-pronged assault. To this end, he ordered his troops to ground and planned an offensive for the next morning, requesting support from a company of the 53rd which would simultaneously attack from the south. In a choice indicative of the lack of alternatives, Captain King's D Company — one of the two companies involved in the 53rd Battalion's fiasco of 27 August — was assigned the task. As direct communication between Sublet and King was not possible, it was agreed that King would move to a spot where he could survey the Japanese positions. From here, his gunfire would act as a signal for Sublet to commence his own attack. King was instructed that this action should not occur before 10.00 am.

Lieutenant Colonel Albert Caro, CO of the 2/16th Battalion, with Captain Frank Sublet on his right. Sublet was Caro's most trusted company commander and later commanded the 2/16th in his own right (AWM026752).

On the morning of 30 August, Sublet was confounded to hear gunfire echoing across Eora gorge prior to 10.00 am. With his own men still preparing for the offensive, Sublet guessed that the noise may have been premature gunfire from King's company. The reality was much worse: the *2/144th* was using heavy machine-guns to fire across the gorge at Maroubra Force Headquarters in Alola. King had become lost in the thick jungle and had yet to reach his attack start point. Sublet decided to launch his offensive alone.

Numerous acts of bravery occurred in the dogged fighting that followed. Perhaps most remarkable was that of Private George Maidment. Witnessing the death of his section leader, Corporal Michael Clarke, Maidment ignored intense rifle and machine-gun fire to collect grenades from Clarke's body before charging up a hill straight towards the Japanese entrenchments. Despite being badly wounded in the chest, he continued to throw grenades until his supply was exhausted. But Maidment was not finished. He then collected a sub machine-gun and stood in the centre of the track engaging the enemy until once again his ammunition was spent. Sublet offered the mortally wounded Maidment assistance, but was 'refused with abuse'. Nevertheless, Sublet later nominated him for a VC, a recommendation that was downgraded and eventually resulted in the award of a Distinguished Conduct Medal — the highest honour below a VC. The downgrade was explained in part by Maidment's mysterious disappearance while being carried back to Myola on a stretcher, and in part by his shadowy history prior to enlistment which included multiple identities and brushes with the law.

While Sublet's offensive was vigorous, it made no meaningful ground against the *2/144th* which was glued to its fighting pits. Around this time Sublet received new orders to withdraw his men through Alola no later than 7.00 pm, as there were grave fears that the Australians would lose control of the village as the night wore on. With events on the Isurava ridgeline largely obscured from those on the Abuari ridgeline, this information must have come as a shock. The catalyst was a major disaster at Isurava Rest House.

Earlier on the same morning of 30 August, the *1/144th* had attacked the 2/14th's former positions in Isurava. Discovering them to be abandoned, they had tentatively pushed forward through the village and along the Kokoda Trail. During the night Kuwada had led the *3/144th* in another attempt to move around the Australians in Isurava by pushing south higher up on Isurava ridge. At daybreak, expecting to find his battalion behind the Australians, Kuwada instead discovered that he was above their left flank in their new position at the Isurava Rest House. A signal was sent for the mountain guns to commence firing on the new position and Kuwada launched his attack. With Maroubra Force under intense bombardment, Potts decided that there was no chance of holding the Rest House and ordered a further retreat.

As preparations for this retreat were underway, the *3/144th* spilled across the Trail behind the Australians, blocking their escape path to Alola. The situation quickly deteriorated when Buckler and Nye's companies in the most northerly positions on the Kokoda Trail — at the rear of the retreating column — came under attack. Maroubra Force was effectively sandwiched between the Japanese attackers. Key ordered Captains Dickenson and Cameron to scale the high ground to the west where Kuwada's attack had originated, and then charge down on the Japanese to clear the route to Alola. This attack did not proceed as planned.

Dickenson became disorientated as he scaled the high ground, and was unsure which direction his company was facing. This was unsurprising given the darkness of the jungle, his inability to see the sun, and the fact that the land is a tangle of tree roots, spurs and ravines. Turning his company to face downhill, he led his men in a frenzied charge towards where he assumed the Japanese to be. Unfortunately the charge was misdirected and, skewing off course, it instead fell on the Australians who were bunched up on the Kokoda Trail waiting to retreat, in addition to the Japanese blocking force. The Australians on the Trail thought they were being attacked by the Japanese and fired back. Large groups of Maroubra Force, including Key and many of his headquarters staff, were separated as men fled off the Trail to escape the savage crossfire. The Japanese blocking force was broken, but the toll of casualties was heavy and many men were isolated from the main body of Maroubra Force.

The impact of this friendly fire is referred to in the 39th Battalion War Diary, and is also mentioned briefly by Raymond Paull in *Retreat from Kokoda*, and in much greater detail by Peter Williams in *The Kokoda Campaign: Myth and Reality*. However, the chaotic final moments of the Battle of Isurava-Abuari appear to have ensured that this unfortunate incident was not widely known. The debacle presents a stark illustration of the extreme difficulty of withdrawing men while under attack by the enemy.

The Kokoda Trail, south of Isurava Rest House and overlooking Alola (N. Anderson, NAA010).

Thus, late in the afternoon of 30 August, as pandemonium ensued near the Isurava Rest House, on the Abuari ridgeline Sublet ordered his men to cease firing and prepare to join the withdrawal. Unable to communicate with all of his sub-units, he simply hoped that the lull in gunfire would alert those platoons not in contact to the impending retreat. Sublet's withdrawal dragged into the night as the two companies moved upstream along Eora Creek to rejoin the remainder of Maroubra Force the next morning.

So ended the Battle of Isurava-Abuari which, while a Japanese victory, was not the outright annihilation that Major General Horii had sought. Horii believed that comprehensively defeating the Australians would open the way for a quick advance across the Owen Stanleys, which was essential if his assault on Port Moresby was to succeed. Delays in the mountains worked to the advantage of the Australians who gained time to move reinforcements forward. In contrast, the Japanese chances of reinforcement were uncertain and almost completely reliant on the outcome of the fighting on Guadalcanal.

The Japanese had expected resistance at Isurava, but not the defiant opposition they had encountered. The arrival of the 21st Brigade added starch to Maroubra Force's defence at the crucial moment. However the disaster at the Isurava Rest House had scattered the 2/14th

Battalion, sending many men into the jungle and forcing them to make their own way back towards Alola in the hope of reconnecting with Maroubra Force. These arduous journeys involved evading capture by a merciless enemy who executed every soldier who had the misfortune of being taken prisoner — including Lieutenant Colonel Key.

Lieutenant Colonel Arthur Key, CO of the 2/14th Battalion. Like all Australians captured during the Kokoda campaign, Key was executed by the Japanese (P05533.028).

Did the Australians stand any chance of winning the Battle of Isurava-Abuari? They certainly had no hope of defeating the Japanese in Isurava, where they were outgunned and outflanked by a fresh battalion with the advantage of occupying the high ground. On the eastern side of Eora gorge, the Australians found themselves on the back foot because of the early failings of the 53rd Battalion. Once that initial setback was overcome — in part because the *2/144th* failed to exploit its early success — it is possible that Sublet may have been able to dislodge the *2/144th* from Abuari ridgeline, but only if King's company had taken part in the offensive of 30 August as planned. That said, the chain of events at Isurava and at the Rest House unfolded so rapidly that the action on the Abuari ridgeline was largely inconsequential by that stage.

Brigadier Potts noted in his post-operation report, 'At no time were the 2/14th and 2/16th Australian infantry battalions ever intact and available for a concerted operation, wholly and solely due to the delays occasioned by supply.' This is the crux of Maroubra Force's defeat at the Battle of Isurava-Abuari: the lack of accumulated supplies at Myola prevented Potts moving his AIF troops to Isurava earlier. As a consequence, by the time he pushed them forward, the Japanese had taken the initiative and the Australians were never able to regain it.

Chater 8

THE FIGHTING WITHDRAWAL

One of the most iconic memories of the Australian experience during the Kokoda campaign was the fighting withdrawal, conducted between 31 August and 5 September. Its purpose was to delay the Japanese until Australian reinforcements could arrive and a suitable position for a pitched defence could be located. A fighting withdrawal involves giving ground to the enemy while maintaining contact to delay their advance and buy time. It is distinct from a retreat in which contact is purposely broken and avoided. By its very nature, a fighting withdrawal is chaotic and it is one of the most difficult military manoeuvres to conduct. This was evident as Major General Horii forced the Australians from Isurava and began to pursue them south across the Owen Stanleys.

Many Japanese soldiers presumed that, having won the Battle of Isurava-Abuari, they now controlled the 'peak' of the Owen Stanleys. This mistaken belief was based on earlier claims by the *Yokoyama Force* that the capture of Deniki meant they held the high point of the range and could easily march down the southern slope to Port Moresby. This misunderstanding partially explains Horii's difficulty in deciphering the vague orders he was issued by *17th Army Headquarters* on 28 August which stated: 'Advance to the southern slopes of the Owen Stanley Range and destroy enemy troops there. Use one section of your strength to secure the front, but amass your main strength on the north side of the range in preparation for future operations.' At precisely which section of the Owen Stanleys Lieutenant General Hyakutake expected Horii to halt his advance was not clear. Horii must have hoped that new orders would be forthcoming since it does not appear that the Japanese soldiers were informed that an immediate assault on Port Moresby had been postponed.

With the Australians on the run from Isurava, Horii handed responsibility for the pursuit to Colonel Yazawa's *41st Regiment*. Yazawa's men were eager to fight; the senior officers of the regiment held little fear of Australians, having previously defeated them in Malaya. With the majority of the *1st* and *3rd Battalions* of this regiment not yet at the front (one company of the *3/41st* was present), the *2/41st* led the chase, commanded by Major Koiwai Mitsuo.

The supply problems that would eventually cripple Japanese aspirations were already apparent and became more marked as the campaign wore on. The ravenous soldiers who pilfered the stores left in Alola by the Australians presented some indication of this. Horii issued a signal calling for restraint and implored his officers to ensure that '… all unit commanders and others in authority, of whatever rank, must exercise the most painstaking control and supervision, so that every bullet fells an enemy and every grain of rice furthers the aim of the formation …'

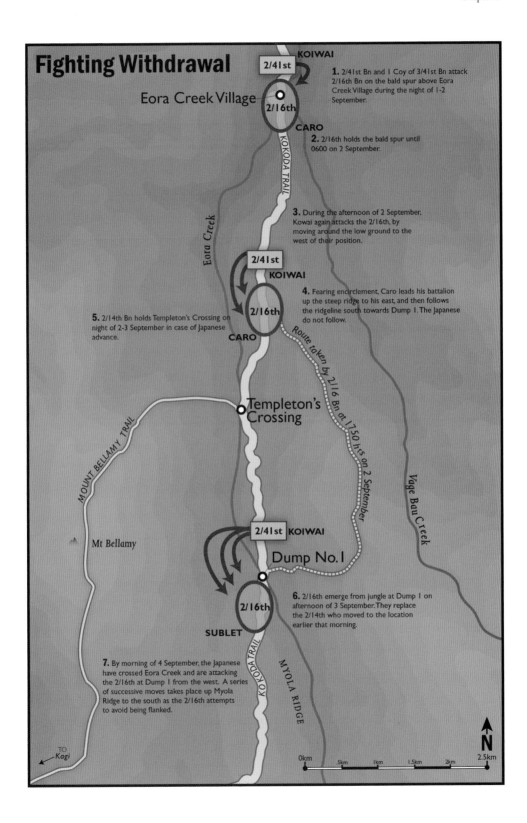

Fighting Withdrawal

KOIWAI

2/41st

Eora Creek Village — 2/16th

CARO

1. 2/41st Bn and 1 Coy of 3/41st Bn attack 2/16th Bn on the bald spur above Eora Creek Village during the night of 1-2 September.

2. 2/16th holds the bald spur until 0600 on 2 September.

3. During the afternoon of 2 September, Kowai again attacks the 2/16th, by moving around the low ground to the west of their position.

2/41st

KOIWAI

2/16th

CARO

4. Fearing encirclement, Caro leads his battalion up the steep ridge to his east, and then follows the ridgeline south towards Dump 1. The Japanese do not follow.

5. 2/14th Bn holds Templeton's Crossing on night of 2-3 September in case of Japanese advance.

Route taken by 2/16 Bn at 1750 hrs on 2 September

Templeton's Crossing

MOUNT BELLAMY TRAIL

Vage Bau Creek

Mt Bellamy

2/41st **KOIWAI**

Dump No.1

2/16th

SUBLET

6. 2/16th emerge from jungle at Dump 1 on afternoon of 3 September. They replace the 2/14th who moved to the location earlier that morning.

7. By morning of 4 September, the Japanese have crossed Eora Creek and are attacking the 2/16th at Dump 1 from the west. A series of successive moves takes place up Myola Ridge to the south as the 2/16th attempts to avoid being flanked.

KOKODA TRAIL

MYOLA RIDGE

TO Kagi

N

0km .5km 1km 1.5km 2km 2.5km

Eora Creek

KOKODA TRAIL

Maroubra Force had supply problems of its own. The fighting withdrawal, commencing at the Isurava Rest House, had begun disastrously. Organising the retreat of four battalions while under relentless Japanese pressure was a task of extraordinary complexity. The inherent difficulties were exacerbated by Captain Dickenson's misdirected attack which had scattered the force and separated many men from the main body. The 2/14th Battalion, in particular, had been badly affected, with much of the battalion's leadership unaccounted for. Dislocated groups and individuals showed incredible fortitude and stamina, making their way through the jungle to rejoin Maroubra Force over the ensuing days and weeks.

By now, the impossibility of Potts' original order to recapture Kokoda was well and truly apparent. Major General Allen had conceded as much when he had signalled Potts with new instructions on 30 August: '… you will endeavour to stabilise your position and maintain patrolling initiative … You are facing a difficult situation but I am confident you will win. Everything we can do is being done at risk of weakness here.' Indeed, moves were afoot in Port Moresby to bolster Maroubra Force as the fighting at Milne Bay had turned decisively in the Allies' favour. The Japanese invasion force had been beaten back in a savage and bloody battle and, with the immediate threat to Milne Bay's airstrips averted, mopping-up operations were all that remained. This allowed Allen leverage in the use of the 2/27th Battalion. Two companies were sent forward along the Trail immediately following Allen's signal. He promised Potts that the remainder of the 2/27th would follow as soon as the 53rd Battalion was extricated, which was necessary to reduce pressure on the Australian supply chain.

A further headache for the Australians at the beginning of the fighting withdrawal involved the groundswell of wounded troops on the Trail. The wounded men slowed the pace of the entire withdrawal and created a nightmare for the medical staff attempting to treat them. Severely wounded soldiers who were incapable of walking had to be carried on stretchers, requiring eight native bearers for every stretcher. It took no fewer than eight days to reach Port Moresby. This was a heavy burden on the native workforce which, while carrying the wounded, was diverted from portering much-needed supplies. Major Rupert Magarey, the Senior Medical Officer of the 2/6th Field Ambulance, argued that air evacuation from Myola presented the best solution. Flying out the most gravely wounded troops would not only enhance their chances of survival, it would also reduce the need to exhaust such a large number of natives in the taxing work of bearing a stretcher the entire length of the Kokoda Trail. Magarey communicated with Colonel Frank Kingsley Norris, the Chief Medical Officer of the 7th Division. Norris was receptive to the idea, as was Potts, who twice sent signals to Allen requesting that the idea be investigated. To their great disappointment, the request was rejected by Air Force Headquarters because of the risks to aircraft landing and taking off from Myola, and the dearth of available aircraft. With air evacuation ruled out, the long haul back to Port Moresby by stretcher remained the only option.

The first destination of the fighting withdrawal was a location approximately 1650 metres south of Alola. From this vantage point the Australians were angered to see the Japanese soldiers in Alola rifling through their abandoned stores and raising a victory flag. A campaign directive issued by NGF had deprived the infantry battalions of their medium machine-guns and mortars, on the basis that carry loads should be reduced and that support weapons were not suited to jungle warfare. The main reason was the belief of senior officers that line of sight was required for the use of medium machine-guns (to range and adjust fire), and that mortars would be ineffective because the bombs would explode in the tree canopy. This directive frustrated the soldiers, who knew that their Vickers medium machine-guns would easily have had the range to spoil the Japanese party. Hugh Challen, Brigade Major of the 21st Brigade, believed that an air attack would be a suitable substitute. He sent a signal to Port Moresby requesting air attacks at first light, then trekked to Eora Creek Village to reconnoitre new positions to which Maroubra Force could withdraw.

Eora Creek Village, often shortened to 'Eora Creek' (but distinct from the Eora Creek watercourse), was a small selection of huts situated on the southern bank of the creek, nestled high in the Owen Stanleys. War correspondent George Johnston referred to it as a grandiloquent title for what was essentially a solitary grass hut (Johnston was being facetious — it is evident from the photographs of Eora Creek Village that there was more than one hut). At this site, the north-flowing Eora Creek turns sharply to the east before buckling north again in an S-shape.

The Kokoda Trail crosses Eora Creek using a log bridge; a short distance later a second log bridge crosses a small tributary that enters Eora Creek from the south-east. The area is hemmed in on all sides by incredibly steep, heavily wooded mountains. This deprives the area of natural light, while the altitude and frequent rainfall makes it cold and perpetually damp. There were few locations along the length of the Kokoda Trail that the Australian soldiers disliked more.

Australian soldiers gain some respite in Eora Creek Village, just days before the fighting withdrawal. This shot was taken by renowned war photographer Damien Parer (AWM150656).

TEMPLETON'S CROSSING

Templeton's Crossing marks a point south of Eora Creek Village where the Kokoda Trail branches into two separate tracks that do not converge again until close to Efogi. The location is cold and mired in mud from the constant rainfall. This was the site of the five-day Battle of Templeton's Crossing from 16 to 20 October 1942.

The Crossing was so named for the crossing of two Kokoda routes, not for any crossing of Eora Creek. This is an important point because it illustrates the error, fashionable in modern times, to refer to two sites along the Kokoda Trail as Templeton's Crossing. The authentic site is often referred to as Templeton's 2, while Templeton's 1 was known as Dump 1 during the Kokoda campaign and was the first crossing of Eora Creek for soldiers who were moving north along the Kokoda Trail.

Lieutenant Bert Kienzle named Templeton's Crossing in honour of his friend Captain Sam Templeton, the popular OC of B Company, 39 Battalion. Templeton was a Northern Irishman and a veteran of the First World War. During the Second World War, the maximum age for enlistment was 40. Like many other men who were older, Templeton falsified his age, claiming to be 39, making him one of the unofficial group known as the 'thirty-nine liars'.

During the very early stages of the campaign, Templeton proved an inspiration to his men. He encouraged them in their difficult passage over the Owen Stanleys and helped stragglers to carry their equipment. Many saw him as a father figure to the young and inexperienced soldiers in the militia and they respected him enormously.

Templeton's fate is shrouded in mystery — he reportedly disappeared during an Australian delaying action near Oivi in July 1942. There are conflicting stories over his eventual demise. Some claim he was killed instantly (a gunshot was heard not long after he disappeared) while others believe he was wounded and taken prisoner for interrogation. Japanese documents appear to indicate that the latter is correct. The documents reveal that, during interrogation, Templeton exaggerated the number of Australian troops in the mountains to discourage the Japanese advance. Templeton's body has never been found.

When Challen arrived at Eora Creek Village he found Major Magarey treating 30 seriously wounded men, all stretcher cases, in a native hut beside the creek. Challen told the doctor of the impending influx of diggers moving along the Trail ahead of the Japanese advance. The hut's exposed position meant that it was at risk of being overrun in the fighting. Magarey's wounded had to be moved as quickly as possible. He returned to his patients and called for attention: 'I want every man who is capable of walking two or three hundred yards with assistance to start off for the top of the hill … we haven't got enough bearers to carry everybody, but this place must be cleared by tonight.' The hill that Magarey was referring to was a distinctive bald spur on the Trail to the south of the native dwellings. This bald spur would feature prominently throughout the campaign.

Magarey's appeal was answered by several men who, in spite of their wounds, immediately rose from their stretchers and struggled up the bald spur with assistance. All but three others — whose wounds were terminal — were carried to a staging post higher up the spur through Magarey's efforts in mustering all available hands to help. By the next morning the stretcher cases were on their way south to Templeton's Crossing en route to Myola. The speed of the Japanese advance required Potts, and in turn Magarey, to continue to adapt his plan. Later, on 1 September, Potts told Magarey he doubted Myola could be held and ordered him to move the wounded soldiers even further back to Efogi.

The first of the expected influx of troops to arrive at Eora Creek Village were members of the 39th Battalion, now asked to fulfil one last combat duty. With the battalion's ranks woefully diminished and numbering fewer than 150 fighting men, the remaining troops were merged into two composite companies. Company 2, led by Captain Bidstrup, was stationed north of Eora Creek and tasked with covering the withdrawal of the AIF men who would move through them and occupy positions south of the creek crossings. Company 1, led by Captain Merritt, camped further back on the southern side of Eora Creek to ensure that the enemy could not bypass the forward company without encountering resistance.

The Australian troops making their way towards Eora Creek Village were a pitiful sight. They were tired and filthy. Words of derogatory encouragement were required to motivate those who had dropped by the side of the Trail in resignation. In spite of the conditions, the Australians generally maintained their sense of humour. Private Ronald Halsall of the 39th Battalion recalled a common analogy used to describe the fighting withdrawal: 'Retreating like hell. We call that the Kokoda Handicap. A horse race that was on the Kokoda [Trail]. We could still have a bit of a joke you know … We'd wake up in the morning and someone would say, "Right ho, line up for the Kokoda Handicap, she's about to start," and away we'd go.'

On the morning of 1 September the roar of aircraft was heard overhead. The Australians looked skywards in the hope that the aerial attack on Alola that Major Challen had requested the day before was about to occur. Instead of fighters, the Air Force had despatched a solitary reconnaissance plane. While this aircraft confirmed enemy targets in Alola, the clouds closed in and obscured the village before the fighters had a chance to attack. The soldiers on the ground were indignant. The perceived lack of air support along the Trail presents a stark contrast to the battle at Milne Bay where the cooperative efforts of the Air Force and Army proved instrumental in defeating the Japanese invasion force.

Damien Parer captured this image of members of D Company, 39th Battalion, moving south during the fighting withdrawal. Their boots sink deep in the mud on the hilly jungle track. At the rear is Staff Sergeant Joseph Long, one of at least nine men who took part in both the Gallipoli and Kokoda campaigns. (AWM013288).

As the AIF battalions streamed into Eora Creek Village, Merritt's company moved forward to cover them as they traversed the Eora Creek crossing. Major John (Ben) Hearman, second-in-command of the 2/16th, soon appeared. He told Merritt that Lieutenant Donald Paterson was on the Trail not far behind him leading Maroubra Force's rearguard. Merritt waited anxiously as the water raged beneath the wobbly log bridge. He intended to destroy it the moment the last of the Australians had crossed.

The speed of the Japanese advance was extraordinary. Warrant Officer Class 2 George Mowat, who was with Merritt, described the task given to Paterson as a 'Suicide job [because the] Japs [were] right on their heels.' In the running battle, the Japanese raced around Paterson's left flank and were able to reach Eora Creek first. They occupied the high ground on the northern side of the S-shape, directly overlooking the log bridges, firing across the creek at Merritt's company. The fire was accurate, and the addition of a Juki heavy machine-gun intensified its deadly effect. Merritt's men were forced to scramble up the hill behind them with no time to destroy the bridge.

This gunfire alerted the rearguard to the fact that the Japanese had beaten them to Eora Creek and thus barred their movement along the Kokoda Trail. Their efforts at holding the Japanese had been courageous but costly. Paterson was dead and several others were wounded, but most of Maroubra Force had managed to get safely across the two log bridges. The surviving members of the rearguard later rejoined Maroubra Force by wading across Eora Creek downstream and then moving south along the same route used earlier by Captain Sublet's companies during their withdrawal from the Abuari ridgeline.

As the first day of spring wore on, the Australians and the Japanese concentrated their forces on either side of Eora Creek Village. Lieutenant Colonel Caro's 2/16th had consolidated on the bald spur on the southern side of Eora Creek, while the 2/14th was holding a position approximately one kilometre further south along the Kokoda Trail in support. The 39th had completed its final combat duty in the Kokoda campaign by holding the log crossings and was withdrawn to Kagi en route to Port Moresby. The men had performed well beyond expectation. Their sister battalion, the 53rd, was not held in the same esteem, and was ordered to proceed directly to Kagi and return to Port Moresby as quickly as possible.

Looking west towards the site of Eora Creek Village. The photograph is taken from just above the confluence of Eora Creek and its tributary. The native hut in the distance has been constructed at the foot of the bald spur (M. Rifat, NAA011).

The *Nankai Shitai* was firmly ensconced on the high ground north of Eora Creek where the troops sited and calibrated their mountain guns. As soon as the Japanese pinpointed Caro's position on the bald spur, their mountain guns opened fire. Fortunately, they caused only minor damage as most of the shells exploded in the jungle canopy above the Australians' heads. But the bombardment was merely a diversion, designed to keep the attention of the 2/16th focused towards its front while Japanese engineers built a better bridge over Eora Creek.

View from the ridge on the northern side of the S-shape of Eora Creek. The Japanese occupied this position during the fighting withdrawal and again during the Battle of Eora Creek. The visible clearing and hut are located on the ground between the two log bridges (N. Anderson, NAA012).

As the Japanese engineers worked, two of Major Koiwai's companies had crossed Eora Creek downstream then swung around and launched an attack on the bald spur from the east. As Eora Creek was their first test of combat in the campaign, these men were cautious and crawled towards the Australians rather than rushing them blindly. Some climbed trees and sniped at the Australians hiding in their foxholes. The focus of their attack was Captain Breton Langridge's D Company holding the forward right position. The fire from the snipers was disconcerting, and Langridge requested permission to withdraw his men, but Caro was firm in his refusal. The position had to be held until 6.00 am on 2 September as Potts had ordered.

The fighting continued into the night. The extreme darkness and driving rain cast an eerie pall over Eora Creek. The Japanese employed deception, calling to the Australians in English to disorient them. As this tactic had been used numerous times by the Japanese, the novelty had worn off and the Australians were well conditioned to the ruse.

Throughout the night, Australian piquets were constantly surprised by Japanese soldiers appearing out of the darkness. Private Cyril Allender of the 2/14th described fighting in such conditions: 'You don't know where it [rifle fire] is coming from. You can't see anybody and it really is not very nice. When you're firing you don't know what you're firing at, you know approximately where they are but you can't see anybody.' Warrant Officer Alan Haddy welcomed the Japanese tactic of infiltration and told his men, 'Wait til they come up close and give 'em curry.'

In what seems strange in an environment with frequent rain and countless streams, Caro's men struggled with thirst. On the bald spur, the 2/16th was removed from the enticing sound of water in Eora Creek below. Small parties of troops were sent to fetch water but became lost in the dark and could not find their way back to the battalion until daylight.

Finally, the nominated time for withdrawal arrived and the 2/16th used the dense mist which hung over Eora Creek to vacate the bald spur. Remarkably, the Australian casualties from the night of four men killed and six wounded were relatively light given the unrelenting pressure on the battalion. In return, Langridge estimated that his company alone had inflicted 100 casualties. That estimate is certainly inflated, but Japanese casualties clearly surpassed those suffered by the Australians. One of the reasons for the higher Japanese casualty rate was the difficulty and high risk involved in conducting jungle operations at night. The Japanese failed badly on this occasion, and night operations were generally avoided by both sides for the remainder of the campaign.

Having withdrawn from the bald spur, the 2/16th headed south along the Kokoda Trail and passed through the 2/14th, which in turn passed back through the 2/16th in a series of overlapping movements to cover the withdrawal. Private Allender recalled of the fighting withdrawal:

An average day was very uncomfortable … either walking or lying and dug in, different places. Different companies were in different places, I mean different platoons are in different places, so you don't know exactly what the others are doing except for where you are yourself. So you don't get, "this is where you have got to be", you [just] dig in and hold your position there and hope that you stay there for the rest of the day. But when things get worse, you only get up and leave again.

Once Caro was certain that contact with the Japanese had been broken after he had vacated the bald spur, he established a new defensive position several kilometres north of Templeton's Crossing. His location was the highest section of the Trail between Templeton's Crossing and Eora Creek Village. To the west, the ground fell away to Eora Creek. To the east, the land rose to a long north-south ridgeline. Potts told Caro to hold this position until 12.00 noon on 3 September.

Twenty minutes forward of this position, Corporal James Willis and six of his soldiers lay in wait for the inevitable pursuit. They did not have long to wait. At 11.00 am a patrol of some 10 Japanese from the *41st Regiment* strolled casually along the Trail. Willis was amazed at the nonchalant manner in which they advanced. Their weapons were slung across their shoulders and they displayed a complete lack of situational awareness. Their indifference proved costly with the Australians wiping out the patrol without suffering any casualties themselves. Willis told his company commander he could not tell whether the Japanese were recklessly naïve or sacrificial.

Private Lionel Smith of the 2/14th commented later: 'There were so many of them [Japanese soldiers] that their officers … didn't mind expending lives, that's what it amounted to … [T]he general idea of the Japanese Army was to surround people and then finish them off … they didn't care about losing lives the Japanese, they were fanatical … They'd never lost and never been repulsed before in all their coming right down the South West Pacific, they only rolled over everything …'

The destruction of the patrol alerted the Japanese to the Australians' new positions and foreshadowed the next stage of the *41st Regiment's* attempt to crush Maroubra Force. Nevertheless, the best way to accomplish this caused friction between the hot-headed regimental commander Yazawa and the cautious battalion commander Koiwai. Instead of attacking the 2/16th immediately, Koiwai held his men, waiting for artillery to arrive to support the infantry. The impatient Yazawa promptly overruled Koiwai, informing him that the attack would commence without delay. Koiwai was frustrated but had no option other than to attack immediately. He directed his men to chip away at both Australian flanks. The initial attacks were held, but Sublet in the front left position soon informed Caro that the enemy had moved around the battalion's entire left flank. Caro feared his battalion was being encircled. If the Trail was cut, the 2/16th would not be able to reach Templeton's Crossing.

A reconnaissance party identified a rough path which skirted the high ridgeline to the east and looped around to Dump 1 (further to the south), avoiding Templeton's Crossing altogether. Caro received permission to withdraw along this route, but Potts ordered him to wait until dusk to allow the 2/14th time to withdraw to and cover Templeton's

Crossing. This was an important precaution in case the Japanese chose to ignore the 2/16th's movement and continued to advance along the Kokoda Trail.

At dusk the companies of the 2/16th left their positions one by one and moved towards the exit path. The vigilant Japanese realised that the Australians were withdrawing and, with two sword-wielding officers at their head, seized the opportunity to attack. It was a vigorous and well-timed assault with the Australians caught off guard at the moment of their greatest vulnerability. The din from the fighting was immense, with light machine-guns and rifle grenades ripping through the foliage. Were it not for an inspired counter-attack led by Sergeant William Duncan's 16 Platoon, the 2/16th's escape would have been impossible.

Having narrowly averted a crisis, the 2/16th pushed south along the crest of the ridgeline until darkness and heavy rain forced the battalion to bivouac for the night. The evening passed without further incident for either the 2/16th or the 2/14th Battalion.

At 5.30 am on 3 September, the 2/16th continued its move towards Dump 1. The men had spent a miserable night high in the Owen Stanleys. Even with respite from enemy attacks, they were beset by problems. Their feet were saturated and their boots had not been removed since prior to the action at Isurava-Abuari. Gastric bugs and diarrhoea were causing weakness and dysentery was starting to spread. The troops struggled on regardless. Every time the human train paused, tired soldiers took the opportunity to rest, lying on the side of the path. In spite of their poor physical condition, their morale remained intact. Warrant Officer John Corbett remembered:

> Morale never dropped in our battalion. I can honestly say that. We were always confident that we were killing more of them than what they were of us and that's what the game was all about. And although we would have very much liked to have had much more men at our disposal … well we couldn't get them, so you had to do the best with what you had.

Finally, at 3.30 pm, the battalion descended the ridgeline and emerged at Eora Creek with Dump 1 on the opposite bank. As the men crossed Eora Creek, they replaced the 2/14th, which had pulled back to Dump 1 earlier that morning and now moved on to Myola. As the final man from the 2/16th was crossing, the Australians came under fire. Caro set a perimeter defence with A Company occupying the front left position, B Company in the front right position, and D Company planted at the rear. The fighting continued into another wet evening but was relatively light.

In Myola, the 2/14th relished a night of peace. The men enjoyed a long-awaited hot meal and changed out of their filthy and tattered uniforms before bathing in the local stream — their first proper wash since 25 August. The battalion's chiropodist was called in to treat the men's sodden feet which were in shocking condition. Immersion in wet boots had caused the feet to swell and acquire a bulbous, misshapen form, much like trench foot from the Great War. In some cases, the socks had become stuck to the skin and, when cut away, the skin peeled straight off the foot.

Damien Parer photographed two Australian soldiers having a cigarette at Myola as the fighting withdrawal worked its way towards the dry lakebeds. They appear remarkably calm (AWM013264).

Myola was the best location for air-dropping along the entire Kokoda Trail. Keeping it in Australian hands remained a cornerstone of Allen's campaign plan. He stressed the importance of the position when he signalled Potts: 'Supply situation demands vital necessity for holding Myola as dropping area … We cannot allow enemy to use Myola. Therefore we must establish a firm base forward of Myola as soon as possible.' Potts was aware of Allen's intent, but was sceptical of its practicality. Maps of the area were poor and did not adequately reflect the ground. Allen wanted offensive actions resumed, and while Potts shared that desire, his highest priority was holding the Japanese and keeping Maroubra Force together. Potts responded to Allen and informed him that he would reconnoitre potential sites forward of Myola the following day, promising to resume offensive actions once he had formed a firm base. Allen was pleased, 'When firm base est[ablished] hope you can cane his ankles.'

On the morning of 4 September, Caro left Captain Sublet in charge of the 2/16th at Dump 1 and left for Myola with the 2/16th Battalion's second-in-command, Major Hearman, to reconnoitre the area with Potts. Sublet sent out several patrols to ascertain Japanese movements. One of these patrols, led by Lieutenant George Hicks, crossed Eora Creek and found freshly made tracks and hastily built shelters. After recrossing the creek on the return leg of the patrol, evidence of an impending Japanese attack was discovered to the west of Dump 1. Hicks spotted at least a company of enemy soldiers forming up and a signal wire was located running southwards. Hicks and his men cut the signal wire and then hurried to inform Sublet.

Sublet deduced from Hicks' information that the enemy was not only planning an imminent attack but also attempting to surround the battalion. The likely target of the signal wire was Myola Ridge (sometimes referred to as Bamboo Ridge), the north-south ridgeline 460 metres behind the 2/16th's position. Sublet wanted the Australians to occupy Myola Ridge before the Japanese and called a company commanders' conference to detail the plan. But it was too late; the conference was interrupted as A Company was hit by a maelstrom of Japanese fire including rounds from a mountain gun. With the 2/16th's left flank in danger of collapsing, the battalion was forced to race for the high ground. Captain Langridge volunteered D Company to protect the move as his company was not directly involved in the fighting. Again the Japanese witnessed the preparations to withdraw and drove at the Australians with greater impetus. Thrusting forward they sliced through Langridge's rearguard and reached Headquarters Company. Fierce fighting staved off any further encroachment and the battalion scrambled to the relative safety of Myola Ridge.

As the attack was unfolding, Potts was with Lieutenant Kienzle and Maroubra Force's senior leadership, formulating a plan to defend Myola. With Allen's orders to hold the position ringing in his ears, all possibilities in front of and behind the lakebeds were being explored. Potts had earlier flirted with the idea of establishing a defensive position between Efogi and Myola, but ruled it out once he realised that the surrounding high ground would afford the enemy too great an advantage. He then moved forward from Myola, scouting the approaches to the dry lakes. With the leading companies of the 2/27th en route from Kagi and expected to arrive later in the day, there was some hope that Myola could be held, although Potts had strong misgivings. Myola was too large, and defending such an extended position would stretch his depleted force to breaking point. When a breathless runner reached Potts' group and informed them that the 2/16th had been forced back from Dump 1, Potts conceded that holding Myola was no longer an option. At 6.00 pm he signalled Allen: 'Strong enemy attack driven in 2/16 Bn ... country utterly unsuitable for defended localities. Regret necessity to abandon MYOLA. Intend withdrawing EFFOGI [sic]. No reserve for counter attack. Men full of fight but utterly weary. Remaining coys 2/27 Bn ... too late to assist.'

With the 2/16th in trouble, Major Hearman hurried forward to Myola Ridge. He took command from Sublet and ordered the battalion to withdraw to Myola. Darkness assisted the battalion to break contact with the Japanese, but it also impeded movement. The diggers literally had to hold onto the man in front for balance and used the small amount of light from the moon to guide their way. When the moon disappeared, the burden of carrying stretchers became too great. The battalion was forced to hold its position on the Trail despite the ever-present danger of an attack from the rear. At 5.30 am the battalion was on the move again and, by 8.00 am, the exhausted troops entered Myola, passing through the 2/14th piquets.

The scene at Myola was chaotic. Every soldier was busy, as the Japanese were expected to arrive at any moment. Potts' earlier evacuation order meant that nothing that could materially aid the Japanese advance could be left behind. If an item could not be carried to Efogi it had to be destroyed. Tins of bully beef were perforated with bayonets and stores were dumped on bonfires. The 2/16th was provided hot food and given clean clothing. This proved a godsend given the appalling state of the uniforms which hung from the men's bodies. Within half an hour the troops were on the move again, headed towards Efogi. Myola was relinquished without a shot being fired.

Contrary to the belief of several senior Army commanders at the time, the fighting over the six days between 31 August and 5 September constituted a successful fighting withdrawal, conducted in a disciplined and professional manner. The sole exception was the initial incident of friendly fire that occurred at Isurava Rest House. While the repercussions of this were immense, such incidents are unsurprising given the tumult of warfare.

There is little doubt that the fighting withdrawal would have been enormously assisted had Air Force Headquarters sanctioned aerial evacuations from Myola. Potts and Maroubra Force's medical staff were bitterly disappointed when their requests were denied. Later in the campaign, during the Australian advance, Allen also requested aerial evacuation from Myola and, again, his request was refused, despite the fact that the 2/6th Field Company had by then worked hard to improve the landing strip. That said, the primary reason cited by Air Force Headquarters was the danger involved, and this was a legitimate concern. The high altitude of Myola, billowing wind gusts, the shortness of the landing strip, the inconsistent and soggy ground surface, and the necessity for steep banking when taking off gave pilots very little room for error. And while there were successful landings at Myola later in the campaign and a small number of wounded were evacuated by air (around 40), on several occasions pilots crashed their aircraft at the lakebeds, validating the concerns and justifying the reluctance of Air Force Headquarters. Nevertheless, this meant little to the commanders and medical staff on the ground who refused to accept the impossibility of aerial evacuation or the idea that a certain degree of risk should not be taken by the Air Force given the magnitude of the problem. As Colonel Kingsley Norris wrote after the campaign:

[A]ir evacuation was neglected. Why this was never adequately undertaken — why after three years of war no adequate ambulance planes were available — why certain casualties had to remain in a forward medical post for eleven weeks after being wounded — these and many other questions remain unanswered.

While the 39th and 2/14th battalions had distinguished themselves at Isurava, the bulk of combat during the fighting withdrawal had been conducted by the 2/16th Battalion. The leadership of the junior officers and NCOs, coupled with the endurance and fortitude of the soldiers, carried them through despite their debilitated condition. The experience of the AIF battalions served them well. For their part, the Japanese forces possessed superior numbers and firepower, and had several opportunities to crush an adversary that was on the run. And yet the *Nankai Shitai* suffered heavier casualties than Maroubra Force throughout the pursuit, draining it of manpower which was not being replaced. In addition, Maroubra Force's success in delaying the Japanese as long as it did gave the 2/27th time to march to Efogi to reinforce the Australians ready for the next set battle at Brigade Hill.

Corporal Henry Evans and Sergeant Leslie Martorana of the 39th Battalion at Eora Creek Village during the fighting withdrawal (AWM013265).

Chapter 9

THE BATTLE OF BRIGADE HILL

The Battle of Brigade Hill was an unmitigated calamity for Maroubra Force and the worst disaster that befell the Australians during the entire Kokoda campaign. Isurava had hurt Maroubra Force, but it was not broken. The Japanese were able to harass the Australians during the pursuit south in the early days of September, but Major General Horii still craved the decisive victory that would eliminate all resistance.

The Battle of Brigade Hill was fought because Brigadier Potts was under immense pressure from Major General Allen to stand and fight given the constant series of retreats following the defeat at Isurava. It was believed that, with the reinforcement of the 21st Brigade's final battalion — the 2/27th — a significant block could be placed on the Japanese advance. This view was influenced by intelligence reaching the highest levels of Allied Command which suggested that the size of the Japanese force facing the Australians had been overestimated and the number of troops that both sides could muster for battle was much closer than reports from the front had indicated.

The view looking south from the 'Kokoda Gap'. Brigade Hill is at the left centre. The villages visible in the photo are, from left to right, Efogi 2, Naduri (both new villages) and Kagi, which moved to its present location after the war (N. Anderson, NAA013).

Descending from the highest sections of the Kokoda Trail through the 'Kokoda Gap' affords a magnificent view to the south over the series of ridgelines that comprises the southern half of the Owen Stanleys. The impressive Brigade Hill is the first in the series, roughly located at the halfway point of the Trail. From the north face of Brigade Hill, Mission Ridge (so named for the abandoned Seventh Day Adventist mission house that straddled it) extends like a nose. The eastern face of Brigade Hill is very steep while the western face is only slightly less so as it drops down to the Fagume River. The closest village is Efogi, which has since moved, but at the time of the campaign was situated on the northern side of Brigade Hill at the foot of Mission Ridge.

While far from ideal, the advantage of Brigade Hill as a site for a prepared defence lay in its clear, treeless approaches from the north which would allow Maroubra Force to observe the *Nankai Shitai*'s advance. Potts also believed that the steepness of the flanks would limit the enemy's opportunities for encirclement. In addition, the two major routes between Templeton's Crossing and Efogi — the Kokoda Trail and the Mount Bellamy Trail — converged north of Brigade Hill. This meant that Potts would not have to split his force to contend with an enemy advancing along multiple paths.

On 5 September the leading elements of the 2/27th rendezvoused with Maroubra Force north of Efogi. Potts ordered Lieutenant Colonel Geoffrey Cooper, CO of the 2/27th, to concentrate his battalion on Mission Ridge. Here the 39th Battalion made its final contribution to the Kokoda campaign, having located prospective defensive positions for the 2/27th to occupy. As the 2/27th assembled it took custody of the 39th's automatic weapons before Lieutenant Colonel Honner led the 185 surviving members of the weary battalion back towards Port Moresby.

The other militia unit, the 53rd Battalion, was still causing consternation. A platoon from this battalion had been tasked with guarding the approach to Efogi at the junction of the Kokoda and Mount Bellamy Trails. To Potts' great frustration, on the morning of 6 September the platoon was discovered to have left the junction unguarded and moved south. A patrol group of 25 men from the 2/27th was rushed forward as a replacement. The patrol, led by Lieutenant Frederick Bell, had barely reached the junction when 300 Japanese were seen approaching from Myola. Bell's men melted into the jungle in preparation for an ambush but were thwarted, as the leading Japanese scouts spotted them and opened fire. Four Australians were killed and four were wounded before the patrol could withdraw. In his report, Bell noted that a number of casualties had also been inflicted on the Japanese.

Elsewhere on the morning of 6 September, the 2/14th and 2/16th moved to join the 2/27th on Brigade Hill, passing through their sister battalion to occupy respective positions behind. Friendly banter at the reunification of the 21st Brigade raised the morale of the tired troops.

Later in the day, Potts was eager to reduce the length of Maroubra Force's flanks and tightened the defensive perimeter by ordering the 2/27th to move higher up Mission Ridge. Accordingly, the Australian dispositions prior to the battle resembled a string of pearls

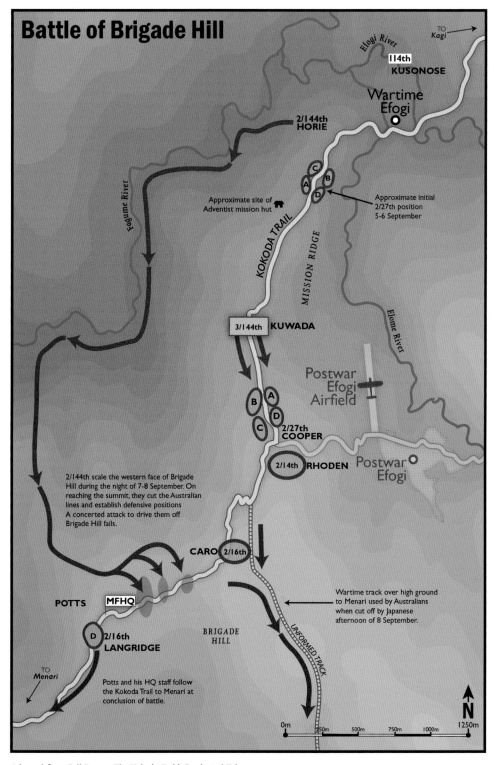

Battle of Brigade Hill

TO Kagi

Efogi River

114th KUSONOSE

Wartime Efogi

2/144th HORIE

C
A B
D

Approximate initial 2/27th position 5-6 September

Approximate site of Adventist mission hut

KOKODA TRAIL

MISSION RIDGE

Fogume River

Elome River

3/144th KUWADA

Postwar Efogi Airfield

B A
D
C
2/27th COOPER

2/14th RHODEN

Postwar Efogi

2/144th scale the western face of Brigade Hill during the night of 7-8 September. On reaching the summit, they cut the Australian lines and establish defensive positions A concerted attack to drive them off Brigade Hill fails.

CARO 2/16th

Wartime track over high ground to Menari used by Australians when cut off by Japanese afternoon of 8 September.

POTTS MFHQ

D 2/16th LANGRIDGE

BRIGADE HILL

UNFORMED TRACK

TO Menari

Potts and his HQ staff follow the Kokoda Trail to Menari at conclusion of battle.

N

0m 250m 500m 750m 1000m 1250m

Adapted from Bill James, *The Kokoda Field Guide*, 3rd Edition, accompanying map.

stretching over two kilometres along the Kokoda Trail. The 2/27th was at the forefront, guarding Mission Ridge, with A Company in the right forward position and B Company in the left forward position. Behind the 2/27th was the 2/14th, with the 2/16th next in line. Potts' Brigade Headquarters was sited further to the rear, with D Company of the 2/16th located farthest to the south to protect the stores and Brigade Headquarters.

Looking south from Kagi, Mission Ridge (at the left of the photograph) extends from Brigade Hill like a nose. The Fagume River cuts the valley in the centre. The Japanese 'Lantern Parade' advanced towards Efogi over the lip of the land in the foreground (M. Rifat, NAA014).

Horii was displeased with the efforts of Colonel Yazawa's *41st Regiment* following its pursuit of Maroubra Force during the fighting withdrawal. With the *41st Regiment* at the vanguard of the pursuit, progress had been limited to an average advance of two kilometres per day. Responsibility for leading the pursuit was now handed to Colonel Kusonose's *144th Regiment*. At the Battle of Brigade Hill Kusonose's forces comprised the *2/144th* and *3/144th*, with artillery support and a company of engineers. Kusonose was an aggressive commander, prepared to take risks for the chance of victory.

On the afternoon of 6 September, activity built to the north of Brigade Hill as Kusonose mustered his forces. The same group of Japanese that Bell's patrol had fought earlier now congregated in Efogi. Further across the valley in the village of Kagi, flames leapt from an enormous funeral pyre as the Japanese cremated the remains of their dead. At dusk the Australians witnessed a peculiar sight later referred to as the 'Japanese Lantern Parade'. The section of the Trail that leads south from Kagi to Efogi is incredibly steep. The ground drops abruptly as the Trail cuts through a series of switchbacks zigzagging down to the Efogi River 400 metres below. This section of the Trail is always damp, and the foliage particularly dense. Descent during daylight hours is precarious. At night it is downright treacherous. Thus the Australians were astonished to see the mountain glow with hundreds of moving lights.

Each Japanese soldier had been provided a burning stick of signal wire to help navigate the descent. The Australians were both fascinated and disconcerted by the display. They regretted that they did not have their Vickers guns with them to fire at the obvious targets, although they took great delight when a flame moved erratically, an indicator that a Japanese soldier had lost his footing and stumbled.

The Japanese 'Lantern Parade' took place on this incredibly steep slope (but further to the west) that leads south from Kagi towards the Efogi River (M. Rifat, NAA015).

The 'Lantern Parade' was the first portent of battle. Potts sent an urgent signal to 7th Division Headquarters: 'turn on all you've got from air on Efogi and Myola at earliest tomorrow morning ... village itself on spur between two creeks MUST be plastered.' The next morning Port Moresby complied as eight B26 Marauders and four P40 Kittyhawks flew overhead and delivered the devastating attack that Potts had requested. Private Kokichi Nishimura of the *2/144th* remembered that the destructive air attack saw the Japanese refer to the area as 'Hell Valley'.

Ascertaining the actual toll of casualties caused by the air attack is difficult and estimates vary wildly. Historian Peter Williams believes that the number may have been as low as 11 killed and 20 wounded, while Major General Horii signalled *17th Army Headquarters* and requested the support of Japanese fighter aircraft reporting that the Allies had control of the air and the attack had caused approximately 100 casualties and deaths. Horii, who was not present at Brigade Hill, may have been reacting to his front-line troops' shocking stories of a bloodbath resulting from the air attack.

The primary value of the air attack lay in the fear it inspired in the Japanese. The morale of the Australians was buoyed and they revelled in watching the Japanese blasted without the means to retaliate. In a sense they regarded this as a form of 'payback' after weeks of helplessness while suffering the relentless bombardment of the Japanese artillery. Potts was satisfied, relaying the following message, 'Bombing and strafing Efogi and Kagi very successful. Troops enormously encouraged. Excellent work, keep it up.'

While the overall number of casualties inflicted by the air attack may have been minimal, it successfully delayed the Japanese assault for several hours. However, when the Japanese mountain guns began firing on the forward Australian positions, it was obvious that their infantry would not be far behind and the 2/27th was soon attacked head-on up Mission Ridge by Lieutenant Colonel Kuwada's *3/144th Battalion*. The fighting was sharp and intense. The 2/27th was unhappy with its position. Unlike the majority of the Kokoda Trail which is shrouded in jungle, Mission Ridge is exposed. The hot conditions saw the men sweat profusely and quickly empty their water canteens. The only source of fresh water was at the head of several small streams to the rear of their position. Runners from the 2/14th were sent to replenish supplies, but the Japanese artillery quickly spotted them from across the valley and peppered them with shells. This prevented the Australians moving freely, which hampered their ability to restock their water throughout the duration of the battle.

Despite the conditions, the 2/27th withstood the frontal assault for the remainder of the day losing 10 men killed in action. However, Potts recognised that the security of his position was entirely dependent on his capacity to prevent the penetration of his flanks. This concern was evident in his signal to Allen: 'Will not give ground if you guarantee my line of communication ... Every endeavour being made to contain one line of approach, but nothing to prevent him by-passing ... Am even using [Captain Thomas] Grahamslaw's police boys for reconnaissance patrols.'

Potts' anxiety was warranted. Bypassing the 2/27th was exactly what Kusonose had in mind. Japanese patrols initially explored the eastern face of Brigade Hill, planning an attack from this direction. The idea proved impractical and was soon discounted, the country simply too difficult. Their focus then turned to the western flank. It was here that Grahamslaw — the senior ANGAU officer present — had led a patrol of native policemen to check for signs of encircling movements. After seven hours the patrol returned and reported that they had discovered no signs of the enemy. Their failure to detect the enemy was to prove costly. Over the next 24 hours, it was on this western flank that Kusonose made his crucial play.

Using the same pin and flank tactic employed at the Battle of Isurava, Kusonose planned to keep the *3/144th* in contact with the 2/27th to pin the battalion to Mission Ridge. Then, as the sunlight faded on 7 September, he sent several companies of the *2/144th* with a Papuan guide along the Fagume River, far to the west of Maroubra Force. Major Horie had earlier been pointed towards a large, distinctive tree on the crest of Brigade Hill and ordered to use this as a beacon to direct his attack. Under cover of darkness, the *2/144th* began scaling the precipitous western face of Brigade Hill. A group of engineers had been attached to the infantry and, once the native footpads disappeared, the engineers cut a track for the attacking force. The final part of the ascent was the most arduous. The moon had disappeared and the Japanese soldiers were forced to climb on all fours. Private Bert Ward of the 2/27th described the Japanese who undertook the climb as 'mountain goats', marvelling, '[It's amazing] how active they were, to be able to keep going. We were flat out! Physically exhausted! And so they must have been!' At last the Japanese reached the summit. As dawn broke they lodged themselves in between the 2/16th and Brigade Headquarters.

Potts' first inkling that something was awry came close to ending his life. At daylight he walked towards a latrine cut into the side of the mountain escorted by Private John Gill of the Guard Platoon. A sharp crack broke the silence and Gill fell, shot dead by a Japanese sniper. In the fracas that ensued, a further two soldiers from Brigade Headquarters were wounded, one mortally. It was now apparent that Maroubra Force shared the summit with an unwanted guest.

So how did the *2/144th* manage reach the top of Brigade Hill without detection? It appears most likely that the Australians were distracted by what was happening on Mission Ridge. Throughout the night, the Australians soldiers had expected action here because they could hear the enemy to their front making an enormous din. The sound of digging and incessant chatter gave the impression that the Japanese did not care about maintaining silence, and perhaps the noise was a ploy to intimidate them. Sergeant Allen Gittos of the 2/16th remarked later, 'The Japs were funny fellows. Through the night we could hear them chopping at the vegetation and moving around yelling to each other as though there was no need to be careful.'

From 4.30 am, furious frontal attacks were launched against A and B companies of the 2/27th. In this extraordinarily steep country, the Australians found that they could simply roll their 36mm hand grenades down the hill in the direction of the noisy Japanese soldiers. These grenades had a seven-second fuse and the Australians took enormous risks for greater effect, holding the grenades for several seconds after pulling the pins, praying for the reliability of the fuse. A and B companies fought desperately to hold the forward position, draining their supply of ammunition and grenades. Once these were expended they quickly consumed their reserves.

While the 2/27th was engaged on Mission Ridge, the *2/144th Battalion* worked to consolidate its position on the summit of Brigade Hill. The men dug in and established machine-gun posts and then attacked north along the Kokoda Trail to the rear of the 2/16th. Frantic fighting prevented Lieutenant Colonel Caro's position being overrun, but a two-company counter-attack could not dislodge the Japanese from Brigade Hill.

The three Australian battalions were being squeezed in a vice, with the Japanese nipping at both their front and rear. In a worrying development, Horie's men cut the two signal wires that ran from 21st Brigade Headquarters to the forward Australian battalions. This limited communication between the battalions and Brigade Headquarters to the temperamental Army No. 108 Wireless Set. While this radio had a nominal range of almost 10 kilometres, that figure was drastically reduced when it was used in the jungle, making it difficult for Potts to converse with his battalion commanders.

At 9.45 am, having made contact by wireless, Potts issued his orders. The 2/14th was to move to Caro's position to help the 2/16th clear the Trail. Cooper was to move one of his companies up Mission Ridge to protect the ground vacated by the 2/14th. Before the wireless stopped working, Potts told Caro he was to take command of Maroubra Force if Brigade Headquarters was wiped out.

Armed with instructions from Potts, Caro called a commanders' conference at noon. If Maroubra Force was to survive, the enemy sharing Brigade Hill had to be expelled. The plan devised was for four companies to thrust at the Japanese from the north. A and B companies of the 2/16th would advance directly along the Kokoda Trail while C Company would advance on the eastern perimeter. On the western edge of the Trail, B Company of the 2/14th under the command of Captain Nye would support the attack. If the Japanese could not be dislodged from Brigade Hill, Maroubra Force would retreat using an alternative path that had been reconnoitred prior to the battle which wove down the south-eastern face of the mountain towards Menari.

But Potts' instructions were not carried out to the letter. Down on Mission Ridge, Cooper was worried by his battalion's dwindling supplies of food, water and ammunition. He was also concerned at his inability to evacuate his wounded men. At 1.00 pm, rather than moving one company up the ridge as per Potts' orders, the entire battalion moved and consolidated in the position formerly held by the 2/14th Battalion. At 1.45 pm, the wireless briefly spluttered back to life and Potts was again able to communicate with his battalions, learning of their impending attack. Evidently Cooper's actions were not widely known because Potts was asked for instructions for the 2/27th — *after* the battalion had already moved back. Ceding Mission Ridge to the Japanese had consequences that would become apparent later in the day.

At 2.45 pm, in driving rain, the 2/16th and 2/14th began their attack on the crest of Brigade Hill. Kokichi Nishimura's platoon, holding the most northerly position on the summit, was obliterated. Nishimura relates that, of the 42 members of his unit in the position at the time, 41 were killed or critically wounded during the onslaught. Nishimura was the sole survivor, albeit with three bullets lodged in his shoulder. Despite the carnage and heavy casualties inflicted on the Japanese, very few Australians were able to penetrate their stubborn defensive block. Horie's men remained anchored to their positions and their machine-guns shot the Australian attack to pieces. Further Japanese reinforcements still scaling Brigade Hill from the west collided with the Australian surge and eroded any remaining chance of success. Among the Australian dead lay Nye and Corporal McCallum, both of whom had distinguished themselves with great bravery at Isurava.

In a last ditch effort to reconnect the Australian lines, Potts ordered a counter-attack from the south. Chosen to lead the attack was Captain Langridge's D Company, previously guarding the brigade supply dump. Such was the gravity of the situation that soldiers from Brigade Headquarters, men who under normal conditions would seldom be required to fight, were attached to the attacking party. In fact, during the fighting of 8 September, only four soldiers from Brigade Headquarters including Potts himself, failed to fire their weapons. It appears Langridge accepted the near certainty of death. He is reputed to have handed his paybook and personal effects to another soldier before leading the charge.

Courage could not break the strong Japanese defence. The attack failed. Langridge and 21 others were killed, with Langridge shouting encouragement to his troops as he died. Gone was Maroubra Force's forlorn hope of holding Brigade Hill. Potts was out of options and out of time.

A sombre tribute to the Australian soldiers who died while trying to reconnect Maroubra Force's line on the crest of Brigade Hill. The flags mark the location where the soldiers were originally buried before their remains were reinterred at Bomana War Cemetery (M. Rifat, NAA016).

With the battle lost, Major Challen arrived on the scene with 38 men he had met in Menari — members of the 21st Brigade's left out of battle contingent who had been moving forward as reinforcements. Their well-timed arrival assisted Potts' plans for an immediate retreat. A small party was left in place to delay the Japanese pursuit while Potts and those with him headed to Menari. Potts had already been informed by the handful of men who had succeeded in getting through the Japanese roadblock that, in the event the surge failed, the isolated battalions would make for Menari via the contingency route.

View of Brigade Hill (in the centre background) from Menari. The slight dip visible in the centre of the summit is the site of the current memorial (M. Rifat, NAA017).

In the closing stages of the battle, there was one final act of immense bravery. Maroubra Force had numerous stretcher cases. Native labour could not be used in such close proximity to the battle, so each stretcher had to be carried by soldiers. With the retreating Australians forced to take an unfamiliar and difficult route, their movement slowed by the stretcher cases, more time was needed to allow the force to escape. Captain Arthur Lee of B Company 2/27th volunteered to form a rearguard while the Australians began the treacherous descent down the mountain.

Cooper's decision to move the entire 2/27th earlier in the day had allowed Kuwada the freedom to advance the *3/144th* up Mission Ridge uncontested. Thus, as Maroubra Force was leaving Brigade Hill, the *3/144th* spotted the withdrawal and pressed hard on the tail of the retreating column. The distance between the attackers and the Australians had shortened to 25 metres when Lee shouted to his small band: 'They're getting all the young chaps. We old buggers have something to account for. Come on boys, give the bastards a full mag.' He and two soldiers then charged the advancing Japanese, spraying them with every round they had, before joining the withdrawal. The Japanese were stunned by the audacity of the move and broke off the pursuit. Lee was awarded a bar to the MC he had earlier been awarded in

Syria. Importantly, the counter-attack won Maroubra Force the short reprieve it needed and enabled the isolated battalions to push on towards Menari.

Despite Lee's bravado, the retreat was disorderly. The 2/27th, furthest to the north and in the most precarious of positions, was the last to evacuate Brigade Hill. Further slowing their escape was the burden of bearing the stretcher cases, each of which required up to 10 soldiers to carry. As a result, the 2/27th became separated from the other two battalions and the Japanese were able to race ahead along the Kokoda Trail, barring their passage to Menari. Forced off the track and wandering through the jungle, the scattered remnants of the battalion took three weeks to rejoin the Australian lines. After much privation, they finally reached safety. However, they were so depleted and exhausted that they were unable to take any further part in the Kokoda campaign. The disaster at Brigade Hill had effectively wiped out the freshest Australian battalion after just one battle.

Hungry members of the 2/27th Battalion line up for a meal at Itiki in October 1942. The troops were lost in the wilderness of the Owen Stanleys after being cut off from Maroubra Force at the conclusion of the Battle of Brigade Hill (AWM027018).

The Japanese flanking attack had produced a stunning victory. This manoeuvre had been attempted previously in the campaign with varying degrees of success, but at Brigade Hill the plan worked magnificently and delivered a complete victory. Kusonose had achieved the singular success for which the *Nankai Shitai* had been yearning.

Much has been made of the defeat at Brigade Hill and the culpability of the commanders involved. The fractured and loose positioning of the Australian units — which made it easier for the Japanese to cleave Maroubra Force in half — was blamed on Potts' perceived preparations for a further withdrawal. Certainly the Australian dispositions were conducive to a continuation of the fighting withdrawal. Further, the independent positioning of the three battalions left Maroubra Force's line communications susceptible to being cut, as they were on the morning of 8 September. Criticism was also levelled at Potts' decision to place the 2/27th at the forefront of his defence, some arguing that it would have been better to have kept this fresh battalion in reserve, ready for a counter-attack. In Potts' defence, he believed that the battered 2/14th and 2/16th battalions might not be able to withstand further Japanese assault. And the 2/27th *did* hold the Japanese frontal attack at bay while under constant artillery fire.

Also scrutinised is Cooper's decision to shift the location of the entire 2/27th Battalion on 8 September, rather than a single company as Potts had ordered. This gifted the Japanese Mission Ridge and, with an unopposed passage to the top of Brigade Hill, the *3/144th* was almost able to sabotage Maroubra Force's withdrawal to Menari later in the day. In fairness to Cooper, the fickle radio communications left him feeling disconnected, and with dwindling supplies, the burden of stretcher cases and the fear of being stranded, his rationale in moving the 2/27th to consolidate with the rest of the 21st Brigade is understandable. And regardless, ceding Mission Ridge was not the decisive factor in the Australian defeat at Brigade Hill. It made breaking contact with the Japanese more difficult, but the battle was lost when Major Horie established the *2/144th* on Brigade Hill and repulsed the Australian attempts to reconnect their lines.

A defeat of this magnitude could not occur without significant consequences. Someone had to be held accountable and that person was Brigadier Potts. On the morning of 8 September, as the battle was reaching its climax, Captain Geoffrey Lyon, a 7th Division Liaison Officer, was moving along the Kokoda Trail towards Brigade Hill. Potts had repeatedly asked that a liaison officer be sent forward to Maroubra Force to convey the challenges that confronted the Force to higher command in Port Moresby. Potts did not believe that the conditions on the ground were truly appreciated by his superiors.

Lyon arrived in the midst of a rapidly deteriorating situation with Potts' attention required elsewhere. He could not have appeared at a worse time. From Menari he spoke with Potts by telephone. The conversation was brief but was to have enormous ramifications. On being told by Potts of the disturbing developments on Brigade Hill, Lyon sent a signal to Allen which painted an extremely dire picture. Allen was alarmed by Maroubra Force's deteriorating position and asked Potts to urgently clarify whether Lyon's ominous assessment was accurate. Potts' short reply was 'Message Lyon Confirmed'.

When Allen relayed this message to Lieutenant General Rowell, the latter decided that a change was required. At best, he believed Potts was physically and mentally exhausted and needed respite, at worst he doubted Potts' ability to defeat the enemy. He called Allen to his headquarters and informed him he was going to replace Potts with Brigadier Porter. Allen wrote:

> I raised no objection because judging from signals from Potts I myself felt that he, Potts, was either tired, or was losing a grip of the situation … I feel the decision to replace Potts by Porter is a sound one, but in fairness to Potts I at this stage, at any rate, have an open mind on the matter whether Potts has shown lack of judgement or has been out-fought. Although it may appear that this is the case I prefer to hear Potts before condemning him.

Rowell and Allen summoned Porter at 1.00 pm on 8 September — before Maroubra Force had tried unsuccessfully to reconnect the broken line — and ordered him to relieve Potts and stabilise the situation. The battle had cost Brigadier Potts his job and the men of the 21st Brigade a commander they respected.

The repercussions of the Battle of Brigade Hill were far-reaching. The Japanese victory shattered Maroubra Force and left the *Nankai Shitai* closer than ever to Port Moresby. Given the toll of casualties and the dislocation of the 2/27th, less than half of those who had fought at Brigade Hill were fit to take part in the Battle of Ioribaiwa just one week later.

Chapter 10
BATTLE OF IORIBAIWA

The final defensive battle fought by the Australians in the Kokoda campaign took place on Ioribaiwa Ridge, only 40 kilometres from, and within sight of, the lights of Port Moresby.

Looking north at Ioribaiwa Ridge from the site of Ioribaiwa village. The wartime village was located on the crest of the ridge (M. Rifat, NAA018).

The disaster at Brigade Hill marked the end of Brigadier Potts' tenure as commander of Maroubra Force. The series of crushing defeats had seen him lose the confidence of his superiors. As Brigadier Porter moved forward along the Trail to take interim command of the force, he was given additional units to assist in his task of defeating the Japanese — the 3rd Battalion (militia) and the 2/1st Pioneer Battalion.

In Port Moresby, moves were underway to further reinforce Maroubra Force with additional AIF units. As far back as the Battle of Isurava-Abuari, Rowell had learnt that the 25th Brigade was sailing towards Milne Bay. He had signalled Blamey at the time, telling him: 'Allen has now had good chance to see 14 Infantry Brigade [protecting Port Moresby] and is by no means impressed with their efficiency and general standard of training. This is no reflection on their courage but units contain a large number of young men not yet properly developed or trained. His view with which I concur is that 25 Infantry Brigade is required here …' With the Battle of Milne Bay then still hanging in the balance, Blamey was unmoved. Following the events of early September, Rowell again petitioned for the 25th Brigade. He signalled Blamey: 'After the experience of the 53rd Battalion I can have NO repeat NO confidence that any … [militia] unit will stand.'

By then the improving Allied position at Milne Bay and the waning fortunes of Maroubra Force had persuaded Blamey to divert the 25th Brigade to Port Moresby. This brigade's first action would be at the Battle of Ioribaiwa. Following the defeat at Brigade Hill, Blamey told Rowell that the 16th Brigade, which had just arrived in Australia after the disastrous Greek campaign, was available if required. This brigade would also shortly join the Kokoda campaign.

On the Kokoda Trail, the soldiers of Maroubra Force were in a dreadful state, suffering the effects of what seemed an endless withdrawal. Captain Rhoden, acting CO of the 2/14th, did his best to maintain morale. He sensed his men's dejection and, in a memorable address delivered on the Trail somewhere between Menari and Ioribaiwa, he implored them: 'Don't give in now, we've got this far and we've done well even though we've lost a lot of people. Australia depends upon us ... don't give in now.' Late in life, Rhoden reflected on his speech: 'I believe it had some effect. But it was no rabble rouser, it was only a sensible, I hope, exposition of where we were and what we'd done and how well we'd done it. It was a reminder call. It wasn't a wake up call, they didn't need waking up. ... I wasn't that type of commander that talked at people, I talked to them.' The speech worked and the morale of the force held.

In the Maguli Range between the villages of Nauro and Ioribaiwa, Potts handed command of Maroubra Force to Porter, informing him that the 21st Brigade was unfit for further operations. The remnants of the brigade were amalgamated into a composite battalion. Potts then returned to Port Moresby while Porter assessed the situation. With the 21st Brigade spent, the only effective units at his disposal were the two units recently added to Maroubra Force. Porter considered the 3rd Battalion (detached from 14 Brigade) incapable of executing any striking role, which left him the pioneers. At this stage however, a breakdown in communications seems to have occurred between Porter and the CO of the 2/1st Pioneers, Lieutenant Colonel Arnold Brown. Porter spoke to Brown while rushing to the front, delivering him a warning order to be ready to move forward at short notice. Brown told Porter that preparations for this move were well in hand, but Porter was aggrieved to discover later that the unit never moved forward, even after he ordered them to do so on 9 September. He noted later, 'This unit failed to carry out any of my instructions as ... [commander of] Maroubra Force, and NO explanation has been offered.'

Whatever the reason for the pioneers' failure to move forward and onto the Kokoda Trail, Porter's options were limited. He decided that the Maguli Range was an unsatisfactory location to hold. The range was too broad and would allow the Japanese to encircle him with little effort. An advance was out of the question given the parlous state of his present force. The only direction to move was backwards, to either of the last two great massifs in the Owen Stanleys.

Imita Ridge was his preferred option because of its closer proximity to Port Moresby (and thereby supply) and its sharp sides which minimised the risk of being flanked. But Allen wanted the Japanese held as far north as possible and ordered Porter to mount his defence on Ioribaiwa Ridge. Ioribaiwa lies to the south of the Maguli Range, separated by the deep ravine cut by Ofi Creek. Porter positioned the composite battalion on top of Ioribaiwa Ridge astride the Kokoda Trail forward of Ioribaiwa Village, while the 3rd Battalion was sited to the east of the composite battalion.

In opposition, Colonel Kusonose again led the *Nankai Shitai* into battle. Riddled with malaria, he was carried forward on a stretcher to the Maguli Range where the *Nankai Shitai* established its headquarters, conducting the battle from his sick bed. The same two battalions from Brigade Hill, the *2/144th* and the *3/144th*, were available for the coming battle.

For several days from 11 September, a similar pattern to the previous Kokoda battles developed as Japanese patrols pushed across Ofi Creek to probe the Australian positions on Ioribaiwa Ridge. To counter the Japanese patrols, the Australians laid booby traps constructed from grenades. This tactic paid dividends, shown by the pools of blood and damaged Japanese helmets and clothing found at the spots where the grenades detonated. The most memorable incident that occurred during this testing period was an ambush on the afternoon of 11 September.

A Japanese patrol descended from the Maguli Range to Ofi Creek and, spying tins of food that the Australians had planted as a trap, the hungry Japanese fell on the food. The Australians, peering down from the lower reaches of Ioribaiwa Ridge, unleashed a storm of gunfire, decimating the patrol. The Australians estimated that 20 to 30 enemy soldiers had been hit by their fire. This ambush is mentioned in numerous war diaries, while historian Raymond Paull notes that it was conducted by Maroubra Force's 'ambush experts', who were later asked to describe their technique to some British officers visiting Port Moresby.

Porter's command of Maroubra Force was brief. Moving up the Trail to take command was Brigadier Ken Eather, accompanied by the 25th Brigade. Eather had impressed as a battalion commander at the Battle of Bardia and it was hoped that this promise would translate into success against the *Nankai Shitai*. Well aware of his superiors' eagerness for an aggressive stance, he marshalled his three fresh battalions ready for an offensive. Eather's plan was to advance on three axes: the 2/25th Battalion would move along the Kokoda Trail; the 2/31st Battalion would advance to the left of the Trail and loop around to attack Nauro from the south-west; while on the right-hand side, the 2/33rd Battalion would approach the same target from the south-east.

Movement was slow as the 25th Brigade came to grips with the unfamiliar terrain. Once the two flanking battalions shifted off the Trail they realised that the foliage was far denser than any they had encountered in their training in the Blackall Ranges in Queensland. Large bodies of troops could not progress through the mass of jungle with any speed.

Thus, by the time Eather's battalions had moved onto Ioribaiwa Ridge on 13 and 14 September (ready to pass around the 21st Brigade and head towards Nauro), the Japanese had located the edge of the composite battalion's line and their mountain guns had begun firing. Kusonose had seized the initiative and compelled Eather to switch his focus; instead of an assault on Nauro, he was now ensnared in the defence of Ioribaiwa.

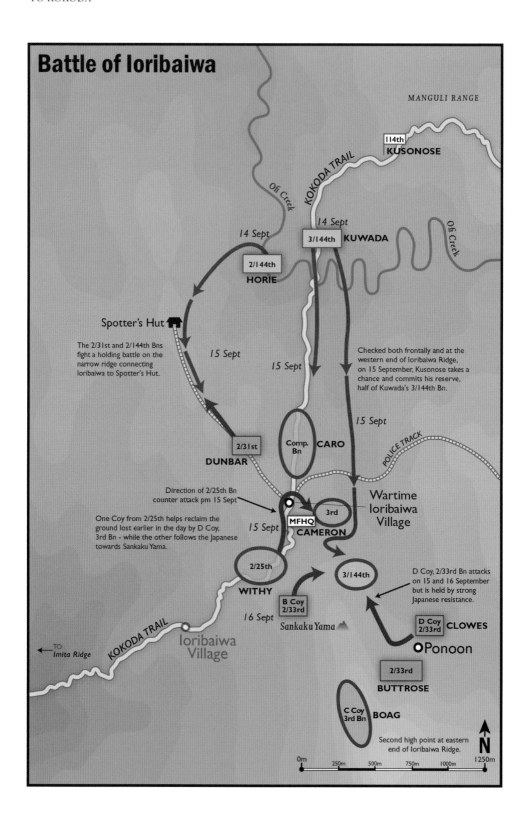

Battle of Ioribaiwa

MANGULI RANGE

114th
KUSONOSE

KOKODA TRAIL

Ofi Creek

Ofi Creek

14 Sept

14 Sept

3/144th KUWADA

2/144th
HORIE

Spotter's Hut

The 2/31st and 2/144th Bns
fight a holding battle on the
narrow ridge connecting
Ioribaiwa to Spotter's Hut.

15 Sept

15 Sept

Checked both frontally and at the
western end of Ioribaiwa Ridge,
on 15 September, Kusonose takes a
chance and commits his reserve,
half of Kuwada's 3/144th Bn.

15 Sept

POLICE TRACK

2/31st
DUNBAR

Comp.
Bn
CARO

Direction of 2/25th Bn
counter attack pm 15 Sept

Wartime
Ioribaiwa
Village

One Coy from 2/25th helps reclaim the
ground lost earlier in the day by D Coy,
3rd Bn - while the other follows the Japanese
towards Sankaku Yama.

MFHQ
CAMERON

3rd

15 Sept

2/25th

WITHY

3/144th

D Coy, 2/33rd Bn attacks
on 15 and 16 September
but is held by strong
Japanese resistance.

B Coy
2/33rd

16 Sept

Sankaku Yama

D Coy
2/33rd CLOWES

KOKODA TRAIL

TO
Imita Ridge

Ioribaiwa
Village

Ponoon

2/33rd
BUTTROSE

C Coy
3rd Bn
BOAG

Second high point at eastern
end of Ioribaiwa Ridge.

0m   250m   500m   750m   1000m   1250m

N

Kusonose hoped to replicate the tactics that had worked for him at Brigade Hill. Half of the *3/144th* was sent forward in a frontal assault, a feint to keep the Australians busy. At the same time, the *2/144th* was ordered to the west in a flanking movement. Kusonose held the second half of the *3/144th* in reserve.

Throughout 14 September, the Japanese frontal attack began making minor inroads into the forward pockets of the composite battalion's line, but could not break through. The *2/144th* was also gaining ground in its sweep on the western side of the battlefield. A track branched out north-west from Ioribaiwa and followed the ridgeline towards Spotter's Hut, a native dwelling some two hours' march away. In some sections the ridgeline was extremely narrow — no more than two metres wide — and it fell away precipitously on either side. It was at this point that the 2/31st, moving towards Spotter's Hut, came face to face with the *2/144th* pushing towards Ioribaiwa. A game of cat and mouse developed as each battalion attempted to use the limited space on the slender ridgeline to flank the other.

After several nights of violent storms, the morning of 15 September broke clear and bright. However, there was little cheer on the western side of the battlefield where the 2/31st spent the day trying to break the stalemate with the *2/144th*. All attempts to advance were greeted with accurate fire from well-concealed snipers, mortars and the mountain guns. The steep slopes on either side of the track allowed the Japanese to barricade any movement. The CO of the 2/31st, Lieutenant Colonel Colin Dunbar, ordered his men back to a wider section of the ridgeline where they bivouacked and plotted a tight defensive line. Neither side could force a way past the other, so they waited for events in other areas of the battlefield to play out.

The composite battalion was having a torrid time manning the central defensive position. These men, who had already endured three weeks of hardship since first being committed at Isurava-Abuari, were now bearing the brunt of Japanese pressure. The Japanese gunners continued to pound their positions and were brazen in the use of their guns. Japanese doctrine emphasised that a gun should be placed at least 800 metres behind the leading infantry. At Ioribaiwa, however, one of the Japanese 37mm guns was moved to within 100 metres of the composite battalion before closing the gap even further to fire from a distance of just 50 metres. The Japanese gun was so close to the Australians that members of its crew were killed by small arms fire. The roar from the artillery was ear-splitting, and men who had shown supreme fortitude in action to this point began to crack. Under such a ferocious bombardment, it was feared that these beleaguered troops could not withstand the unremitting attacks much longer.

With Kusonose's attempt to encircle on the western side of the battlefield checked, he threw caution to the wind and ordered his reserve half-battalion to encircle the eastern flank. Committing his reserve at this early stage of the battle was a risky ploy and Kusonose had underestimated the length of the Australian lines, making the move even riskier. This was an easy mistake to make because Kusonose was ill and initially unaware that the Australians had been reinforced. He was also unaware that the Australian line was not continuous.

Historian Bryce Fraser has analysed the dispositions of Maroubra Force as they appear in the *Official History* and discovered that they have been incorrectly recorded. By 15 September the Australian units on Ioribaiwa Ridge were, from right to left, the 2/33rd Battalion, the 3rd Battalion, the composite battalion and then the 2/31st Battalion. The 2/25th Battalion was tucked in behind these positions as a reserve. However, as Fraser has correctly pointed out, unlike the depiction in the *Official History*, there was a gigantic gap in the Australian lines that stretched from the 2/33rd Battalion stationed in the village of Ponoon, to the right-hand edge of D Company of the 3rd Battalion which was defending much closer to the Kokoda Trail. Essentially, the 2/33rd Battalion was divorced from the main Ioribaiwa defensive position.

The gap in the Australian line was the result of several factors. The initial orders for the 2/33rd Battalion were to bypass Ioribaiwa and attack Nauro from the south-east, thus the battalion was close to Ponoon searching for a route known as the Police Track which would take it towards Nauro. Second, the maps used by the Australian commanders were grossly inaccurate. Some were sketches based on observation and roughly drawn by hand, while others were drawn from aerial photographs, with some sections of the map left incomplete because the camera's vision had been obscured by clouds. As a result, numerous topographical high points and features were mistaken, or had been left off the maps altogether. A specific example of the confusion this created appears in the reference in the Australian primary records to a 'high point' east of (wartime) Ioribaiwa Village. In fact, there are two. The one closest to the Kokoda Trail is a distinctive pyramid-shaped protrusion that the Japanese called *Sankaku Yama* (Triangle Mountain). Further to the east near Ponoon, there is a second taller, flat-topped peak. Because there was no distinction made between these two points on the maps used at the time, several Australian officers were given ambiguous directions to move east to the 'high point', without knowing which specific high point was their destination.

Kusonose's attempt to encircle Maroubra Force's right flank was not directed far enough to the east and, instead of flanking the Australians, its trajectory took it straight into the yawning gap between the 3rd and 2/33rd Battalions. However, the Japanese miscalculation may have delivered them an unlikely success, as the 3rd Battalion made a critical error. While digging fighting pits in its allocated defensive zone, 17 Platoon of D Company was surprised by a scouting party at the head of the Japanese flanking move. Inattentive sentries allowed the scouting party to sneak up on the Australians. The error was compounded by the fact that the soldiers digging the pits did not have their weapons close at hand so the platoon was quickly overpowered and forced from the area. But, unlike the 53rd Battalion's capitulation at Abuari, on this occasion the militia steadied and prevented the Japanese completely overwhelming the line. Nevertheless, the Japanese had now wedged themselves on Ioribaiwa Ridge and were ready for the Australian reaction.

The response came in the form of a two-pronged counter-attack. Lieutenant Colonel Charles Withy, CO of the 2/25th Battalion, personally led two of his companies from their position in reserve and attempted to drive the Japanese off Ioribaiwa Ridge. In support, a company from the 2/33rd closed in on the Japanese flanking movement from the east.

The 2/25th's counter-attack was moderately successful. One company helped 17 Platoon regain the ground it had lost earlier, but the second company could not push the Japanese off Ioribaiwa Ridge. Instead, they pursued the Japanese who turned to the east and headed towards the steep slopes of *Sankaku Yama*.

The 2/33rd's contribution to the counter-attack was less successful. The CO, Lieutenant Colonel Alfred Buttrose, ordered his A Company to support the 2/25th. This company found the terrain too difficult to move through and, after two hours of trying, abandoned its attempt. Buttrose hoped his D Company might fare better. Led by Captain Tim Clowes (brother of Major General Cyril Clowes who commanded Milne Force), D Company moved west from Ponoon, deeper into the Ofi Creek ravine, and ran straight into the left flank of more Japanese working their way up Ioribaiwa Ridge. After a searing firefight, Clowes was unable to clear the Japanese so he pulled his company away with several casualties and a number of soldiers missing. The inability of A Company to attack in concert with Withy reduced the effectiveness of what should have been a two-pronged assault, and made life difficult for Clowes who was later forced to attack alone. As night fell, so did the rain, and the drenched Australians were ordered to renew their attacks the next morning while the Japanese clung to their toehold on Ioribaiwa Ridge.

Men of the 2/14th Battalion enjoy a rare moment of rest under a makeshift shelter close to their positions on Ioribaiwa Ridge. Lance Corporal Harold Atkinson (left) cleans his Thompson sub machine-gun while Sergeant Harold Phefley writes a letter home (AWM026727).

On 16 September, the previous day's action was repeated. Duelling continued on the narrow ridge between the 2/31st and the *2/144th* while, in the centre, the Japanese made further ground, although the composite battalion continued to hold on. The decisive action occurred at the eastern end of the battlefield. The company of the *3/144th* which had earlier lodged itself between the Australian battalions attempted to summit *Sankaku Yama*. Controlling this salient would afford commanding views across Maroubra Force's entire position. The Australians themselves had tried several times to climb to the top, but had been defeated by the unscaleable cliffs.

Eather now felt vulnerable. He was unable to communicate easily with his units to the east, most of his native carriers had been tasked with ferrying the wounded off Ioribaiwa Ridge (which did not leave enough for forward duties) and, with gunfire emanating from the slopes of *Sankaku Yama*, the idea took hold that the Japanese were gaining ascendancy over the Australian position.

Sankaku Yama ('Triangle Mountain') as seen from the Kokoda Trail on top of Ioribaiwa Ridge (M. Rifat, NAA019).

Shortly after, as B and D companies of the 2/33rd went into action trying to knock the Japanese off Ioribaiwa Ridge, Eather's confidence evaporated. He discussed the situation with Porter, who agreed that Maroubra Force needed to disentangle itself and make a fresh start. Eather called Allen and sought permission to retreat to Imita Ridge if necessary. Allen urged Eather to fight on, but reluctantly told him that the choice was his and warned that no further withdrawals would be sanctioned. He is rumoured to have said: 'There won't be any withdrawal from the Imita position, Ken. You'll die there if necessary. Do you understand?' Rowell echoed these sentiments, telling Allen, 'Confirm your orders to Eather. Stress the fact that however many troops the enemy has they must all have walked from Buna. We are now so far back that any further withdrawal is out of question and Eather must fight it out at all costs. I am playing for time until 16 Inf Bde arrives.'

Having secured permission, Eather gave the general order for retreat. Unlike the chaos of the earlier withdrawals from Isurava and Brigade Hill, the withdrawal from Ioribaiwa was well-organised and orderly. By nightfall, all but a rearguard battalion had relocated to Imita Ridge. The battle-weary Japanese had secured their final victory in the Kokoda campaign, against an adversary far superior in numbers.

Eather's decision to abandon Ioribaiwa is contentious. Criticisms have focussed on the disparity between the reasons he gave Allen prior to the withdrawal, and those he listed in his post-battle report. The signals during the battle appear desperate, and highlight Eather's fears that he was being encircled and might not be able to hold the Japanese on Ioribaiwa. By contrast, the post-battle report appears more rational, and portrays the decision as one that was based on careful consideration. It paints the decision to withdraw as a strategic move. In the post-battle report, Eather reasoned that withdrawing to Imita would allow the Australians to respond to Japanese artillery with their own artillery and would shorten the Australian supply line. He also describes Imita Ridge as a better defensive position. All of these factors were known prior to the battle and were Porter's reasons for favouring Imita Ridge over Ioribaiwa Ridge for a set defence.

There is no reason to doubt that the concerns Eather expressed in his signals during the battle were genuine. The composite battalion holding Maroubra Force's centre was on the verge of collapse. The inability to adequately communicate with his units and reliance on inaccurate maps contributed to the confusion that pervaded Eather's headquarters and there is a sense that he felt he was operating blind. Yet to a certain extent his anxiety was unwarranted, as he still had a fresh reserve with half of the 2/25th Battalion uncommitted and ready to move where needed.

It seems probable that at least some of the reasons cited as justification for the withdrawal in Eather's post-battle report were contrived after the fact. That said, in the overall scheme of the Kokoda campaign, the withdrawal to Imita Ridge was militarily sound because Porter's initial assessment that Imita offered greater advantages than Ioribaiwa was accurate. Maroubra Force could have remained on Ioribaiwa, but for what tactical or strategic purpose? Holding an unimportant ridgeline that was recaptured by the Australians before the end of the month in any case would have resulted in an unnecessary loss of life. Allen's own preference appears to have been the decisive factor in choosing Ioribaiwa as the place to make the stand, rather than the judgement of the commander on the ground.

Withdrawing to Imita Ridge shortened the Australian supply line while lengthening the Japanese supply line at a time when the *Nankai Shitai* was facing its own looming supply crisis. Devastating floods between the beachheads and Kokoda had turned roads to quagmires and washed out bridges, making rivers, particularly the Kumusi, impossible to cross. The resulting difficulties in moving supplies forward, coupled with Australian air superiority that harassed the enemy north of the Owen Stanleys at every opportunity, had wreaked havoc with the Japanese supply lines. Retreating to Imita Ridge allowed the Australian 25-pounders at Owers' Corner to bombard the Japanese positions on Ioribaiwa, heralding the first time in the campaign that Japanese guns could be answered with an equivalent response in firepower. The effect of this on the morale of the Australian troops was enormous.

The 14th Field Regiment's 25-pounder guns being hauled through the jungle in the vicinity of Uberi on the Kokoda Trail. Members of the regiment are assisted by the 2/1st Pioneer Battalion (AWM026855).

But, most importantly, withdrawing to Imita allowed the Australians to regain freedom of offensive movement. This was essential, as it was the fundamental basis of Eather's orders. Eather could not execute his orders to capture Nauro while stuck in a defensive slugfest over Ioribaiwa with an enemy that was not accustomed to giving ground easily.

Once the Japanese had attacked first at Ioribaiwa, the Australians were girdled and forced into reactionary manoeuvres. From Imita Ridge, aggressive patrolling from a stable base of operations could be resumed. Therefore, even if Eather's decision-making had been influenced by pressure during the heat of battle, in the overall scheme of the campaign, the correct decision was made.

Nevertheless, the withdrawal to Imita Ridge caused panic and dismay at GHQ in Australia. The unexpected nature of the move so soon after the commitment of the 25th Brigade sparked a crisis of command. Other commanders would soon discover that they too would join Potts in the bloodletting of Kokoda leadership.

JAPANESE ARTILLERY

Throughout the Kokoda campaign the Japanese held one distinct advantage over the Australians: artillery. The Japanese use of artillery pieces in each Kokoda battle was a force multiplier, and the Australians were never able to match the Japanese ranged weapons.

The Japanese had 16 artillery pieces in Papua, 13 of which were used during the Kokoda campaign. These consisted of six 75mm guns, four 70mm guns and three 37mm guns. They used their artillery in three roles: indirect fire support, direct fire support, and close support of the infantry.

The physical effort involved in moving these weapons across the Kokoda Trail was immense. Although the guns could be disassembled and carried in pieces, one 75mm gun alone weighed 540 kilograms. The greater weight, however, was the ammunition, with each shell for the same gun weighing eight kilograms. Approximately 940 men were responsible for carrying the guns, ammunition and other paraphernalia across the Owen Stanleys.

While it is difficult to ascertain the exact percentage of killed and wounded, conservative estimates suggest that the Japanese artillery was responsible for around 35% of casualties. What cannot be quantified is the impact of the artillery on Australian morale. The helplessness felt by the men who were subjected to relentless bombardment without the means to retaliate sapped both their number and their spirit.

The Type 92, 70 mm Infantry Gun (Mark Wahlert).

IMITA RIDGE

Imita Ridge was the final defensive position occupied by the Australians. It was a better defensive position than Ioribaiwa because it reduced the length of the Australian supply lines and allowed the Australians to use their own artillery — the guns of the 14th Field Regiment.

Imita was never attacked. The Japanese surge south was over. As the situation on Guadalcanal turned in favour of the Allies, General Horii was ordered to withdraw the *Nankai Shitai* north to protect the beachheads. Lacking a word in the Japanese language for 'retreat' the dispirited Japanese soldiers were ordered to 'advance to the rear'.

The most enduring memory of Imita Ridge is the Golden Stairs, cut by Australian Army engineers into the southern side of the ridge to help soldiers reach the summit. In reality, the stairs hindered rather than helped and made climbing more difficult. The *Official History's* description of the Golden Stairs illustrates why: 'each step battened at its edge by a rough log, sometimes broken and therefore treacherous, and cradling mud and water from the afternoon rains.' The Golden Stairs no longer exist.

There are many tough ascents on the Kokoda Trail, including the one in this iconic photograph. The photograph has traditionally been credited as the best image of the Golden Stairs, in line with its original caption. Recent analysis suggests that the caption may be incorrect and instead, the photograph may depict the climb to Ioribaiwa Ridge (Army Museum of Western Australia, AMWA30357).

Chapter 11
IMITA RIDGE

The *Nankai Shitai* was delighted with its triumph at the Battle of Ioribaiwa and revelled in its success. The glistening ocean and visible lights of Port Moresby were an elixir for the Japanese soldiers' tired, emaciated bodies. They were determined to push on. It would take only a matter of days for them to realise the stark reality of their situation.

The 2/33rd was assigned the task of protecting the Australian withdrawal from Ioribaiwa. The procession leaving Ioribaiwa for Imita Ridge moved on into the night as stretcher cases and a violent storm slowed progress. Brigadier Eather ordered Lieutenant Colonel Buttrose to delay the Japanese for four days. Buttrose decided to accomplish this by arranging a chain of company-sized ambush sites along the Kokoda Trail. Each successive company was to inflict as much damage as possible on any enemy that approached, and then pull back through the next company which would be located 15 minutes' march further south.

The distinctive double-humped Imita Ridge as seen from Ioribaiwa Ridge (M. Rifat, NAA020).

B Company was to establish the initial ambush position on Ioribaiwa Ridge in the area that had housed 25th Brigade's food dump during the Battle of Ioribaiwa. The Australians destroyed everything of value that could be salvaged by the enemy. Bayonets were used to puncture bully beef tins and spare clothing was set alight. Booby traps were set by placing live grenades among the abandoned stores. Nevertheless, Buttrose soon realised that B Company's ambush position was too exposed and ordered the company to the rear of the chain. With this rearrangement, responsibility for the initial ambush passed to A Company which was in an overwatch position south of but within sight of the food dump.

The Australians were restive as they waited for the inevitable Japanese appearance. At 6.00 pm, the first two Japanese soldiers tentatively approached the food dump. Captain Kenneth Lawson, OC A Company, was to signal the start of the ambush by firing the first shot. He waited for more Japanese to congregate, but the two Japanese soldiers did nothing, apparently wary of the danger. The tense standoff lasted 10 minutes before a stray shot from an impatient Australian caused a domino effect and several of Lawson's platoons began firing wildly at the food dump.

The ambush opportunity was squandered. In the commotion, not a single Japanese soldier was confirmed hit. Lawson followed his earlier orders to pull his company back, section by section, to a rendezvous located 15 minutes to the south of C Company. Having reached the rendezvous, Lawson realised that Sergeant Alexander Tobin's platoon was missing. A runner was sent and located the platoon in its original ambush position. Unlike the rest of A Company, Tobin's platoon had maintained fire discipline and refrained from shooting as the men had not sighted a single enemy soldier. Tobin's platoon was withdrawn, leaving C Company the next in turn to confront the Japanese advance the following morning.

C Company was positioned in a large kunai patch on the southern side of Ioribaiwa Ridge. One platoon was positioned on the left, two covered the Kokoda Trail on the right, and extra firepower was provided from the rear by three 2-inch mortars. The rain had cleared, but the Japanese did not advance, most likely hesitant after the firestorm that had erupted at the food dump earlier. Buttrose opted to force the issue and ordered a patrol to lure the Japanese forward. Three soldiers from D Company led by Lieutenant Richard Cox were given the unenviable task. They timidly crossed the kunai patch and inched into the jungle, expecting at any moment to be shot by the Japanese who they felt certain were watching their every move. No shots were fired, but Cox was confident he had captured the enemy's attention. He turned the patrol around and hastily moved back to the Australian lines.

The ploy had the desired effect. At 6.45 am approximately 50 Japanese soldiers from the *3/144th* emerged from the jungle and moved into the kunai patch, oblivious to the potential danger. The ambush was triggered when Captain Larry Miller, OC C Company, shot the sword-wielding Japanese officer at the head of the party. The rest of C Company then followed suit, pouring a tremendous amount of fire into the startled Japanese. The noise was deafening, described as an 'orchestra of fire' as rifles, machine-guns, mortars and grenades blasted away. C Company expended its entire supply of ammunition, firing close to 3000 rounds.

Miller was certain that the patrol had been obliterated, concluding that there was little chance that any of the Japanese could have survived such a brutal assault. He ordered his men to withdraw through D Company, the next company along the Trail.

Whether C Company's ambush caused the devastation that Miller claimed is questionable. The 2/33rd's unit historian, Warrant Officer William Crooks, wrote that, with the exception of Miller, none of the other men in C Company could confirm that enemy soldiers had actually been hit. This appears to corroborate the Japanese account which states that only two men were wounded, one of whom later died. A Company's botched ambush at the food dump had already demonstrated that sheer weight of firepower did not necessarily translate to high casualties if the fire was random.

This was the furthest south the *Nankai Shitai* ever advanced on the Kokoda Trail. The next 2/33rd company in line waited expectantly but no further Japanese movement eventuated. The Japanese were content to hold their ground on Ioribaiwa Ridge. Buttrose moved his battalion across Ua-Ule Creek to rendezvous with the remainder of the 25th Brigade on Imita Ridge.

By 17 September Maroubra Force had consolidated on Imita Ridge. Brigadier Eather began planning to advance northwards once more. The units under his command were finally in one location, uncommitted to action and of considerable strength. At his disposal were the three battalions of the 25th Brigade, the 3rd Battalion, 24 men from the 2/6th Independent (Commando) Company and the 2/1st Pioneer Battalion which had now moved forward onto the Trail. In total, Eather had 132 officers and 2492 men available to him.

Shifting to Imita Ridge had finally given Maroubra Force some respite after weeks of continual pursuit and harassment. The beleaguered 2/14th and 2/16th battalions resumed their separate identities and marched off the Trail and back to their base at Koitaki to recuperate. The troops who remained were able to take stock and properly reorganise before initiating offensive operations.

22 September 1942. The 21st Brigade is relieved from duty after a torturous month in the Owen Stanleys and is sent to Koitaki for rest. Here, a wounded Australian soldier has his cigarette lit by Salvation Army Chaplain Albert Moore, padre to the 2/14th Battalion. The soldier on the stretcher is Lieutenant Valentine Gardner, D Company, 2/14th Battalion (AWM013287).

Eather was active during the week that followed, organising several patrols of approximately 50 men of all ranks. These patrols were ordered to advance along different trajectories through the jungle chasm that separates Imita Ridge and Ioribaiwa. The sorties were designed to locate Japanese positions and determine their approximate strengths. A patrol from the 2/25th was the first to contact the Japanese near Ioribaiwa, engaging them in several sharp skirmishes. Small actions continued to occur during this period as the Australian patrols skirted the Ioribaiwa ridgeline testing the Japanese defences.

The *Nankai Shitai* spent its days on Ioribaiwa fortifying its position, erecting stockades and constructing shelters and trenches to protect the men from Allied air attacks of which they remained fearful following the air attack near Efogi. The chronic lack of food was all-consuming. Scavenging parties were sent out and ordered to collect as much food as possible to supplement the failed supply line. However, for the most part, the days following the Battle of Ioribaiwa were relatively sedate.

The lull was broken on 27 September when Eather called his battalion commanders via telephone hook-up and told them to prepare for an all-out assault on Ioribaiwa the following day. Satisfied with the intelligence garnered by his patrols, Eather gave each of his battalion commanders explicit instructions concerning his role in the planned offensive. Eleven days had passed since Ioribaiwa had been ceded and the 25th Brigade was itching for a chance to lock horns with the Japanese once more.

The next morning Maroubra Force moved out, expecting stern resistance from the Japanese. As they closed in on Ioribaiwa, however, they discovered that the ridge was deserted. From each of his battalions, Eather received the same message: no Japanese encountered.

In fact, the order to relinquish Ioribaiwa had been communicated to Major General Horii several days earlier. On 23 September, Lieutenant General Hyakutake at *17th Army Headquarters* had signalled him stating: 'the army will adjust the front line in the area of South Seas Force operations to strengthen the defences at Buna.' He added, 'The commander of the South Seas Force will assemble his main strength in the Isurava and Kokoda areas and secure these as a base for future offensives ...' The instructions dampened Horii's satisfaction in gaining Ioribaiwa, but they were based on sound reasons.

The situation on Guadalcanal had again swung in favour of the Allies following the Japanese defeat at the Battle of Edson's Ridge. Japanese high command realised that Guadalcanal might be the decisive campaign of the Pacific War and nominated it as the most important strategic theatre. As a result, it soaked up resources — namely manpower and materiel — originally earmarked for the *Nankai Shitai* in Papua. The siphoning of resources deprived the *Nankai Shitai* of the support it required for a successful crossing of the Owen Stanleys in sufficient strength to break the Port Moresby garrison. In addition, the Japanese intercepted signals traffic which prompted fears that the Allies intended to attack Giruwa directly, possibly with paratroopers. The Japanese were eager to garrison the beachheads to protect them from naval and aerial attack.

Even without these factors, there were more immediate problems for the *Nankai Shitai*. Horii had exhausted his supply chain. Aerial bombardment of the Japanese supply line between the beachheads and Kokoda coupled with major flooding along the Kumusi River had brought the movement of supplies to a halt. Getting supplies across the swollen Kumusi was a particular problem. The bridges that crossed it were in constant need of repair and, despite the best efforts of the Japanese engineers to keep them operational, the destruction of a bridge had a crippling effect on the flow of supplies to the front line.

A makeshift wire bridge crossing the Kumusi River at Wairopi. Although this photo was taken much later in November, the picture illustrates the width and swift flow of the river, and the difficulty in moving supplies across the flimsy bridge (AWMP02423.033).

The Japanese seldom resupplied their force in Papua from the air, which meant the bulk of supplies were carried forward by manual labour. To assist with this task, 2000 indentured natives and 2360 horses had accompanied the Japanese from Rabaul. A further 300 native carriers were drawn from the tribes of northern Papua. Both the natives and animals were mistreated and overworked. Many succumbed to sickness. When a native could no longer work through injury, or illness, he was deemed excess to requirements and was often murdered. The cruel treatment meted out to the native carriers prompted many to desert. Without new carriers to replace those who died or deserted, the Japanese struggled to maintain their supply train, particularly as the force advanced further south. With their troops starving and deprived of basic levels of sustenance, the *Nankai Shitai* had no reasonable chance of success.

Finally, the constant casualties from fighting and sickness had drained the *Nankai Shitai*'s numbers. By contrast, Maroubra Force was continually reinforced and, with several fresh battalions now in and forward of Port Moresby, any last ditch effort by the Japanese to surge towards the capital was likely to result in a heavy defeat. The Japanese had reached the zenith of their advance.

As Australian war correspondent Osmar White concluded, 'The Japanese fell back through the range from Eoribaiwa [sic] because their efforts to establish supply were doomed to failure from the start. They fell back because they were exhausted, diseased and starved.'

PREPARING FOR THE JUNGLE

Prior to the Kokoda campaign, the Australian Army was far from proficient in jungle warfare. Malaya was the only campaign of any length in which Australians had fought in the jungle, and in that case, because the 8th Division had been captured when Singapore surrendered, the benefit of experience was lost to the remainder of the Army. In contrast, the *IJA* was vastly experienced, having been engaged in full-scale war for five years prior to the Kokoda campaign, and having fought previously in jungle environments in Malaya and Burma. The *IJA* was arguably the finest jungle-fighting outfit in the world.

The Australians needed to adapt to jungle warfare and adopt measures and infantry minor tactics to deal with the new operating environment. One example was the need for camouflage. When Japanese troops attacked A Company, 39 Battalion, on the Kokoda escarpment on 9 August, they were caked in mud, wearing green uniforms, and had attached foliage to their bodies to blend into the natural environment. Private Ronald Halsall of the 39th Battalion recalled, 'The first thing the Jap would do was grab a bush and hold it up in front of them, and when you weren't looking they'd go a few yards this way. And sometimes we'd say gee that bush wasn't there before.'

In contrast, the first units of the Australian Army that fought on the Kokoda Trail were still wearing khaki uniforms. It was worse for the 21st Brigade as prior service in Syria had seen the men's webbing bleached white by the desert sun. The stark white webbing stood out clearly against a jungle green background. At a press conference held in mid-September after General Blamey's first visit to Port Moresby, war correspondent and Blamey critic Chester Wilmot asked the general whether he thought that green uniforms were necessary for the jungle of New Guinea. Blamey answered, 'Not at all. It is true that those [khaki] uniforms were designed specifically for the jungles of India but I have never seen any evidence that the jungle of New Guinea is any different to the jungle of India. I think the uniforms the soldiers are wearing are quite adequate … ' Wilmot responded, 'Well I can provide several thousand witnesses who have actually fought in New Guinea who can provide evidence to the contrary …'

Blamey may not have conceded the point then but, by the time the 25th Brigade arrived at the Kokoda Trail, the troops were wearing green uniforms. However, even then there were setbacks. The green uniforms issued were simply khaki uniforms cooked in stoves with green dye added at the last minute. The rushed job caused the dye to run when wet, which in turn saw the soldiers suffer skin complaints such as eczema.

Another tactic to which the Australians had to adapt was the Japanese use of deception. The Japanese would often call to the Australians in English to intimidate and trick them. At first the ploy was disconcerting, but as the campaign progressed, the Australians learnt to ignore it. A novel way to overcome the ruse occurred at the Battle of Myola Ridge. Here, during an Australian attack by the 2/33rd Battalion, the Japanese shouted English phrases to the Australians such as 'Withdrawal! Withdrawal!' The attacking patrol commander improvised and gave directions to the Australian soldiers in Arabic, a language that the diggers had learnt in a basic form during earlier service in Syria. During the same battle, the Australians altered their tactics based on their observations of enemy routine. Attacks were planned to occur between 8.00 and 9.00 am once the Australians realised that the Japanese often had breakfast at this time and were consequently less vigilant.

Jungle fighting also required the use of a different offensive formation to the one that had long been part of Army doctrine. On the open battlefields of Syria, it was common for a platoon to move with a 'two up, one back formation' so that, on contact, the bulk of the unit's firepower was at the front where it could be brought to bear on the enemy and could 'compensate for the absence of cover'. In the jungle, it was better to move in single file with a single section up and two sections back. The idea was to limit the damage sustained in the event of an ambush and allow the commander flexibility to move his men where they were needed — information he would not have until contact had been initiated.

As the Kokoda campaign progressed, numerous commanders wrote papers on jungle fighting detailing observations based on their experience. Brigadier Selwyn Porter made some interesting points in a report he wrote in October 1942. He considered that the Australian experience of modern warfare in North Africa, Europe and Syria had caused the Army to develop a false sense of security based on the belief that rapid mobility would be possible and instant fire and air support would always be readily available. He noted that jungle fighting was different, and was firmly of the belief that the Australians should 'Learn from our [experienced] enemy; but we should learn to counter his successful methods, rather than copy them ... because to imitate Japanese tactics will result in our doom.' This assessment was based on his belief that the Japanese were willing to sacrifice men for an advantage, an attitude he was convinced that the Australians should not or could not emulate. Having made these observations, Porter listed some important lessons that had been learnt in just over two months of jungle warfare, and which remain relevant to this day. These included:

- Ambush is superior to patrol hunting because, in thick jungle, two patrols may miss each other even though their paths might cross very close.

- Patrols striking at enemy positions are only useful if a follow-up force can quickly move behind the striking force to occupy any ground gained.

- Commanders need to be close to their forward companies because the line of sight difficulties and communication limitations will hamper their ability to control a battle from some distance away.

- Junior officers and NCOs have to make tactical decisions on the spot, and even individual rifleman have to act as their own leaders to an extent because, in jungle warfare, it is often impossible to know what is occurring in the next section, let alone elsewhere in other platoons or companies.

- In hilly, densely vegetated country, the rate and scale of movement needs to be contracted because of the intense fatigue involved.

Early in the Kokoda campaign, General MacArthur had been forthright in expressing his poor opinion of the Australian Army's jungle-fighting ability. On 6 September he had written to General George Marshall, Chief of Staff of the US Army and stated, 'the Australians have proven themselves unable to match the enemy in jungle fighting. Aggressive leadership is lacking.' This accusation may have borne some truth up to that point in time, as one Australian unit after the next had been committed to stem the tide of the Japanese advance along the Kokoda Trail and each had been successively forced to withdraw.

However, as the campaign evolved, the Australians gradually improved and adapted to the unique conditions, developing the tactics required for success in jungle fighting. For example, when the first AIF unit (the 21st Brigade) reinforced Maroubra Force in August, it was rushed forward and, as a result, made many of the same mistakes as the militia. The men were still wearing khaki uniforms and did not take forward support weapons such as 3-inch mortars and medium machine-guns. In coming to grips with the Kokoda campaign, they realised that they were fighting two enemies, the Japanese and the jungle, both equally intimidating.

By the time the 16th Brigade moved up the Trail in October, it was far better prepared. The men had had the benefit of jungle training in Ceylon where they had acclimatised to jungle conditions and had learnt skills such as the ability to live on limited rations. Just prior to their embarkation for Port Moresby, lessons were conducted on Japanese tactics. This pre-planning made a substantial difference, and equipped the 16th Brigade to cope with both the environment and the enemy. By the end of the campaign the men had adapted well and had become proficient jungle fighters.

The Kokoda campaign, and the Battle of the Beachheads which followed, was instructive for the Australian Army which learnt that training methods and packages would need to be adopted to prepare for fighting in a jungle environment. One benefit of the harsh lessons learnt during the campaign was the establishment of the Land Headquarters Training Centre (Jungle Warfare), now known as the Land Warfare Centre, at the end of 1942. As the jungle was the environment of operations for the remainder of the war, it was vital that lessons from the campaign be captured and widely disseminated.

A patrol from the 2/31st Battalion moves in single file along the banks of the Brown River between Menari and Nauro (AWM027081).

Chapter 12
THE CAUTIOUS ADVANCE

Following the decision to abandon Ioribaiwa, Horii reorganised his force. A new group known as the *Stanley Detachment* (primarily formed from the *2/144th*) would construct and man a redoubt in the Owen Stanleys while the remainder of the *Nankai Shitai* moved further to the north. Horii hoped that, once the situation on Guadalcanal improved, the majority of the *Nankai Shitai* could re-link with the *Stanley Detachment* for a fresh assault on Port Moresby.

A Japanese shell dump found on Ioribaiwa Ridge following its recapture by the Australians on 28 September 1942. The shells are from the 75mm mountain gun (AWM026832).

With Ioribaiwa secured on 28 September, Australian patrols pushed further forward along the Kokoda Trail. They crossed the Maguli Range and arrived at the now deserted Nauro. The Trail on either side of Nauro showed signs of a hasty retreat, that of the Australians in early September and the Japanese in late September. The smell of decomposing bodies hung heavy in the air.

One small group of diggers camping in the Maguli Range several weeks later made a horrific discovery as they passed through the site of the abandoned Japanese headquarters. At the end of a day's march they bedded down in darkness in an area where the odour was particularly strong. The next morning the troops lifted their groundsheets to pack them away. To their horror, they discovered body parts protruding from the ground. These belonged to half-buried Japanese corpses — the Australian troops had just spent the night sleeping on top of dead Japanese troops.

Looking north from Nauro, the swampy Brown River valley is covered in clouds. The chain of ridgelines that bisects the southern half of the Kokoda Trail forms a backdrop. The first barrier to the north is 'The Wall'; beyond this is the village of Menari (M. Rifat, NAA021).

North of Nauro, the constant rain had churned the Trail to a soup. The swampy terrain was littered with Japanese bodies and equipment. Both armies had been careless with hygiene in this area, and had defecated at random with no regard for proper sanitation. This befouled the streams and creeks from which the men drank, causing the spread of dysentery. The Australians made a concerted effort to clean the area, but the bacterial infection had already taken hold and many men fell ill.

Private Harold Newman of the 2/33rd Battalion stops for a drink on a patrol between Nauro and Menari. The danger in this region was not from an enemy bullet, but from the spread of dysentery as the whole area was heavily befouled (AWM027079).

MALARIA AND DYSENTERY

The high wastage of manpower to tropical disease is a feature of jungle warfare. This was true of the Kokoda campaign, in which two of the most debilitating illnesses were malaria and dysentery.

Malaria is an infectious disease caused by a parasite. The disease is transmitted to humans through the bite of infected female *Anopheles* mosquitoes. Symptoms include high fevers and anaemia, and complications can lead to organ failure.

Bacillary dysentery is a bacterial infection of the colon, typically spread via contact with the faecal matter of an infected person. Symptoms include diarrhoea, vomiting, fever and dehydration.

Three years before the Kokoda campaign, the then Director General of Medical Services, Major General Rupert Downes, the Army's most senior medical officer, received a report warning of what could be expected if fighting spread to New Guinea. The report stated:

> [Australian soldiers would] … incur a heavy morbidity rate from malaria, and perhaps a mortality rate from the same cause … The other great cause of morbidity will be bacillary dysentery with a heavy mortality in troops in poor physical condition.

Despite this warning, efforts to counter these dual perils were not given the priority they deserved. A training pamphlet, *Tropical Warfare*, containing vital information on the medical aspects of jungle warfare, was not released until November 1944, too late to help Australian forces engaged in the Kokoda campaign.

Predictably, without effective measures in place, and hygiene discipline among the Australian soldiers not always what it should have been, malaria and dysentery took a heavy toll, with as many as 2800 non-battle casualties evacuated during the campaign.

To be fair, the effective management of both malaria and dysentery was difficult under the tough conditions of the campaign. These problems were compounded by a worldwide shortage of anti-malarial and anti-dysentery drugs and locally available protective netting and clothing. However, the methods used to prevent and treat both diseases improved over the course of the Pacific War.

During the Kokoda campaign, treatment and suppression of malaria revolved around a regime of anti-malarial drugs: quinine, Atebrin and plasmoquin. Paludrine did not become readily available until 1946.

Fortunately, because the *Anopheles* mosquito does not commonly inhabit high altitudes, malaria was not as prevalent in the Owen Stanleys as it was in the waterlogged lowlands of Papua such as the beachheads and Milne Bay.

Dysentery undoubtedly posed a greater danger to the health of Australian soldiers and is particularly virulent when victims are also suffering from malnutrition and exhaustion, two conditions that dogged the troops on the Kokoda Trail. According to the *Official Medical History*, upwards of 2000 Australian troops with dysentery 'were admitted to medical holding units and disease was whittling away the force'.

Two Kokoda veterans describe the effect of dysentery on those afflicted:

Corporal Gilbert (Stewart) Simmons, 2/25th Battalion:

> I had dysentery [north of Templeton's Crossing] and I went down to the doctor, told him all about it, I was passing blood and so forth [and he said], "Out." And I said, "Oh doctor, I got to walk all the way back to Owers' Corner?" And he said, "Yes you have." And I said, "Oh I don't want to do that. Can't you give me something?" "Soldier, get out of here. Don't you know what caused Napoleon to be defeated in the battle of Russia?" And I said, "The Russian army." And he said, "No, amoebic dysentery. What you've got, now get out." Oh god, how I got back to Owers' Corner, I was ill and that sick.

Lieutenant Dennis Williams, 2/2nd Battalion:

> [Bruce MacDougal had dysentery], but he was one of those fellows that never gave up on anything. And he shed his trousers because they'd been soiled so often that he couldn't possibly keep them clean. So he marched with his boots, no socks of course, and his shirt and his pack, so he looked like some weird caricature of a medieval warrior, with nothing but his shirt tails. And that's how he marched for, oh several weeks, until somehow or other, he scrounged another pair of trousers, but they didn't do him much good either. Because as I said, he was mad with malaria for a start, and had this ghastly dysentery. But he never stopped, he was a man and a half.

Preventative measures were instituted to improve hygiene discipline and sanitation. This included isolating men showing symptoms of dysentery and enforcing stricter water controls to ensure that latrines were established away from creeks used for drinking water. While these measures were partially effective in minimising the spread of dysentery, those already infected required medication in the form of the drug sulphaguanidine. The efficacy of this drug was highlighted by Sir Alan Newton, the Chairman of the Defence Department's Medical Equipment Control Committee, who later claimed, 'If this drug had not have been available, there might have been a different end to the … [Kokoda campaign].'

Supply, the perennial problem of the Kokoda campaign, was Brigadier Eather's primary preoccupation. Forward of Uberi, he had 900 carriers to assist the 25th Brigade. The relatively small number of battle casualties during this time reduced the burden, as no carriers were required to act as stretcher-bearers. However, the number of carriers decreased daily through desertions and sickness. The lack of ANGAU officers proficient in the native languages of Motu or Tok Pisin aggravated the problem. Many carriers deserted because of the hard, constant labour and because they missed their families. Lieutenant Kienzle did his best to sustain their motivation and commitment. When a Rabaul carrier who had suffered horrific wounds at the hands of his Japanese masters was discovered, Kienzle paraded him before the Papuans to illustrate the difference in the protagonists' treatment of their native workforce. Kienzle noted in his diary that this graphic display served its purpose and there was a marked increase in morale among the Papuans. The air-dropping of supplies was also essential and Eather ordered the construction of a dropping ground at Nauro. Nevertheless, difficulties in supply retarded the advance throughout early October.

Lieutenant Colonel Allen Cameron briefs a group of soldiers from the 3rd Battalion before they depart on a long-range patrol from Menari. Cameron was the Kokoda campaign's 'everywhere' man. He temporarily acted as CO of both the 39th and 53rd battalions in the early part of the campaign after the COs of those units were killed, and later returned as CO of the 3rd Battalion (AWM027010).

With Guadalcanal still in the balance, the Allies sought to secure Papua as quickly as possible. GHQ was concerned that the Japanese would divert troops from Guadalcanal to Papua if they were successful in the island campaign. General MacArthur's strategy for securing Papua involved a three-pronged advance on the Japanese bastion at Buna-Gona. The priority axis of advance was along the Kokoda Trail. Securing Kokoda and its airfield with great haste was thus a priority as this was the easiest way to supply the two brigades moving along that axis. Concurrently, a battalion from the US 126th Regiment was to advance on the second axis along the Kapa Kapa Trail which crossed the Owen Stanleys to the south-east of the Kokoda Trail. The first of the American troops began their march on 6 October. They were woefully unprepared for the trek, as the Kapa Kapa Trail is longer and more difficult than the Kokoda Trail. Their CO had a heart attack within days of setting out, and the whole journey took almost a month and a half to complete. The Americans remembered it as a 'living, wide-awake nightmare'. The third axis of advance was along the northern coastline of Papua, with the 2/10th Battalion, which had fought at Milne Bay, airlifted to Wanigela to advance up the coast. A sense of urgency was palpable throughout the whole of October.

As the Australian advance rolled forward with 3rd and 2/25th Battalion patrols at the vanguard, they reached the village of Menari and discovered that this, too, had been abandoned. The patrols then scaled the southern face of Brigade Hill to the scene of the earlier battle. It was a solemn occasion. Unburied Australians lay where they had been killed a month earlier, in some cases still grasping weapons in their hands. Some Australian bodies were found lying on stretchers — evidence that wounded and sick soldiers had been murdered where they lay. Still, there was no sign of the main Japanese force.

On 3 October the 16th Brigade, which had arrived in Port Moresby on 21 September, entered the campaign. Under the command of Brigadier John Lloyd, the troops set off along the Kokoda Trail at the same time as Deputy Prime Minister Francis Forde and Generals MacArthur and Blamey were at Owers' Corner inspecting the beginning of the Trail. In front of the gathered press, MacArthur famously told Lloyd, 'By some act of God, your Brigade has been chosen for this job. The eyes of the Western World are upon you. I have every confidence in you and your men. Good luck and don't stop.'

Australian Deputy Prime Minister Francis Forde and Generals Douglas MacArthur and Thomas Blamey on their arrival in New Guinea. Forde's safari suit prompted many larrikin quips from the Australian soldiers (AWM013427).

The Australians finally located the Japanese on 8 October, some 11 days after they had vacated Ioribaiwa. While the main body of the 25th Brigade was located between Menari and Efogi, Eather had pushed out several long-range patrols north of Efogi with instructions to find the enemy. A patrol led by Lieutenant Archibald Barnett from the 2/25th moving along the Kokoda Trail was the first to find the Japanese on the southern tip of Myola Ridge, the same thin, north-south running ridgeline that the 2/16th had fought along during the fighting withdrawal. In a short engagement the patrol lost one man killed in action while two others were wounded, including Barnett, who was shot in the stomach.

Parallel to this action, on the Mount Bellamy Trail between Kagi and Templeton's Crossing, a 3rd Battalion patrol led by Sergeant Bede Tongs was also hunting the Japanese. At 10.00 am the patrol heard gunfire from the direction of Myola and assumed that Barnett had found the Japanese. Tongs guessed it would not be long before his own patrol also contacted the enemy. This suspicion was strengthened when his forward scout stopped abruptly. There were signs of recent Japanese activity. The patrol pushed warily forward. Not 200 metres further on they found Japanese soldiers guarding the Trail. Both routes to Templeton's Crossing were blocked. The *Stanley Detachment* would need to be rooted out.

* * * *

Throughout early October, while Maroubra Force was searching for the Japanese in the Owen Stanleys, significant events were unfolding away from the front line. Lieutenant General Edmund Herring had replaced Lieutenant General Rowell as GOC NGF following the latter's spectacular falling out with General Blamey (see Chapter 18). Herring arrived in Port Moresby and assumed command on 1 October. Both Herring and Major General Allen were present at Owers' Corner on 3 October when MacArthur, Blamey and Forde inspected the start of the Kokoda Trail.

Owers' Corner, 3 October 1942. Colonel Charles Spry points out locations of heavy fighting in the Owen Stanleys to (from left): Lieutenant General Edmund Herring, new GOC NGF, General MacArthur and Major General Allen. This is the closest that MacArthur and Herring came to the fighting on the Kokoda Trail (AWM150813).

Over the next two days the two commanders met repeatedly, with Allen eager to impress upon Herring the difficulties of supplying his division on the Kokoda Trail. On 5 October Allen moved 7th Division Headquarters forward to Uberi, confident that Herring understood his difficulties. Optimism had increased within NGF Headquarters and at GHQ. It was their belief that the supply train was not overly stretched at that point (Maroubra Force remained close to Port Moresby), while the 16th Brigade had recently arrived as reinforcement, encouraging the idea that the advance along the Trail would move quickly. It would not take long for the perennial supply problem to poison Herring and Allen's relationship.

On 2 October Brigadier Eather had signalled the urgent need for air-dropping to commence as a result of several factors. First, the further Maroubra Force moved north, the more reliant it became on carriers. This was because the Pack Transport Company — whose men and animals worked tirelessly throughout the campaign — could only operate as far north as Imita Ridge. From this point, the only options to move supplies forward were air drops or native carriers. Second, because of the severe shortage of carriers, those present were overworked and sickness and desertion continued to erode their numbers. By 4 October, when the Australians had advanced a sufficient distance forward of the Maguli Range, new dropping grounds were cleared and air-dropping resumed, albeit with disappointing results.

Near Uberi, October 1942. Men of the Pack Transport Company leading horses and mules loaded with supplies along the Kokoda Trail between Owers' Corner and Imita Ridge (AWM027022).

The disappointing results gravely concerned Allen and he raised the issue with Herring. On 7 October he advised Herring that, in order to stockpile 21 days' reserve to support the advance (which he believed was Herring's intention), 50,000 pounds (2.2 tonnes) of supplies had to be air-dropped daily as the minimum requirement to sustain the force. This figure was sufficient to cover the 30% wastage that ensued from this method of supply. Less than 25,000 pounds of supplies had been recovered from the first two days of air-dropping because the Air Force did not have sufficient aircraft available to deliver that amount of goods, and the art of air-dropping had yet to be refined. Many dropped supply boxes missed the small targeted dropping zones at the southern end of the Trail while others, which had been poorly packed, were destroyed on impact with the ground. Allen intimated that, unless the required amount of supplies was dropped, he would have to amend his plans and withdraw his troops to Imita Ridge, which could leave Maroubra Force susceptible to counter-attack.

As a consequence, the air supply program intensified over the following days. However, on 11 October, Herring and Blamey took the matter of air-dropping into their own hands. Ignoring a signal from Allen that stated the exact position of his units and his desire for supplies to be dropped at these locations, Blamey signalled Allen, 'You have been furnished with supplies as you required and ample appear to be available. In view [of] lack of serious opposition advance appears much too slow … Dropping arranged only at Myola.'

This was an enormously risky strategy and Herring later explained the rationale:

> 7 Division was advancing against a retreating enemy and we wanted the rearguards driven in as fast as humanly possible … [Allen] would not see that owing to the terrain and the shortage of carriers the building up of reserves at one spot tended to hamper the advance we all wanted and not expedite it. For first of all it took some time to build up the reserves … and they could only be of use if carried forward as the troops advanced … With the shortage of carriers they could only be carried forward by the troops themselves. What NGF wanted to do was keep dropping as far forward as possible, so as to reduce the problem of carrying and make as many of the fighting troops available for battle as was possible.

Herring and Blamey were using the supplies as a carrot to coax Allen to accelerate the advance. Despite the bullish approach, there was logic in Blamey's direction and Herring's rationale. Nevertheless, there were also two major flaws in this strategy. First, while dropping supplies at Myola would sustain the force on the Kokoda Trail, it would not supply troops advancing along the Mount Bellamy Trail as they would be required to back-track. Second, and more important, the first sentence of Herring's statement mischaracterises the Japanese movements in the Owen Stanleys as those of a retreating army that could be easily overrun. This is a theme that persists throughout the Kokoda campaign as Allen is subject to increasing criticism for his perceived slow rate of advance.

In fact, the Japanese were not retreating, because they had *already* retreated. The *Stanley Detachment* had used the 11 days between its retreat and its next contact with the

Australians to construct a formidable and layered defensive position high in the Owen Stanleys. While both blocking positions on the two routes to Templeton's Crossing had been discovered on 8 October, there was still no accurate information concerning the size of the Japanese force that occupied them. The misconception that Allen was advancing against a retreating enemy compounded his predicament. It was only after the war that Herring admitted that the Japanese had a 'very great capacity' for preparing and holding defensive positions, and this was a significant factor which 'everyone had to learn, from General MacArthur downwards.'

On 12 October Allen responded to Blamey's signal concerning the dropping of supplies at Myola, escalating the tone of correspondence. Each man was becoming increasingly exasperated that the other was not appreciative of his position. Allen argued:

> My outline plan . . . is designed to capture Kokoda as soon as possible. Apparently it has been misunderstood. Nothing is being left undone in order to carry out your wishes and my brigade commanders have already been instructed accordingly. The most serious opposition to rapid advance is terrain. The second is maintenance of supplies through lack of native carriers. Reserve supplies have not repeat not been adequate up to 11 Oct. Until information of recoveries today am unable to say whether they are yet adequate. Rate of advance does not entirely depend on air droppings. Equal in importance is our ability to carry forward and maintain our advanced troops. Notwithstanding that men carry with them up to five days' rations, maintenance forward of dropping place is still necessary. This country is much tougher than any previous theatre and cannot be appreciated until seen. From all reports the worst is north of Myola. The vigour with which we press the enemy is dependent on the physical endurance of the men and the availability of supplies. Our men have pressed so far with vigour consistent with keeping the men fit to fight.

Allen then conferred with Brigadier Eather, telling him where he should position the 25th Brigade's battalions. He provided Eather an outline of his plans to recapture Kokoda using the 16th and 25th brigades. Because the strength of Japanese opposition blocking the routes to Templeton's Crossing was yet to be determined, Allen's plan was overly optimistic, probably a result of the pressure exerted from above. Blamey liked to hear what he wanted to hear and could not abide excuses. Allen's prediction that the terrain north of Myola was the worst on the Kokoda Trail was hardly likely to appease given that it foreshadowed an even slower advance when Blamey already considered that the advance lacked haste.

The fact that Allen had described his difficulties in accumulating reserve supplies for a second time suggests that Herring had not explicitly told him that he did not want the advance delayed while a reserve of supples was accumulated. And this was not something that Allen should have been expected to presume as, in mid-August when Brigadier Potts was in a similar position to Allen, Potts had been ordered by the then GOC NGF Rowell to delay all offensive moves forward of Myola until sufficient reserves of supplies had been stockpiled.

As Maroubra Force prepared to clear the twin obstructions barring Templeton's Crossing, Herring was plotting and wasted little time in sounding out Major General George Vasey as a possible replacement for Allen. Vasey initially rejected the overture, confiding to his wife that he had no inclination to become 'stuck in those hills'.

Major General Allen and Brigadier Eather in discussion on the Kokoda Trail. The third man is Lieutenant Dalrymple Fayle, ADC to Allen (AWM026750).

Chapter 13

TO TEMPLETON'S CROSSING

As issues between Major General Allen and his superiors bubbled away below the surface, Brigadier Eather activated his plan to secure Templeton's Crossing. The 2/25th Battalion would advance along the Mount Bellamy Trail, while the 2/33rd Battalion would move along the Kokoda Trail with the 3rd Battalion behind it in support. The 2/31st Battalion would remain in Efogi in reserve, ready to move where needed.

Members of the 2/31st Battalion rest away from the front line in the Owen Stanleys, ensuring that their Bren gun is within easy reach (AWM027013).

By 10 October the Australians had reoccupied Myola. Surprisingly, the most important supply base for the Australians along the entire Kokoda Trail was captured as it had originally been lost — without a shot being fired. Once Myola was occupied, the immediate concern became reestablishing the lake bed as a base for operations. Work details were sent to cut the kunai grass and clear the ground so that air-dropping could commence. Shelters were also constructed to shield the men from the nightly rain and cool temperatures that caused them great discomfort at such a high altitude.

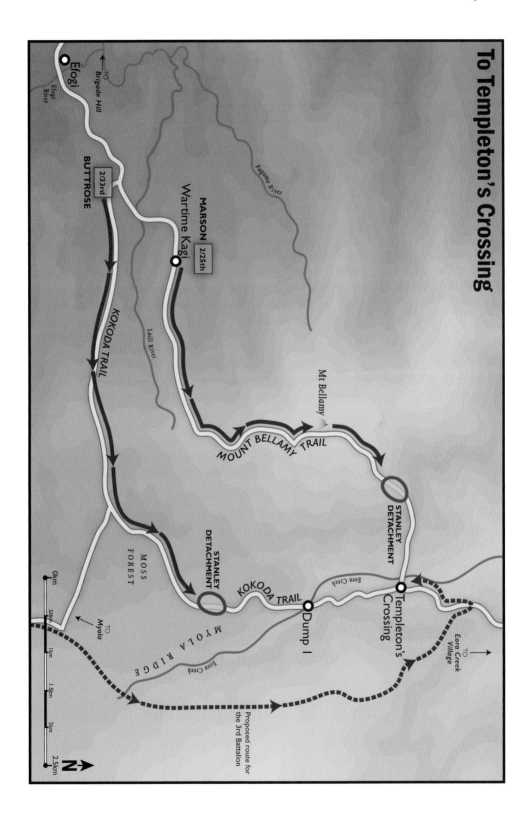

On the same day, Lieutenant William Innes led his platoon from C Company, 2/33rd Battalion, on a fighting patrol to Myola Ridge where the Japanese had earlier been located. The density of the jungle and the sharp ravines that fell away on either side of Myola Ridge made it an excellent location for a delaying defence. Innes' arrival was greeted with gunfire, and a runner was sent back to Lieutenant Colonel Buttrose informing him that contact had been made.

The next day, 11 October, Brigadier Eather ordered the 2/33rd to capture Templeton's Crossing. Buttrose had already ordered Lieutenant Doug Copp, OC C Company, to lead his remaining platoons forward to join Innes and smash the Japanese post. Copp left Myola at 9.00 am and by noon he had reached Myola Ridge, completing C Company's strength. Innes had been busy scouting the Japanese position along both flanks, gaining as much information as possible. He told Copp that the position appeared strong and spread in depth along the ridgeline. Small interconnected rifle pits provided mutual fire support. Large trees had been felled and the trunks used to cover the firing pits. Narrow slits were all that were visible, allowing the Japanese to fire at the Australians while presenting a very small target in return. This cover was particularly effective against grenades as the logs provided overhead blast protection and only an accurate throw that penetrated the firing slit would harm the occupants. Copp decided to hold his attack until the next morning. Innes' 14 Platoon was to move out to the west for half an hour and then strike back at the ridgeline, while 13 and 15 platoons would attack the Japanese directly from the south. Moving into position in the thick jungle proved difficult but, by 10.00 am the next morning, C Company was ready to attack.

On the morning of 12 October, Buttrose and the remainder of the 2/33rd moved out to join C Company. They left Myola at 8.00 am and were still marching forward when Copp's offensive began. The men of 14 Platoon swarmed towards the defensive mounds they had identified as Japanese targets. The other two platoons heard the firing and moved in, making some slight headway and gaining a foothold on the southern tip of Myola Ridge. Clearing the bunkers required courage and daring, as Australian soldiers literally ran right up to the firing pits and attacked them at point blank range in tactics reminiscent of the 1st Brigade's attack at Lone Pine 27 years earlier. When members of 14 Platoon heard Japanese voices further to the north, they realised that the Japanese position was larger than expected. Copp directed his men to hold their ground, having realised that the Japanese position was too large for a single company to defeat.

The condition of the Trail, now turned to a morass by the perpetual rain, slowed Buttrose's progress towards Copp. When the battalion finally consolidated at the southern end of Myola Ridge at 1.00 pm, Copp told Buttrose that his attack had achieved some success, but there were still significant Japanese fortifications some 275 metres in front and beyond to the north. Reconnaissance was difficult because the camouflaged Japanese firing pits were hard to locate. The whizzing rifle fire confirmed the close proximity of the enemy.

Buttrose decided that the battalion would attack at 2.00 pm. Captain Thomas Archer's B Company would push through C Company and attack directly along Myola Ridge. Captain

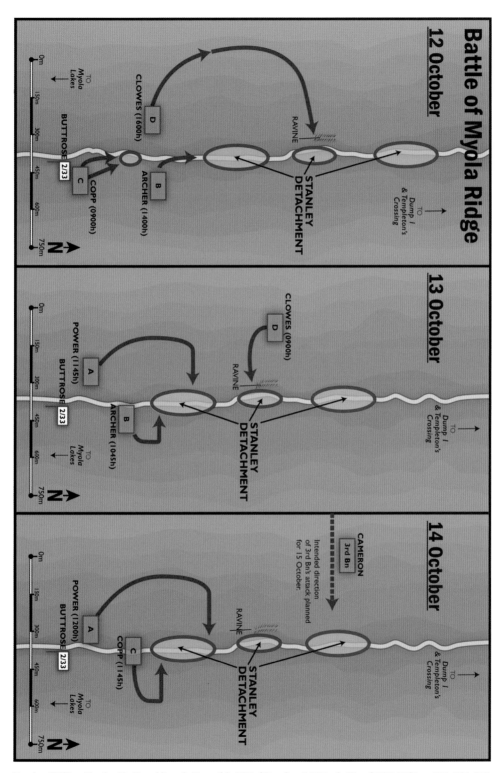

Based on William Crooks, *The Footsoldiers, the Story of the 2/33rd Battalion A.I.F. in the War of 1939-1945*, pp. 201, 206, 209.

Clowes' D Company, would swing to the west and move 550 metres northwards along the left flank of the ridgeline (the estimated depth of the Japanese defence). Clowes would then slice onto the Trail, his company's rifle fire the signal for Archer to attack.

D Company found the terrain extremely difficult to navigate, and pushing forward the 550 metres proved more difficult than expected. The dense jungle foliage blocked natural light and restricted the men's visibility as they trudged northwards in single file. The land was cut by ravines and criss-crossed by enormous trees that had fallen and now barred the way. D Company had not reached its forming-up position when firing erupted from B Company. Clowes wondered what had caused the firing, as Archer was not supposed to attack until his signal.

The size of some of the trees along the Kokoda Trail is evident from this photograph taken on the approach to Myola Ridge. The man at the bottom centre of the picture (wearing orange) is dwarfed by the trees above him (D. Crosbie, NAA022).

Realising that B Company had been engaged by enemy forces, Clowes hurriedly searched for a suitable place for his men to form up. He continued northwards until he stumbled into a clearing. Finally able to see his entire company, he used hand signals to launch an attack. The company pivoted to the east and, in a single straight line, worked its way up the steep side of Myola Ridge. After much exertion the troops reached what they thought was the cusp of the ridgeline. Here they could see the Trail and the Japanese soldiers who were stunned by their sudden appearance. However, to their dismay, they discovered that they were separated from the enemy by a six-metre ravine. As his men scrambled to traverse the ravine, Clowes found it impossible to keep his attacking line in formation and his platoons became mixed together.

The Australians sprayed Tommy gun fire as the Japanese soldiers fled for the safety of their firing pits. The Australians carrying light machine-guns hit the ground and scanned for targets. The Japanese responded quickly. Within 10 minutes a Juki was pouring accurate fire on D Company. Worse, many Australians were stuck in the ravine still trying to clamber out. This made them easy marks for the Japanese who showered them with grenades. Realising the attack would not succeed, Clowes ordered his men to retreat to the original forming-up position. Once there, D Company formed a perimeter for the night, wary of a Japanese counter-attack.

The premature firing that Clowes had heard earlier from B Company was prompted by the vigilance of the Japanese on the southern tip of Myola Ridge. When Innes' 14 Platoon at the forefront of the Australian perimeter was pulled back to allow B Company freedom of movement, the ground that Innes gave up was believed to be clear of Japanese. This assumption was wrong. The Japanese had seen Innes and followed his platoon, occupying ground much closer to the 2/33rd's position. As a result, when Archer moved forward to his start position with every intention of waiting for Clowes' gunfire signal, his company walked straight into an ambush. The leading scout, Private Gordon Ludbrook, was killed instantly. B Company immediately retaliated. Archer used all three of his platoons in tight sweeping actions to the left. As they identified and moved in to destroy the firing pits, they were shot down by Japanese concealed in other pits they had not seen. The rain intensified and, with the Owen Stanleys now draped in darkness, Archer was unable to secure the contested ground. He ordered his men to retreat 180 metres and hold their position for what would be a wet and uncomfortable night.

On the drizzling morning of 13 October, Clowes intended to launch a fresh offensive. His basic plan was to attack slightly to the south of the troublesome ravine. Again his company scrabbled up the slope, but the Japanese had strengthened their defences along the western edge of Myola Ridge in anticipation. A wall of grenades and several Jukis and light machine-guns hammered them as they approached. As casualties mounted, Clowes pulled his men off the ridge and then led them back to Battalion Headquarters.

At the south-eastern tip of Myola Ridge, Archer led the bulk of his B Company in a renewed attack. Overall movement was slow, although mobility was improved this time as the troops left everything behind except their weapons and ammunition. When gunfire echoed through the jungle from the direction of D Company, Archer advanced towards the enemy with greater urgency, eager to support Clowes' attack. Watchful Japanese saw them coming through the foliage. Grenades and Tommy guns were used in the mad scrap that developed, as individual Japanese fighting pits were neutralised. Archer was unable to direct his men as most were crawling on the jungle floor and line of sight between each section was non-existent. When the promised support of mortars failed to eventuate — the mortar crews were fearful of hitting their own troops — Archer ordered his men to retreat.

The section of the Kokoda Trail that crosses Myola Ridge is a tangle of moss-covered tree roots (D. Crosbie, NAA023).

A third attack on the same morning finally found success. Lieutenant Kevin Power led a patrol in the direction that D Company had taken, but marched only 270 metres north. The Japanese were preoccupied with Archer's attack, allowing Power and the 50 men with him to burst onto Myola Ridge with complete surprise. Within minutes, Japanese soldiers were being shot as they sat and ate in a lean-to. Even better, a Juki that had harassed the Australians over the preceding days was decommissioned with hand grenades. With great discipline, the Japanese composed their defence and began to inflict casualties on the attackers. Power feared his patrol was surrounded and ordered his men to pull out, having held the Trail for an hour in the face of terrific odds. At least 20 Japanese bodies were counted as his men scampered back down the ridge. For his bravery and coolness under pressure, Power was awarded the MC.

Buttrose was disappointed that the sole success in clearing Myola Ridge had come with Power's enterprising attack. The Japanese resistance was strong and, by moving their Jukis and light machine-guns from position to position, they were able to react quickly to the different points on the ridge where the Australians appeared. Buttrose needed more firepower. He requested an air strike, but held little hope it would materialise given the low cloud cover. He conferred with Brigadier Eather who agreed to send the 3rd Battalion — under the command of the ubiquitous Lieutenant Colonel Cameron — approximately 900 metres to the north-west of the 2/33rd to support the offensive. Manoeuvring into position would take Cameron time, but Buttrose was eager to keep applying pressure, so new attack plans were drafted for 14 October. Copp's C Company would attack the apex of the ridge once he heard the sound of gunfire from Power who was to repeat his patrol's surprise attack.

By midday the next day, Power had led his men to their new starting position, having moved further north to change the direction of the attacks. This time the Japanese were ready for him. Having absorbed attacks from this western flank over several days, the element of surprise had well and truly disappeared. Power's men neared the lip of the ridge where they were met with a blitz of gunfire and grenades. The withering fire prevented any Australian from reaching the top of the ridge. Complicating matters were deceptive shouts from the Japanese, who called out English phrases such as, 'Hey Bob, over here, I'm wounded.' In response, Power called off the attack in Arabic, the basics of which members of the 2/33rd had learnt during their earlier service in Syria.

Copp was faring no better at the forefront of the Japanese defence. His men had rushed forward and up onto the southern tip of Myola Ridge. With the Trail in sight, the Japanese opened fire and the Australians fell quickly. In less than five minutes, 17 men had been killed or wounded. Copp's two platoons were not strong enough to overrun the position. He pulled his men back, but not before the Japanese had caused further damage by creeping towards the remainder of the battalion and letting loose with a clutch of hand grenades.

Buttrose was becoming increasingly frustrated. With Power and Copp's attacks foiled, he ordered Lieutenant Herbert Warne's platoon forward. But before Warne could manoeuvre his men within range of the enemy he was shot dead. The day ended badly with the dismal weather and heavy casualty list eating away at the Australians' morale. There was one bright point. News was received that Cameron was ready to support the 2/33rd and would attack Myola Ridge from the west at 11.00 am the next morning.

When the highly anticipated attack was launched on 15 October, the two Australian battalions stormed Myola Ridge only to find it deserted. The Japanese had retreated during the night. The Battle of Myola Ridge ended with a whimper.

The pursuit began without pause. The 2/33rd pressed forward along the Trail, the 3rd Battalion close behind. By nightfall they had reached Dump 1 at the first crossing of Eora Creek, the same location at which the 2/16th had fought on 4 September during the fighting withdrawal. As the troops bivouacked for the night they were subjected to sporadic Japanese gunfire from across Eora Creek, the last resistance they faced until they reached the second line of the *Stanley Detachment's* defence at Templeton's Crossing. Despite another dreary night in wet and cold conditions amid the dreadful stench of rotting corpses, the Australians were optimistic of soon reaching their objective.

The next morning the two battalions marched northwards. The proximity of the Japanese forces was evident from the fresh boot prints left in the mud and the fires that smouldered along the way. Templeton's Crossing and the fight to win it back was close.

While the 2/33rd had been clearing Myola Ridge, the 2/25th Battalion had been checked on the Mount Bellamy Trail. On 12 October the battalion had been ordered to leave Kagi and move towards Templeton's Crossing. Early on the morning of 13 October, progress was halted when the forward scouts came under enemy fire. Despite being lashed from both sides of the Trail, the fire from enemy concealed on the steep face of Mount Bellamy was particularly strong and accurate.

25 Brigade Advancing along Kokoda Trail near Templeton's Crossing, painted in 1944 by Official War Artist George Browning. Browning based his painting on eyewitness accounts and his own notes on the terrain at Templeton's Crossing which he toured in 1944 (AWM ART23615).

As the 2/25th pushed on, the men made a grotesque discovery: a parcel of human meat. The battalion doctor confirmed that the meat was human. The remains belonged to two Australian scouts killed during an earlier 3rd Battalion patrol. The starving Japanese had resorted to cannibalism.

By this stage, the battalion's 49-year-old CO, Lieutenant Colonel Withy — an experienced officer who had seen action at Gallipoli — had been evacuated from the campaign with a severe skin condition. The battalion's second-in-command, Major Richard Marson, was now leading the battalion. He ordered A Company to dislodge the enemy on Mount Bellamy, while B and C companies advanced along the Trail with D Company in reserve. A Company believed it had cleared the left flank, but the battalion was unable to advance much further before constant sniping from this area forced Marson to bivouac for the night. The next morning patrols were sent to scour the area for the enemy.

Corporal Gilbert (Stewart) Simmons of the 2/25th Battalion described his experience of patrolling the Trail:

> I'll never forget the first time I was forward scout [on a patrol] … the officer called me over and he said, "Stewie, there is a bridge up there somewhere". And he used to have a certain time because you were very lucky to survive, so you had a certain time, then somebody else took over, see. And you couldn't do anything, you only walked up the track. You were the bloke they were going to shoot at, then you'd know there were Japs there.

While the patrols engaged in several small firefights, the battalion remained unable to push through to its objective. On 15 October Marson received the news that the Japanese had abandoned Myola Ridge. The 2/25th pushed forward, hoping to find its avenue of advance also open. Progress was eventually barred by a stockade of timber and wire. Presumably this obstacle formed a substantial impediment as it prompted Marson to order his men to retire to their previous position. It was not until 4.15 pm the next day that the 2/25th was finally able to reach Templeton's Crossing and link up with the 25th Brigade.

The movement of the 2/25th Battalion from Kagi to Templeton's Crossing has prompted criticism from Historian Peter Williams who wrote, 'It does seem that, in the period 12-15 October, little attempt was made by the 2/25th to obey the order to take Templeton's … [Crossing].' He added, '[It is] true that the 2/25th, who faced a third [of] their number of Japanese, for some reason had not made a whole hearted effort.' The reference to the 2/25th's opposing a force a third of its size is based on Williams' assertion that the majority of the *Stanley Detachment*, or 520 of its original strength of 667, had fortified Myola Ridge, while a much smaller force of 147 defended the Mount Bellamy Trail.

Brigadier Eather was unaware of the size of the two Japanese blockades. At Myola Ridge, the depth of the defence and the estimated number of Japanese troops defending it was raised several times as attempt after attempt to capture the ridge foundered. On Mount Bellamy, it appears Eather assumed that at least a similar number of Japanese were entrenched — if not more — because twice he ordered Buttrose to reach Templeton's

Crossing so that he could then march south down the Mount Bellamy Trail to wipe out the enemy blocking Marson's path. Given that the 2/25th was facing the smaller number of enemy, it would have made more sense for Marson to be given the order to press the attack so as to break through and help the 2/33rd on Myola Ridge.

In fairness, determining the strength of an enemy in the jungle is extremely difficult. However, the country and terrain that Marson reported as restricting his movement was no worse nor dissimilar to the country with which Buttrose was forced to contend. Williams has therefore raised a valid question, and it is difficult to understand why Marson found it more difficult to reach Templeton's Crossing than Buttrose, given Marson's numerical advantage over the enemy and relatively low number of casualties suffered (two killed and 11 wounded for the four days it took to reach the objective) in comparison to those of Buttrose during the same period (10 killed and 43 wounded).

Williams suggests inadequacy of command as a potential reason for the apparent slow movement of the 2/25th, concluding that 'All was not well in that battalion'. As evidence, he points out that two COs were replaced within a month and a third (Marson) soon after because he was wounded. This is slightly misleading as it contains an implicit suggestion that the COs may have been replaced because of poor performance. This was not the case. Command of the 2/25th Battalion changed multiple times throughout October 1942 because of illness and war wounds, and once Marson recovered from the minor shrapnel wound he suffered later at Templeton's Crossing, he resumed command of the 2/25th Battalion and held it until the end of the war.

There are few detailed accounts explaining what occurred on the Mount Bellamy Trail. However, the 2/25th's rate of advance was certainly slower than that of the 2/33rd. Eather should have urged Marson to hasten his advance as the 2/25th should have reached Templeton's Crossing first and might then have assisted the 2/33rd in breaking the stronger deadlock it faced on Myola Ridge.

****

Mid-October saw a lull in criticism of the rate of advance as Maroubra Force was committed to action and began to ram through the first tier of the *Stanley Detachment*'s defence. With Myola secured, work parties improved the dropping ground and airstrip and collected the dropped supplies. The incentive for Blamey and Herring to air-drop supplies forward of the troops as an enticement to accelerate the advance had disappeared, as no dropping grounds existed north of Myola until the village of Alola could be reoccupied. While the supply situation had improved slightly with Myola in Australian hands, any delay in capturing Alola was likely to cause the vexed issue of supply to again rear its head.

Allen had not exaggerated when he described the section of the Kokoda Trail north of Myola as the worst along its entire length. All the *Stanley Detachment*'s positions were concentrated in this region because of the suitability of the topography. The section of the Trail that plunged off the northern edge of Myola Ridge to Dump 1 was particularly difficult. Here the Trail that had been constructed by Lieutenant Kienzle only two months earlier clung to the sheer muddy drop. The constant wear from thousands of boots and the area's torrential rain had seen its condition rapidly deteriorate. As the action shifted to Templeton's Crossing, all supplies dropped at Myola had to be ferried down this mountain to reach the forward troops, and the wounded had to be carried back up the steep slope to reach the medical dressing station at Myola. The further the Australians advanced north, the more difficult it became to supply the force and extract the wounded. This would inevitably slow the advance, a certain recipe to erode GHQ's limited patience with Allen.

Mist hangs heavy over Myola Ridge (D Crosbie).

Chapter 14

THE BATTLE OF TEMPLETON'S CROSSING

With the *Stanley Detachment*'s decision to withdraw from its first defensive line, both routes to Templeton's Crossing were now open to the Australians. The 2/33rd, 2/25th and 3rd battalions all reached the Crossing on 16 October. It was in this vicinity that the Japanese sited their second defensive line. The convergence of the two routes from Efogi made it a natural position to fortify.

Templeton's Crossing looking north. The huts are modern constructions. The second layer of the *Stanley Detachment*'s defence in the Owen Stanleys was 450 metres north of this position on the high ground visible to the rear of the photo (M. Rifat, NAA024).

The new commander of the *Stanley Detachment* was Lieutenant Colonel Tsukamoto. Major Horie had been recalled to Japan to complete a promotion examination. He wasted no time in leaving the battlefield, galloping to Giruwa on horseback. Tsukamoto was disgusted at Horie's departure midway through the campaign, commenting that he never wanted to see his face again.

The exact location of the Japanese was pinpointed 450 metres north of the Crossing by Captain James Beckett, OC D Company, 3rd Battalion. As soon as the enemy was located, Beckett's company was caught in a firefight and went to ground.

The Australian battalion commanders convened to agree on dispositions: Major Marson would hold the area west of Eora Creek, Buttrose would occupy the Trail and ground around the Crossing, while Cameron would consolidate the 3rd at the rear of Captain Beckett's position. The thrust of the Australian attack would be provided by the 3rd Battalion, using the high ground to the east of the Crossing. This was the same north-south running ridgeline

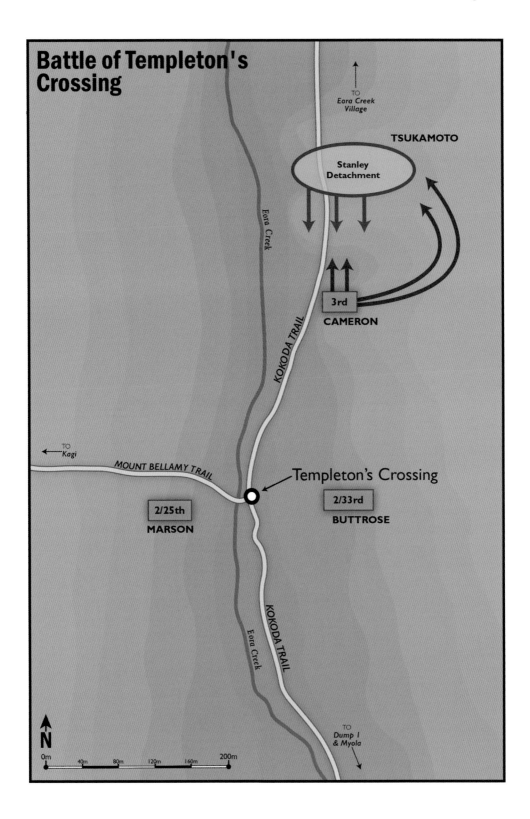

Battle of Templeton's Crossing

TO
Eora Creek Village

TSUKAMOTO

Stanley Detachment

3rd

CAMERON

Eora Creek

KOKODA TRAIL

TO
Kagi

MOUNT BELLAMY TRAIL

Templeton's Crossing

2/25th

MARSON

2/33rd

BUTTROSE

Eora Creek

KOKODA TRAIL

TO
Dump 1 & Myola

N

0m   40m   80m   120m   160m   200m

that the 2/16th had followed to avoid Templeton's Crossing on 2 September in its escape from the Japanese during the fighting withdrawal.

Once the Australians had moved to their respective positions, Marson sent a patrol along the west bank of Eora Creek to discover whether the Japanese were on both sides of the creek, and to locate a mortar that was proving a nuisance to his battalion. This latter assignment assumed greater urgency when a blast from the indiscriminate bombing hit Battalion Headquarters and wounded Marson. He was evacuated from the battlefield the next day and Major Alfred Millroy assumed command. Marson would return to lead the 2/25th a week later, having recovered from his wounds.

The following day, 17 October, saw the majority of fighting fall to the 3rd Battalion. Beckett began the morning by gauging the level of resistance along the length of his front line. Those companies of the battalion as yet uncommitted swept around Beckett's right flank into attack positions. B Company, with Captain William Atkinson at the helm, scrambled to the immediate right of Beckett, while A and C companies, led by Captain Thomas Boag, looped up and around the ridgeline seeking to hit the Japanese rear.

By 1.30 pm, Atkinson's men had climbed to their forming-up position and were ready to attack. Word had filtered through the ranks of the 25th Brigade of the discovery several days earlier of the two cannibalised men from the 3rd Battalion on the Mount Bellamy Trail. The Australians seethed with anger and were eager to exact retribution, none more so than Sergeant Tongs, who recalled the date as the birthday of his younger brother who had been taken prisoner by the Japanese during the fall of Singapore. Tongs later remarked: 'I knew that we were going to fight the Japanese that day … so I determined that my brother Reg would be avenged and we'd also heard about the cannibalism of two A Company scouts and that had to be dealt with also … that day was one of a very aggressive attitude.'

Just before B Company commenced its assault, an enemy machine-gun post with a fan-shaped firing lane was identified as a potential obstacle to the success of the operation. Tongs decided to eliminate the threat. He crawled towards the post on his hands and knees, the whole time looking warily at the barrel of the gun. The two Japanese manning it, finger on the trigger and scanning for targets, failed to see Tongs approach. Acting quickly, he threw a grenade which landed in the post and blew the enemy apart. Tongs remembered, 'I belted like a Stawell Gift runner, back to the platoon and when I got back [they were ready] for an attack and … the company commander [Atkinson who] wasn't far away sang out to me, "Get that attack going Sergeant Tongs." I didn't take much notice, I only yelled, "Get stuck into the bastards!"'

With the machine-gun post spectacularly destroyed, B Company yelled and screamed as they attacked. Private Noel (Nace) Hogan recalled, 'The noise of our boys was enough to scare anyone without gunfire at all.' Alternating between fire movements and blazing from the hip, B Company gained almost 200 metres of ground before consolidating on a spur. Hogan commented, 'Heartened by the sight of enemy dead the spirits of the boys rose to great heights, everyone seemed to forget everything and they simply burst into weapons pits and huts.'

Lieutenant Colin Richardson was severely wounded during the attack, shot in the chest by a sniper hidden in a tree. The bullet punctured his lung and blew a hole out through his back. Richardson propped himself against a tree as Atkinson tried to reach him to bandage the bloody wound. While Atkinson was busy treating Richardson, the same Japanese sniper targeted him. Miraculously the bullet missed, travelling through the gap between his back and haversack. Private Dudley Downes, alert to what was unfolding, stepped calmly from cover and killed the sniper, having spotted him from the smoke emanating from the muzzle of his rifle.

Richardson was in a morbid state. Geoffrey Mutton, the 2/33rd's Medical Officer, saw him and thought he was dead, but did his best to provide a better dressing. Lacking appropriate supplies, Mutton later recalled in a letter to Richardson: 'I did have half a dozen rusty safety pins in the bottom of my pouch. So I did what I could to patch you up with the pins and then the priest gave you the last rites and we had to leave you.' Richardson woke at Company Headquarters the next morning, surrounded by the bodies of Australians killed in action. Several soldiers in the vicinity were astonished that he was still alive. Richardson's hazy recollection of the incident was of an approaching soldier who said:

> "I'll get you a smoke sir." And oh anyhow he rolled a ... cigarette and started it going and he gave it to me and was putting it up to my lips. I'd smoked at that time and I took one breath and gave it to him back and I said, "I don't think I'll be needing this mate. You keep it."

Richardson was then evacuated to Myola and, despite the ordeal, he survived.

Papuan porters (the legendary 'Fuzzy Wuzzy Angels') carry wounded Australian soldiers on stretchers across a creek somewhere between Templeton's Crossing and Myola. While this photograph was taken during the fighting withdrawal, the same journey had to be made as casualties accrued during the Battle of Templeton's Crossing. The photograph's original caption reads: 'Australians in New Guinea pay a high tribute to the courage, endurance and comradeship of the New Guinea natives who are playing a very important part in the Allied efforts to drive the Japanese from the country' (AWM013256).

While the 3rd Battalion's D and B companies spent the remainder of the afternoon parrying Japanese counter-attacks, the other two companies, which had swung further to the right, also found success. In tandem they pushed up the high ground before turning left and following the ridgeline to the north. Captain Boag knew that the Japanese were below him to his left, however large cliffs prevented any deviation from his current course until a defile was discovered that provided access to the Japanese flank. Here Boag split his companies: C Company would stream down the ridge towards the enemy while A Company would guard the defile to protect the retreat.

C Company charged down the ridgeline making the noise of 'a pack of elephants', reaching a Japanese camp and taking the enemy soldiers completely by surprise. Lieutenant Eric Bourne claimed it was 'like shooting rabbits'. When the dust settled, the Australian troops told Boag they thought that they had inflicted 30 casualties without loss. Boag pulled his men back up the ridgeline, planning to attack again the next morning.

As this front-line fighting was occurring, Brigadier Eather had arrived at Templeton's Crossing and established his headquarters within the perimeter of the 2/33rd's position. He was acutely aware of the proximity of the enemy as mountain gun and mortar rounds exploded within the perimeter. As the day drew to a close, Eather expected his exhausted brigade to be relieved the next day by the 16th Brigade, currently approaching Templeton's Crossing.

Members of the 16th Brigade moving up the Kokoda Trail towards the front line (AWM027055).

But on 18 October the relief of the 25th Brigade was postponed as the Australians suffered a reversal. At 10.00 am A and C companies of the 3rd Battalion moved to replicate their attack from the day before but became disoriented. They ploughed through the jungle in the direction they supposed would lead to the Japanese position, but instead burst into the perimeter of their own B Company. The debacle did not end there. Captain Peter Blundell of the 2/25th Battalion was ordered to circumnavigate the battlefield with A and D companies of the 2/25th to exert additional pressure on the Japanese by attacking from the right flank of the 3rd Battalion. Half an hour before the 1.00 pm deadline, Eather was concerned that nothing had been heard from Blundell, but assumed that the attack might still occur because gunfire was heard from the direction he had taken.

The attack did not materialise. Blundell became lost and suffered casualties while unsuccessfully trying to manoeuvre his men into position. This bungled attack had messy repercussions. Blundell blamed the 3rd Battalion for not providing guides. Cameron's Situation Report disputed this assertion and claimed that guides had been provided. Eather himself was dissatisfied when a report from Blundell failed to yield any useful intelligence. When he later received a request from the 2/25th Battalion asking that Blundell be relieved of his command, Eather agreed. Blundell's performance throughout the campaign was considered unsatisfactory and to have adversely affected the morale of his men. He was recalled to 7th Division Headquarters before being repatriated to Australia.

With the Australians failing to execute both major offensives planned for the day, the Japanese capitalised and grasped the initiative, launching several fierce attacks against Cameron's D and B companies. This forced Brigadier Lloyd to alter his planned use of Lieutenant Colonel Cedric Edgar's 2/2nd Battalion which had arrived at Templeton's Crossing during the day. Although originally ordered to relieve the 2/33rd, the troublesome developments along the 3rd Battalion's front instead prompted Lloyd to order Edgar to move forward at first light on 19 October to strengthen the Australian front line.

The next morning Edgar pushed his battalion forward of the 2/33rd up the heavily contested ridgeline to the east. Several strong 2/2nd patrols were thrust forward to test the Japanese and assist the 3rd Battalion. Cameron's men were exhausted, and along with the other battalions from the 25th Brigade, were urgently in need of rest. Nevertheless they held their positions, and were confident that they were gradually wearing the enemy down, their belief supported by the fact that the Japanese counter-attacks were becoming more sporadic.

The remainder of the 16th Brigade arrived during the afternoon and the hammer strike that would secure Templeton's Crossing was planned. Eather and Lloyd agreed that the 16th Brigade would manage operations from the next day. The 2/25th and 2/33rd would be replaced by the 2/3rd Battalion, the 2/1st Battalion would push forward to replace the besieged 3rd Battalion, and Edgar's battalion would bear the brunt of offensive actions. Sergeant Tongs described the arrival of the 16th Brigade: 'I looked up the back and the scrub had cleaned up a bit with fire and so on … and here was this 2/1st Battalion, the 2/1st coming through. They were dressed in their jungle greens and these blokes all looked about

8 foot tall. They're coming through the jungle only behind us and we all breathed a sigh of relief.'

Tongs recalled a 2/2nd Battalion lieutenant coming to him to ask, '"How close are they?" And I said, "Oh about 20 paces." Anyhow they lined up to attack them and they kept going and then fired some rounds and then they came back again and this platoon commander bloke said, "By God, they are close aren't they ... anyhow we'll get them tomorrow.'"

That evening was bitterly cold and heavy rain fell. The no-nonsense Edgar discussed tactics with his company commanders, giving them clear instructions on their lines of attack. The Battle of Templeton's Crossing had reached its climax.

Australian soldiers cleaning their rifles before going into action against the Japanese (AWM013466).

On 20 October the 2/2nd Battalion was to crush the *Stanley Detachment* in an offensive that would involve the entire battalion. A and C companies under Captains Donald Fairbrother and Courtney Swinton were to attack from the immediate right of the 3rd Battalion to cement the Australians' most crucial flank and provide rear support to the main thrust. That main thrust was to be executed by B and D companies under Captains Ian Ferguson and Clive Baylis. Their orders were to scale the heights of the eastern ridge and, from there, drive the Japanese off the two parallel spurs that jutted out westwards from the ridgeline and formed the strongholds of Tsukamoto's position.

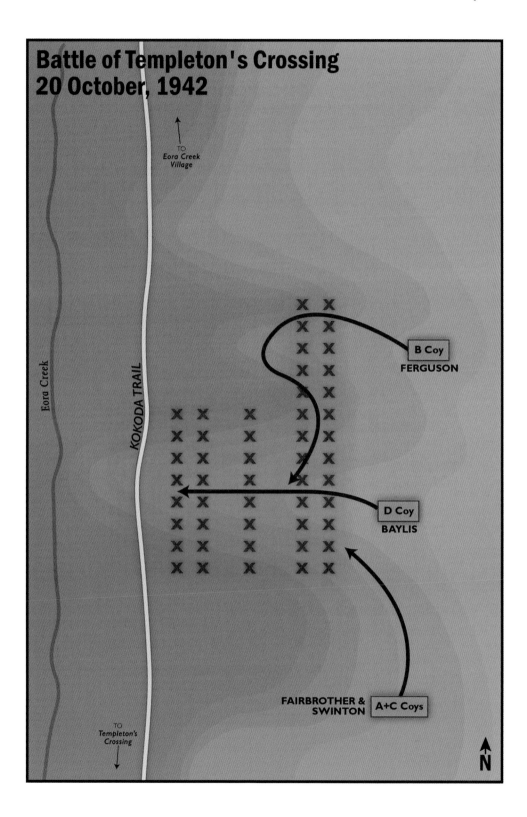

Battle of Templeton's Crossing
20 October, 1942

The morning of the attack was cold and dim. The men ate breakfast and calmed their nerves with hot milk. Lloyd was present at Edgar's battalion headquarters and wished the men well. The forming-up position was not far beyond Cameron's front line, an estimated 160 metres. The Australians heaved their way into position and swivelled to face down the slope, Ferguson's B Company on the right and shorter of the two spurs, Baylis' D Company on the left. Both officers configured their companies to attack with a platoon on either side of their allocated spur and a reserve platoon moving at their rear. The men were instructed to move in single file with scouts well forward.

At 11.00 am the attack began with both companies advancing in unison. The troops moved as quietly as possible, mindful that the enemy was nearby. They advanced 180 metres before the first Japanese outpost fired at them. On contact, the Australians fanned out and eliminated the outpost with grenades. A further 140 metres down the ridgeline the first of the main Japanese positions was encountered spread across both spurs. It comprised four light machine-guns and at least 15 firing pits. They were expertly camouflaged and virtually undetectable. B and D companies approached to almost point blank range before the Japanese opened fire.

The withering fire decimated B Company's leadership. Two of the three platoon commanders were killed and the third was wounded. Ferguson was saved from certain death when he tripped over a tree root and gunfire aimed at him killed the two men behind him. The dogged opposition was silenced with sheer persistence. Ferguson and Baylis split their platoons into pincers to squeeze the Japanese. Actual sightings of the enemy were few and far between, so the attackers directed their rifle fire at the presumed locations of the defenders.

Ferguson soon reached the end of his spur. The Japanese fought desperately to maintain their grasp on the feature, but B Company was unyielding. When they killed the two officers orchestrating the defence, the leaderless Japanese fled off the spur. B Company had captured its objective but at a significant cost; the ferocity of the Japanese defence left many dead or wounded. Their reward was the capture of an impressive arsenal of weapons and intelligence. Edgar ordered Ferguson to move his company to his left to the rear of Baylis who was still propelling his way down the longer spur.

As the afternoon wore on, the final Japanese defensive line on D Company's spur was reached. Here the defence was most stubborn, and Baylis worried that his company might not have the strength to break it. He requested mortar support which was forthcoming, albeit completely ineffective. A battalion observation post was sent forward to direct the mortar bombing, although poor communications equipment meant that the relayed instructions were unclear and none of the bombs landed in the right area.

The Australians' communications equipment generally performed poorly in the jungle and hampered their ability to coordinate attacks. Signaller Carlton Parrott of the 2/2nd commented that, '[T]rying to convey messages back to the battalion headquarters …was impossible. The 108 sets, we found out, didn't work in the jungle at all. They were useless. So we were having a lot of strife there.'

Even more perilous was a problem with the mortars. Many of the mortar rounds had been air-dropped at Myola and impact with the ground had rendered some defective. When this faulty ammunition was used the round would often prematurely detonate in the mortar tube. Entire mortar crews were being maimed by their own ammunition.

With the mortars of little use, Baylis requested that a company from the 2/1st strike directly north at the spur, effectively pressuring the Japanese from two directions. Edgar responded that assistance could not be organised that day and told Baylis to continue the attack alone. Baylis stuck to the same plan, albeit on a smaller scale. He ordered his second-in-command, Captain Jack Blamey, to lead 16 Platoon around the spur to assail it from the same direction from which he had wanted the 2/1st to attack. The manoeuvre worked. Faced with unremitting fire from two directions, the remaining Japanese surrendered the spur. B and D companies consolidated their gain and formed a two-company perimeter for the night.

While Baylis and Ferguson were attacking the two spurs, the rest of the 2/2nd had also spent the majority of the day embroiled in hard fighting. At 10.00 am A and C companies had marched towards their forming-up positions. They were still short of these when Captain Fairbrother's leading platoon was fired on. He immediately set his platoons the task of encircling the Japanese but, in doing so, one by one they became bogged down by strong opposition. Captain Swinton tried to help A Company and moved his men to secure the flanks and the rear of the attack. The platoons of the two companies worked well in mutual support but the number of casualties grew steadily. Wounded men trudged from the battlefield back to medics behind the front line. Signaller Parrott recalled:

> The wounded from A Company were coming past me, and one bloke called Jimmy Shanahan, from the coal fields of Newcastle, he come staggering past bleeding. He said, "Oh Carl, I've been shot. Shot in the heart." … He could still stand up, he was very agitated, as he would be. And the bullet had hit his plastic meat ticket and had gone in near the nipple of the left breast, and it had come out the back, immediately behind that. And he'd sit down one minute and then he'd stand up. "I should be dead," sort of attitude. And I thought he should be, too … I took him back a bit and showed him where the regimental aid post was … This went on through the day. The funny thing about it, the next morning, only before we moved forward to follow the Japanese down to Eora Creek after they retreated, Jimmy Shanahan come back up the track. I was amazed to see him. I said, "What's doing, Jim?" He said, "Oh, the doctor said the bullet hit the meat ticket and deflected, went into my chest, hit a rib, went right around my body and come out the back, it went straight through, but look at me now." His whole chest was black and his back was black with bruising. I said, "What are you doing?" He said, "I'm going back to my platoon." I said, "You're bloody mad, Jim." I said, "What did the doctor say?" He said, "To stay there … [but] I'm going back to my platoon."

In the midst of the battle, soldiers such as Shanahan returned to their platoons not only because they did not want to let their mates down, but also because they were not sure where else to go.

Fairbrother and Swinton could not crush their opposition before dark, so they ordered their men to withdraw and form a strong bivouac position. This was skilfully conducted, with each section covering the other as they withdrew in stages. A stiff fight was still expected the next day as, throughout the night, the Australians could hear incessant Japanese chatter.

It was not to be. On 21 October troops from the entire 16th Brigade closed in on the *Stanley Detachment*'s stronghold from multiple directions. They found it empty. Tsukamoto, lacking time to seek permission from Horii, had ordered his men to vacate Templeton's Crossing during the night. Ferguson and Baylis' stampede down the twin spurs had exacted a heavy toll and dashed Tsukamoto's hopes of holding the position. The *Stanley Detachment* hurried towards Eora Creek Village, its final line of defence in the Owen Stanleys.

Winning Templeton's Crossing cost the Australians 54 dead and 68 wounded. In the aftermath, the 2/2nd found further evidence of Japanese cannibalism, provoking increased fury among the Australians. It pointed to the utter desperation of the remnants of the *Nankai Shitai*, now critically short of all supplies.

The outstanding feature of the Battle of Templeton's Crossing was the leadership and initiative displayed at the junior officer level. Captains Fairbrother, Baylis and Ferguson all received the MC for their exemplary leadership, and they were ably supported by their lieutenants and NCOs, many of whom fell during the drive down the twin spurs. The 2/2nd Battalion had completed what Brigadier Eather's 25th Brigade had begun.

＊＊＊＊

While the Australians had been fighting to prise Templeton's Crossing from the Japanese, the Allied situation on Guadalcanal had become desperate. The Japanese were amassing troops ready for a major assault on Henderson Field (the main airfield on Guadalcanal) which was held by the Allies and was crucial to the security of their position. Vice Admiral Robert Ghormley, Commander South Pacific Area, was pessimistic and weary, unsure whether he could maintain the US Marines' fragile hold on the island. If the Japanese secured Henderson Field and thus Guadalcanal, precious resources could be diverted to reinforce the *Nankai Shitai* on the Kokoda Trail. Admiral Chester Nimitz, Commander-in-Chief, Pacific Ocean Areas, was concerned that the situation had become critical, and decided to replace Ghormley with Vice Admiral William Halsey, a renowned fighting man he expected to reinvigorate the situation. This occurred on 18 October. MacArthur may have feared that, without a rapid victory in Papua, his own position as a Pacific commander was in jeopardy.

Even before learning of Ghormley's demotion, MacArthur had signalled General Blamey on 17 October and told him: 'extremely light casualties indicate no serious effort yet made to displace enemy ... You will attack enemy with energy and all possible speed at each point of resistance. Essential that Kokoda airfield taken at earliest. Apparent enemy gaining time by delaying you with inferior strength.' Blamey then forwarded this signal to Allen.

The assertion that the Japanese were gaining time by delaying with a smaller force was correct. The Australians had certainly enjoyed a numerical superiority at the Battle of Templeton's Crossing. The major point of contention however, according to Allen's ADC Lieutenant Dalrymple Fayle, was the accusation that the men had not been seriously trying. Fayle commented later, '[This] deeply hurt and visibly affected [Allen], not, as he said, for his own sake, but for the wonderful men who had been fighting.'

On the very day that MacArthur's signal was sent, Captain Boag's two companies of the 3rd Battalion had delivered a destructive blow to the Japanese at Templeton's Crossing and laid the foundation for the ensuing attack that would win the battle. Further, the same mischaracterisation of the Japanese retreat across the Owen Stanleys earlier made by Herring is also evident in MacArthur's signal. Unlike the Australian fighting withdrawal which involved daily skirmishes as Maroubra Force gradually pulled back, the *Stanley Detachment*'s defence in the Owen Stanleys was static. Contrary to MacArthur's comments, the Australians *were* attacking the Japanese with energy and speed and at their *only* point of resistance.

Allen's response reaffirmed the difficulty of supply. He wrote that, with the limited number of carriers he had available, no more than three battalions could be kept forward of Myola in contact with the enemy. He also remarked that casualties alone were not the sole indicator of success and asked that judgement of his performance be held until either the report of a liaison officer (Lieutenant Colonel John Minogue, who was currently making his way forward to Allen for this purpose) or another senior staff officer had been considered.

Blamey contacted MacArthur in response to Allen's signal. He agreed with MacArthur that progress had been slow and assured him that he had been urging Allen to pursue a more rapid advance. For the first time he also made an effort to defend Allen, pointing out that there were many impediments to a swift advance.

However, several days later on 20 October — ironically the day on which the 2/2nd had shattered the last pillar of Japanese resistance at Templeton's Crossing — MacArthur, now aware of Ghormley's demise, impatiently ordered Blamey to pressure Allen to 'deploy his superior forces in concerted action with a view to the early capture of this important locality.'

The next day, as it became clear that the Japanese had abandoned Templeton's Crossing and the Australian advance resumed, MacArthur pressed Blamey more forcefully:

> Operational reports show that progress on the Trail is NOT, repeat NOT, satisfactory. The tactical handling of troops in my opinion is faulty. With forces superior to the enemy we are bringing to bear in actual combat only a small fraction of available strength enabling the enemy at the point of actual combat to oppose us with apparently comparable forces ... It is essential to the entire New Guinea operation that the Kokoda airfield be secured promptly.

MacArthur's signals must have influenced Blamey, as he then signalled Allen, telling him:

> During last five days you have made practically no advance against a weaker enemy. Bulk of your forces have been defensively located in rear although enemy has shown no

capacity to advance. Your attacks for most part appear to have been conducted by single battalion or even companies on narrow front. Enemy lack of enterprise makes clear he has NOT repeat NOT sufficient strength to attack in force. You should consider acting with greater boldness and employ wide circling movement to destroy enemy in view of fact that complete infantry brigade in reserve is available to act against hostile counter-offensive.

In reality, the minor advance over the preceding five days had been due to the fact that the Australians were embroiled in a major battle at Templeton's Crossing. The tactical criticism ignores the reality that the Australians were using the same tactics the Japanese had used successfully during their Kokoda campaign victories. They had used some of their force to pin and hold the enemy while another force flanked the position and attacked from either the side or rear. The density of the Papuan jungle and the broken landscape made broad, encircling manoeuvres unfeasible. Moving large bodies of troops along the formed but narrow paths in the Owen Stanleys was difficult, but moving troops off such paths was near impossible.

Allen and his brigadiers had already contemplated broad manoeuvres. While the 2/33rd was struggling to break through the *Stanley Detachment* during the Battle of Myola Ridge, Eather had sent patrols to investigate the possibility of sending the 3rd Battalion on a broad movement around the eastern side of the Myola Lakes, with the intention of reconnecting with the Kokoda Trail near Templeton's Crossing and then marching south along the Trail to attack the Japanese from the rear. A more ambitious plan involved sending the 2/31st Battalion north along a parallel track west of the Kokoda Trail that would bypass most of the Japanese positions altogether. Neither of these ideas could be implemented because of the paucity of signal wire, which was crucial for maintaining contact between the battalions. There were also insufficient carriers to keep the battalions supplied as it was, let alone if the number was fragmented and sent on wide-ranging missions.

MacArthur had told Blamey on 20 October that occupying Kokoda airfield was imperative 'in order to provide satisfactory supply and evacuation'. Blamey had voiced a similar conviction when he told Allen that his problems on the Trail would be eased once Kokoda was captured. These statements confirm that the supply train and means of evacuating wounded troops were unsatisfactory during the campaign, validating Allen's protestations. Once again, it reinforces the folly of comparing the Australian advance to that of the Japanese. Perhaps if the Australians had been pursuing the Japanese each day, relying on such a plan would have been practicable. But the Australian advance was not fluid. Gritty fighting was needed to dislodge the enemy from prepared and fortified positions. This was time consuming, and the Japanese were often prepared to fight to the last man to hold a position that had no discernable value. Consequently, a plan that relied on the capture of forward points to sustain the force was overly optimistic and lacked flexibility to deal with setbacks.

When Allen received the critical signals, his initial response, albeit one that he was advised against sending, was, 'Come up yourself and fight the bloody battle with what I have and see if you can do any better.' Instead he tempered his words. The signal he finally sent responded that he 'was singularly hurt to receive General MacArthur's signal … since I feel that the difficulties of operations in this country are still not fully realised.'

Tellingly, Allen's reply also included the line, 'I have complete confidence in my brigade commanders and troops and feel that they could not have done better.' This last line is important for two reasons. First, it illustrates the difference between Allen, who defended and had confidence in his subordinates, and MacArthur, Blamey and Herring, who doubted and second-guessed them. Second, Allen's unequivocal confidence in his brigade commanders, particularly Brigadier Lloyd, was to prove his own undoing during the coming Battle of Eora Creek.

Brigadier John Lloyd, Commander 16th Brigade. Lloyd was a decorated veteran of the Great War and respected for his undoubted personal bravery. However, his decision-making at the Battle of Eora Creek prompted criticism from his battalion commanders (AWM122335).

Chapter 15

THE BATTLE OF EORA CREEK – THE FIRST TWO DAYS

The Battle of Eora Creek was the most confusing battle fought during the Kokoda campaign. The extremely complex terrain of the battle site made it difficult for even the participants to understand what was happening for large periods during the fighting. Throughout the week-long battle there were repeated occasions on which sub-units were lost and out of contact and commanders felt they were operating blind. The first two days of the battle in particular are difficult to follow because platoons and companies were being separated from their parent battalions and sent off on individual tasks with no real overarching coordination. The primary records are littered with contradictions and there are glaring discrepancies in the first-hand accounts. As a consequence, descriptions written since the battle have varied from author to author, depending on which sources they have chosen to follow.

Japanese war correspondent Seizo Okada described Eora Creek Village as 'the remotest heart of the great mass of mountains'. The defensive qualities of the site were already well known as a battle had been fought in the canyon during the fighting withdrawal. Since then, the Japanese had spent the better part of two months using the advantageous terrain of the site to fortify two defensive zones. The upper zone was constructed on the towering Eora Ridge to the west of Eora Creek Village. This position, described in the *Official History* as a 'forest fort' was directly linked to the village of Alola by a supply path. It was built on the only water available on Eora Ridge and gave the Japanese command of the highest ground within the vicinity of Eora Creek Village. It is unlikely that the Australians knew of the existence, let alone the extent of this upper defensive position when the battle began. The lower defensive zone was situated on the same ridge that overlooks the S-bend in Eora Creek from the north that the Japanese had occupied during the fighting withdrawal. The lower zone enabled overwatch of the log bridge crossings over Eora Creek and the tributary, and also blocked the Kokoda Trail to Alola. The two defensive zones were linked by rough tracks between them. The Japanese defence at Eora Creek would be conducted by Lieutenant Colonel Tsukamoto and the *144th Regiment*. Tsukamoto had succeeded Colonel Kusonose as Commander of the *144th Regiment* when illness had forced the latter's evacuation from the Kokoda Trail.

With Templeton's Crossing secure, the 16th Brigade wasted no time in pressing forward towards Eora Creek Village. The men had no illusions as to what lay ahead. The 25th Brigade captured a native carrier from Rabaul who told the Australians there had been 300 Japanese at Templeton's Crossing and a further 200 were at Eora Creek. In fact, there were far more than 200 Japanese waiting for the Australians.

The advance to Eora Creek Village from Templeton's Crossing followed two parallel paths. The bulk of the force moved along the Kokoda Trail led by Lieutenant Colonel Paul Cullen's 2/1st Battalion, closely followed by half of the 2/3rd Battalion. Simultaneously, the remaining two companies of the 2/3rd led by the battalion's second-in-command, Major Ian Hutchison, moved north along a rough track following the ridgeline east of Templeton's Crossing, followed by the 2/2nd Battalion. Brigadier Lloyd's objective was Alola. The further north the Australians moved, the more difficult supply became. Occupying Alola was essential because it would allow air-dropping to resume north of Myola and would ease the pressure on the supply train.

The two advances stalled when the leading scouts were shot by Japanese ambushes. Both Hutchison and Cullen moved troops to flank the Japanese, but the fading light made movement difficult and both subsequently pulled their men back into bivouac positions intending to try again at dawn. However the Japanese withdrew during the freezing night and, by morning on 22 October, the Australians realised the paths were clear and resumed their advance.

The advance along both routes was laboured, particularly on the higher eastern track which was extremely narrow. Lieutenant Dennis Williams described the march forward:

[W]e were in a place where the war was fought on a series of ridges that were very narrow, and very often, a one or two man front. So when we were advancing across, you weren't having five hundred men moving in unison at the front, you were only two men, first and second scout. And the trouble was, that when we were in really close contact with the Japanese, that when you bump into them, the first bloke inevitably got shot. So it was a kind of lottery for who would have to go out and take up the front running. And there'd be, not another lottery but a fairly carefully worked out place that a forward scout had a certain number, an hour or two hours to do, and then he was replaced. So everybody had a go at it, and it was a bad luck if you were a forward scout when you actually bumped into the Japanese and, at a range of about five yards, he couldn't miss, so he shot you. And then of course the whole business would go into action, and we'd sort of surround him and throw hand grenades and shoot, until either he was dead or he ran away to fight again. Then you took up the march and so on, and that was jungle warfare, that was pretty well what it was down to.

At a point just south of Eora Creek, Hutchison's troops swerved westwards off the high track and rejoined the Kokoda Trail in front of Cullen. The 2/3rd was now at the vanguard, with Captain Colin Brown's A Company the first to reach the bald spur above Eora Creek Village at 10.30 am. This was the same bald spur that the 2/16th had defended while protecting Maroubra Force's fighting withdrawal almost two months before.

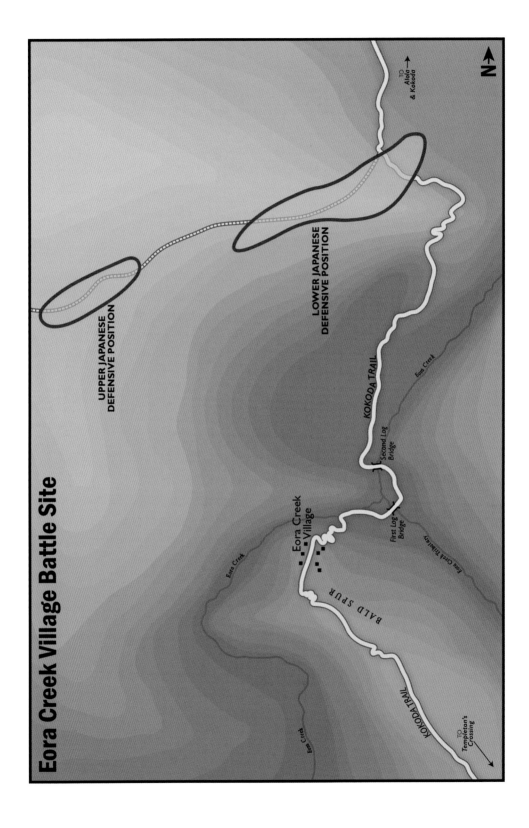

Eora Creek Village Battle Site

The bottom of the bald spur is just visible in this photograph taken from the east at Eora Creek (M. Rifat, NAA025).

The American-born Brown and several other men inched down towards the native huts at the foot of the spur. They were uneasy, wary of being ambushed in the exposed position. A member of the group, George (Bill) Langham, warned: 'Better not stand too long as this could be a trap for us.' No sooner had he uttered the words than the Japanese opened up with heavy machine-guns and mortars. The diggers scrambled to find whatever cover they could, but four were hit, including Brown and Langham. The rest of A Company peered towards them from higher up the spur, presuming their comrades to be dead. Rescue was out of the question as any attempt was likely to incur further casualties. However three of the wounded were still alive and 'lying doggo', employing a degree of battlefield cunning. As soon as darkness set in they were on their feet, scrambling up the spur to safety. The Battle of Eora Creek had begun.

Despite their unanticipated defeat at Templeton's Crossing, the Japanese had constructed a formidable defence at Eora Creek. The log bridges over both Eora Creek and the tributary that fed it from the south-east were left intact to encourage the Australians to advance over rather than around them. While both bridges were heavily defended, avoiding them would involve scaling the near-vertical heights that rose straight from the creek bed to enclose the canyon. These features naturally funnelled the attacking Australians directly towards the Japanese defences.

When Cullen and Lieutenant Colonel John Stevenson, CO 2/3rd Battalion, arrived at Eora Creek both immediately recognised the strength of the Japanese position. Both favoured detours around the log bridges rather than a direct assault. To this end, both commanders moved units to the flanks. Stevenson sent his D Company to the high ground east of Eora Creek and assembled the rest of his battalion on the eastern side of the bald spur. Cullen ordered Captain Arthur Sanderson's A Company down the western side of the bald spur to cross Eora Creek upstream. Sanderson was then to swing around to the north and drive down on the lower Japanese defensive position as quickly as possible. Sanderson's company was the third from the 2/1st Battalion to head in this direction. Prior to reaching the bald spur, Brigadier Lloyd had ordered Captain Archibald Simpson's D Company to cross Eora Creek, bypass Eora Creek Village, and head directly towards Alola. When Simpson set off, Headquarters Company followed in error, unaware of its mistake until the following day.

The Battle of Eora Creek was Brigadier Lloyd's defining moment of the Kokoda campaign. He had achieved success at Templeton's Crossing by executing the final phase of a plan put in place by Brigadier Eather. Now in outright command, Lloyd had the opportunity to seize the initiative and influence the outcome of the battle.

A view of the ground between Eora Creek and Eora Creek tributary from the direction of the bald spur (N Anderson).

But the battle did not begin as well as Lloyd might have hoped. Earlier that morning he had been informed that the bridgeheads and the high ground north and west of Eora Creek had been secured. When he arrived at the bald spur and was told that the earlier information was incorrect, he was understandably irate as he had issued orders which he now realised were flawed. This may have included the directive given to Simpson, who would find it difficult to reach Alola if the key positions at Eora Creek were not held by the Australians.

As the remainder of the 16th Brigade arrived at Eora Creek, traffic on the Kokoda Trail began to bank up at the top of the bald spur. The Australians were unaware that they were visible to the *Stanley Detachment* observing them from the ridge opposite. The Japanese waited until the Australians were heavily bunched before smothering them with mortar and mountain gun fire. The Australians scrambled to escape through the devastating rain of fire.

Among the casualties were three medical orderlies who were killed while treating men who had been wounded earlier. The 2/3rd's RMO, Captain Maurice Goldman, was hit in the spine by a shrapnel blast while Stevenson was also hit, sustaining an injury to his ear. In spite of the pain and discomfort, he remained in command of his battalion.

Extreme pressure for rapid success was consuming Major General Allen and percolated down the chain of command. With several companies already manoeuvring to the east and west of Eora Creek, Lloyd saw no value in diverting more troops along circuitous routes. He demanded a frontal attack. Stevenson was tasked with securing the log bridges so that Cullen could cross and attack the enemy.

Having witnessed the Japanese firepower that was fixed on the bridges, Stevenson and Cullen were highly sceptical of Lloyd's plan. Even if the bridges could be secured, the size of Cullen's force available for the subsequent offensive would be inadequate, comprising only C Company and B Company (minus a platoon), with the remainder of his battalion already committed to other tasks. Cullen's preference was to move his whole battalion behind Captain Sanderson's A Company to gain the high ground to the west.

The reluctance of the battalion commanders turned to resentment as Lloyd refused to consider any alternative plans. Cullen was particularly aggravated by the impression that Lloyd considered him a coward for questioning his orders. Cullen thought Lloyd was tired and clinging obstinately to a decision that was tactically poor and unnecessarily risky, later noting that 'The Kokoda Trail, [is] no place to go over when you're 50.' Cullen's assessment was slightly askew as Lloyd was 48 years old.

This stand-off then produced one of the most intriguing episodes of the Battle of Eora Creek. Cullen (who later went on to become a major general) gave many post-war interviews on his experiences during the Kokoda campaign, and frequently described an incident that occurred on 22 October before he and his men attempted to cross the log bridges. According to Cullen's recollection, following his conversation with Lloyd, he returned to the log bridges to conduct further reconnaissance. Here he came across an officer from the 2/3rd Battalion, a Lieutenant Ken Burke, who told Cullen that he had taken command of his company because of casualties. Cullen then told Burke that Lloyd had ordered the 2/3rd to capture the log bridges. Burke was reportedly angry at this order, and told Cullen he was unwilling to attack the bridges in spite of Lloyd's order because, as Cullen could see for himself, the Japanese had already killed 13 men from his battalion who lay dead at the first bridge. In his later recollections, Cullen claims that he had to crawl through the bodies to reach the bridge. The 13 dead Australians lying at the log bridge is a powerful image, and the substance of this story has been repeated in several publications including Paul Ham's *Kokoda* and Brian Freeman's *Lost Battlefield of Kokoda*.

But the accuracy of the story is questionable. The War Memorial's Roll of Honour, which lists the names and details of members of the Australian armed forces who have died in war, records a single soldier from the 2/3rd Battalion as having been killed on 22 October. In fact Maroubra Force as a whole — including the 25th Brigade, which was not present at Eora Creek — lost a total of only 10 men killed in action on this day. Further, there is no Captain or Lieutenant Ken Burke listed in the 2/3rd Battalion's nominal roll. There was a Lieutenant Burke in the 16th Brigade, a Lieutenant John *Kenneth* Burke of the 2/2nd Battalion. But the 2/2nd Battalion was located behind the bald spur, nowhere near the log bridges, so this Burke cannot be the man to whom Cullen refers. These anomalies stand out because of the explicit detail in which Cullen describes the incident, and the consistency with which he told the story in several different interviews. If this incident occurred as described, Cullen has exaggerated the number of Australian soldiers killed at the first log bridge, and must have mistakenly referred to someone else as 'Burke'. Questions over the accuracy of this story suggest that Cullen's account of the Battle of Eora Creek should be treated with caution.

Nevertheless, what was certain was that the bridge crossings were bottlenecks which would funnel the Australians into a death trap. Cullen again appealed for a flanking attack rather than a head-on assault. Lloyd remained steadfast: the frontal attack would proceed. He was adamant that the 2/3rd would capture the first bridge, but ordered Cullen to attack with the 2/1st even if the 2/3rd could not complete its mission. Cullen resigned himself to the fact that the frontal attack had to be launched.

As daylight waned and rain blasted the canyon, Lieutenant Colonel Stevenson passed responsibility for securing the bridges to Captain John Gall who was now commanding A Company of the 2/3rd Battalion following the earlier wounding of Captain Brown. Whether Gall crossed or baulked at crossing the log bridges is another mystery of the opening stage of the Battle of Eora Creek. The *Official History* account of Gall's movements is at odds with the Battalion War Diary.

According to the *Official History*, Gall 'tried an outflanking approach ... in preference to a direct approach over the bridges.' This is *precisely* what Cullen and Stevenson had wanted, but had been expressly overruled by Lloyd. In this version of events, Gall and two platoons crossed Eora Creek to the left of the two bridges (presumably somewhere near the foot of the bald spur or further to the west), and a third platoon attempted to cross to the right of the bridges. The two platoons that attempted to cross Eora Creek to the left of the bridges were successful, but intense gunfire forced Gall to lead the two platoons up and onto Eora Ridge, away from the direction of the bridges. The fate of the group that crossed to the right of the bridges was far more traumatic as will be described shortly.

In contrast to the *Official History*, the 2/3rd Battalion War Diary records that Gall, plus two platoons and a section from his third platoon, *did* cross the bridges. The war diary states that Gall considered further crossings dangerous, and decided to head for Eora Ridge with two platoons, leaving a section of the third platoon behind at the second bridge to fend for itself. The 16th Brigade War Diary supports this rendition and adds that 'the bridgehead was secured by moonlight early this morning by A Coy 2/3 Bn.'

Which version is correct? One problem with the accounts in the war diaries is the discrepancy in timing. The 2/3rd Battalion War Diary records the crossing of the bridges as having occurred at 8.30 pm on 22 October. The entry in the Brigade War Diary appears on 23 October, at least three and a half hours after the time claimed by the Battalion War Diary.

The more serious problem concerns factual accuracy. Gall may have crossed the bridges, but his instructions were to secure the bridgeheads. Irrespective of where his A Company crossed Eora Creek, it certainly did not secure a bridgehead for the 2/1st as ordered. The war diary entries appear unreliable while the most accurate version of events seems to be the description provided by the *Official History*.

Cullen suspected that the bridgehead had not been secured for his 2/1st and remained agitated over his orders to attack the bridges. When the rain finally ceased at 2.30 am and visibility improved with the emergence of the moon, he busied himself reconnoitring the bridge crossings with his adjutant, bodyguard and Intelligence Officer. To his consternation, he could not see any of Stevenson's men and assumed the bridgeheads had not been secured. The 2/1st Battalion would have to storm the bridges alone.

The Japanese had constructed a bunker to guard the first crossing, with a machine-gun pointing down the line of the bridge. Cullen and his companions crawled across the bridge towards the bunker, expecting to be shot at any moment. They were amazed at the lack of opposition. Sidling up to the bunker, they quickly dropped a grenade through the firing slit to account for any enemy. The hand grenade, muffled by the sound of the roaring creek, dispatched the inattentive sentry. Cullen now saw the opportunity to push his men across both bridges with the Japanese apparently caught off guard.

The log bridge crossing over the Eora Creek tributary. Lieutenant Colonel Cullen and his adjutant, Captain Geoffrey Cox, neutralised the Japanese bunker that guarded this crossing (M. Rifat, NAA0026).

The Intelligence Officer skewered paper on sticks, staking them into the ground to mark out a path to the first bridge. Captain Peter Barclay's C Company was then roused and prepared for action. Following the pieces of paper they moved quietly down the bald spur, through the village and over to the first crossing. When the first bridge was crossed without incident, the troops made for the larger second bridge. Two platoons crept across before the Japanese finally realised what was happening, opening fire on the shadowy figures from the ridgeline above.

The log bridge crossing over Eora Creek. The wartime bridge was in roughly the same location (M. Rifat, NAA027).

Sergeant Robert Armstrong, in command of the third C Company platoon, was forced to lead his men across the second bridge without the benefit of surprise. Armstrong recalled, 'Most of the boys had never been in action before and were jittery. I went across the bridge first to see if [Lieutenant] Jim McCloy's platoon were clear, and then I got my platoon across — each section at a time between bursts of fire.' Amazingly, only two of Armstrong's men were wounded while making the dangerous journey. 'Crossing those bridges was really a terrible experience,' Cullen remembered.

As soon as Captain Barclay's C Company had crossed Eora Creek, it ran into a small group of Australian soldiers huddled on the right-hand side of the bridgehead. This was the section from Captain Gall's company that, according to the differing accounts, had either crossed Eora Creek to the right of the bridges or had crossed the bridges and been left behind when intense gunfire drove Gall towards Eora Ridge. Meeting this section provided the 2/1st Battalion the first indication that the 2/3rd had indeed attempted to secure the bridgeheads. Notwithstanding the ambiguity of how they actually crossed Eora Creek, this little group had endured a traumatic night. As soon as the men had reached the opposite bank they were spotted by the Japanese who opened fire, forcing them to hug the ground. Unable to move and in a perilous position, the section leader asked for a volunteer to brave the enemy's withering fire and return to Lieutenant Colonel Stevenson to report their predicament. Private Francis Richardson volunteered. Springing to his feet, Richardson had dashed just five metres towards the bridge when a shot rang out. The bullet slipped under Richardson's helmet and struck him near the eye, killing him instantly.

Richardson was a bit of a larrikin. He had been court-martialled on several occasions for a litany of charges including drunkenness, failure to pay for food and drinks, swearing at a superior officer, and behaviour unbecoming of a member of the AIF. However, like the ruffian Private Maidment, whose heroism had stood out at the Battle of Isurava-Abuari, Richardson's selfless act proves that indiscipline and valorous deeds are not mutually exclusive.

With both bridges crossed, C Company tried to follow the Kokoda Trail as it wove away from the bridgehead and into a basin-like area that the Japanese had prepared as a killing ground. The surrounding jungle had been bashed flat so that the defenders could saturate the area with gunfire. Moving in the darkness, all three platoons of C Company became disoriented and navigated well away from the Trail. When dawn broke, 15 Platoon found itself well to the west of the second bridge with 13 Platoon nearby. Captain Barclay had been killed during the developing firefight, so Lieutenant McCloy took command of both platoons. On the right-hand side of the Trail, Lieutenant David Pollitt's 14 Platoon was faring no better. Daybreak illustrated the hopelessness of their situation. Having followed the course of Eora Creek downstream, Pollitt reached a dead end. Steep cliffs prevented any further movement northwards or to the west, and with the creek on his right, his men were extremely vulnerable. The situation worsened when Japanese appeared on the cliffs above and pelted the Australians with grenades. One of the grenades blew fragments of shrapnel through Pollitt's body. Lance Corporal John Hunt, doing what he could to protect his mates, hoisted himself up the cliff face and killed several Japanese who had appeared poised to wipe out the entire platoon. With that accomplished, the 14 Platoon men then shouldered their wounded and slowly retraced their steps towards the second bridge crossing.

With C Company fighting bitterly to maintain a footing on the Japanese side of Eora Creek, loud shouting and gunfire reverberated across the canyon from Eora Ridge to the west. This was Captain Sanderson's A Company, 2/1st Battalion which, until this moment, had been out of contact, its fate unknown. Sanderson's story deserves its own telling.

The day before, acting on Lieutenant Colonel Cullen's orders, Sanderson and his men had clambered down to Eora Creek from the bald spur and searched for possible crossing points. It took an enormous effort to plunge into the frothing water and climb Eora Ridge opposite which rose from the creek at a sharp angle. The crossing was so difficult that 7 Platoon, which was leading with Sanderson in tow, soon realised that 8 and 9 platoons were no longer behind it. Despite waiting and searching for the missing platoons, the company remained broken up once darkness fell. Worse, an unarmed Japanese soldier had seen 7 Platoon's position. Before he could be killed, the soldier ran off and was assumed to have reported the Australian presence on Eora Ridge, negating any element of surprise for Sanderson's attack.

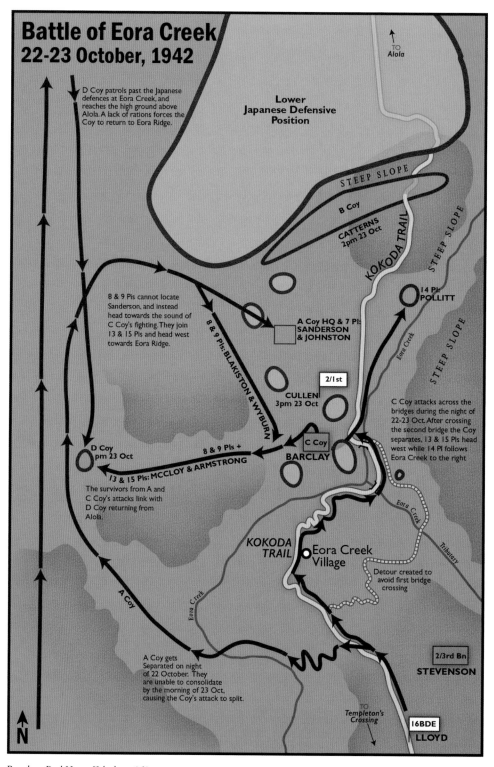

Battle of Eora Creek
22-23 October, 1942

TO
Alola

D Coy patrols past the Japanese defences at Eora Creek, and reaches the high ground above Alola. A lack of rations forces the Coy to return to Eora Ridge.

Lower
Japanese Defensive
Position

STEEP SLOPE

STEEP SLOPE

B Coy

CATTERNS
2pm 23 Oct

KOKODA TRAIL

STEEP SLOPE

14 Pl:
POLLITT

8 & 9 Pls cannot locate Sanderson, and instead head towards the sound of C Coy's fighting. They join 13 & 15 Pls and head west towards Eora Ridge.

8 & 9 Pls: BLAKISTON & WYBURN

A Coy HQ & 7 Pl:
SANDERSON
& JOHNSTON

Eora Creek

2/1st

CULLEN
3pm 23 Oct

C Coy attacks across the bridges during the night of 22-23 Oct. After crossing the second bridge the Coy separates, 13 & 15 Pls head west while 14 Pl follows Eora Creek to the right

D Coy
pm 23 Oct

8 & 9 Pls +

C Coy

BARCLAY

13 & 15 Pls: MCCLOY & ARMSTRONG

The survivors from A and C Coy's attacks link with D Coy returning from Alola.

Eora Creek

KOKODA
TRAIL

Eora Creek
Village

Detour created to avoid first bridge crossing

Eora Creek

Tributary

Eora Creek

A Coy

A Coy gets Separated on night of 22 October. They are unable to consolidate by the morning of 23 Oct, causing the Coy's attack to split.

2/3rd Bn

STEVENSON

TO
Templeton's
Crossing

16BDE

LLOYD

N

Based on Paul Ham, *Kokoda*, p. 360.

Even after these setbacks, Sanderson resolved to attack the next morning, regardless of whether the rest of the company could be found. The diggers were vocal in their disapproval. Normal platoon strength was 34, but 7 Platoon numbered no more than 17 men. The troops considered a half-platoon far too small to have any impact on the larger Japanese force. Sanderson countered that Cullen was relying on them to attack the next morning, and attack they would.

At dawn on 23 October, with his company still fragmented, Sanderson remained adamant that the attack would proceed. He led those who remained with him in a gallant charge through the jungle, advancing towards what he guessed to be the Japanese position. The optimistic attack soon met enemy opposition, and the Australians shot the Japanese in large numbers, particularly Sanderson, who was armed with a German Mauser he had acquired in Libya during the Western Desert campaign. But their success was fleeting and soon the Japanese had surrounded the small party. Sanderson, who had been directing his charges with toots of his whistle and curses at the enemy, was mowed down, sprayed in the back by a Japanese machine-gunner.

With the platoon commander, Lieutenant Keith Johnston, and seven others also dead, 7 Platoon's attack faltered. The survivors fled, slipping through the encirclement wherever they could. Some moved back up the mountain in the direction from which they had come while another group sprinted straight for Eora Creek, struggling to cross the swirling and powerful water. Private Stephen Sheldon, a soldier of small stature, did not have the strength to fight the current and was pulled under the water and presumed drowned. So ended this sorry foray, the value of which will be analysed shortly.

The commotion from Sanderson's charge was also heard by another group, the missing platoons from his A Company which had spent an unhappy night on Eora Ridge searching unsuccessfully for their leader. On hearing gunfire from the direction of the bridges, they realised that Sanderson had attacked without them. Lieutenants Charles Blakiston and Ronald Wyburn rallied their men and raced towards the fighting. When they reached the basin near the second bridgehead they looked in vain for Sanderson, instead making contact with Lieutenant McCloy and Sergeant Armstrong's platoons from C Company. The four platoons united but were unable to make any further impression on the stiffening opposition. They turned to the west and fought their way out of the basin back up Eora Ridge to the same location where A Company had started its fractured attack.

With half his companies fighting for survival, Cullen was eager to get more men across Eora Creek. This was no easy task, as any movement across the log bridges was now attracting mass bombardment from the Japanese mountain guns. A detour was needed. This was created by pushing through the jungle east of the bald spur to cross the Eora Creek tributary further upstream. While this negated the need to cross the first bridge, the second bridge still had to be traversed. This proved a nerve-wracking endeavour during daylight hours. Nevertheless, by midday Captain Basil Catterns had moved his B Company across, collected the survivors of Lieutenant Pollitt's 14 Platoon and, to avoid congestion, pushed away from the bridgehead and along the Kokoda Trail.

Moving along the Trail northwards out of the basin, Catterns hit the fringe of the lower Japanese defensive zone. B Company could make no further progress and was ordered to dig in. The ground was so steep that the Japanese were virtually on top of the Australians, able to fire down and throw grenades at them — they were 'sitting ducks'. Cullen, devoid of further units to bolster Catterns' numbers, asked Brigadier Lloyd for reinforcement. The request was granted and, at 4.00 pm, Captain Nicholas Lysaght led B Company, 2/3rd, across the creek. Cullen wanted Lysaght to immediately attack around Catterns' vulnerable left flank, but the approach of dusk and the absence of rations persuaded him to delay the attack until early the next morning.

Thus ended two of the most terrible, muddled and bloody days of the entire campaign. No fewer than 34 Australians had been killed and many more wounded. The optimistic plans of Lloyd and Allen, which had required the capture of Alola by 23 October, were a fantasy. Lloyd had noted on 22 October that 'The enemy at Eora Creek is well dug in, with well sited positions, and his clearing from this area may prove a difficult task.' Given this assessment, it is difficult to comprehend how he thought that the small forces he had committed during the first two days of the battle would be sufficient to dismantle such a strong position. Intelligence prior to the battle indicated that Eora Creek was defended by a minimum of 200 men with the support of artillery, heavy machine-guns and mortars.

Cullen's assessment was that, while Lloyd was undoubtedly a brave soldier, his grasp of infantry tactics was outdated and he lacked an appreciation of jungle warfare. This assessment, fair or otherwise, does not make allowance for the weight of unrealistic expectations which MacArthur, Blamey, Herring and Allen were all placing on Lloyd to deliver battlefield success.

The pressure for quick results most likely influenced Lloyd's tactics and his desire for the bridges to be crossed and secured. That the bridges *were* crossed appears to vindicate his plan. But there was an alternative plan that could have achieved the same result within the same time-frame with reduced casualties. This alternative was suggested to Lloyd ad nauseam by his battalion commanders. By concentrating his brigade on the high ground of Eora Ridge, Lloyd could have replicated the successful plan used at Templeton's Crossing. Given that this was the area from which the decisive stroke at Eora Creek eventually came, Lloyd should have considered the proposal on 22 October when it was first presented. As it eventuated, because the 2/1st Battalion, which was used in the frontal attack, was under strength, by the time it had traversed the two log bridges, it was in no position to inflict any substantial damage on the entrenched Japanese. As Frank Sublet later observed in his history of the campaign, 'Cullen had been thrown into the battle [by Lloyd] in a very weakened state' and the commitment of Lysaght's company only 'reinforced failure'.

Senior command's need for instant gratification may have been the ultimate driver of Lloyd's poor decision-making during the first two days of the battle, but that alone was not the reason for the mishaps of 22/23 October. Lloyd faced additional constraints in the form of inefficient communications equipment and obsolete maps.

There was no adequate communications network available to the Australians during the early days of the battle. The heavy wireless sets became waterlogged and failed, and telephone cable was in short supply. The Japanese were using small, compact wireless sets and had lightweight aluminium telephone cable which made the Australian communications equipment look 'prehistoric by comparison'. As a consequence, the Australians relied on runners to relay information, which made real-time coordination between separate units practically impossible. The woeful inaccuracy of the available maps further compromised Lloyd's ability to command and control the battle.

The actions of Captains Gall and Sanderson also need to be examined. Assuming Cullen's exchange with 'Lieutenant Burke' actually occurred, it is probable that Cullen was referring to Gall. It was Gall who had been ordered to reconnoitre the bridges, putting him in the right location for the exchange to have taken place. And, as in Cullen's story, Gall had taken command of his company following the wounding of its regular commander, Captain Brown. If Cullen had actually spoken with Gall before the bridges were rushed, why then was the coordination between the 2/1st and 2/3rd battalions so poor? In two days of madcap fighting, this was the one clear instance in which tight coordination between battalions could have been arranged, and yet it was not. When it came to crossing the bridges, the 2/1st Battalion had no idea where Gall was or how he had arrived there. As the 2/1st Battalion War Diary states, 'at no time were any of the 2/3 Bn seen, and apparently they had gone elsewhere'. It was only good fortune that allowed the 2/1st Battalion to cross the log bridges without mass casualties.

Finally, to Captain Sanderson's attack. It was undoubtedly courageous and is a favourite tale in Kokoda folklore. But, ultimately, it cost Sanderson and 10 others their lives and achieved very little. The question then, is whether Sanderson should have consolidated his company before attacking. Some written accounts of the battle claim that Sanderson's orders were to sweep around the high ground on the west to coincide his attack with the crossing of the log bridges. If this was true, then Sanderson was right to attack when he did because he needed to support the rest of his battalion.

However, it is clear from the primary records that these were *not* Sanderson's orders. His instructions from Cullen on 22 October were to 'take his Coy across the creek on the left, up the ridge above the Japanese, and to attack them from above — either when he got there, or if that was too late in the day, then to attack early the following morning'. Sanderson, in fact, was not even aware that the bridge crossings were going to take place. His company had already set out for Eora Ridge *before* Lloyd's idea to storm the bridges was conceived. The moment Sanderson and his men crossed Eora Creek they lost their ability to communicate with the rest of the Australians. They remained out of contact until their headlong charge down into the basin on the morning of 23 October.

Sanderson's character emerges in accounts of his actions. Prior to the Kokoda campaign, every officer in the 2/1st Battalion had removed his rank insignia and chosen to carry rifles rather than pistols to reduce the risk of Japanese sharpshooters recognising them as officers and selectively picking them off, a task at which they had proven particularly adept.

Sanderson was the exception: 'If I'm going to die', he was reported to have said, 'I'm going to die as an officer.' This attitude was emblematic of Sanderson's larger-than-life personality and representative of his approach to leadership once he assumed command of A Company on 18 October. Therein lies another issue. Sanderson was not an experienced company commander — he was a quartermaster — and had only acted as company commander for five days after replacing A Company's regular commander who had been evacuated ill.

Even without experience, Sanderson must surely have known that 17 men were not going to defeat such a numerous opponent. He may have taken Cullen's orders to attack as soon possible too literally, when he might have had a greater impact on the outcome of the day's fighting if he had consolidated his company and attacked in larger numbers. While Sanderson's attack was exceptionally brave, it was also unnecessary and somewhat reckless.

During the first two days of the Battle of Eora Creek, the Japanese had proven the value of well-sited defence and occupation of the tactically important high ground on the battlefield. Their ability to inflict such heavy casualties on the Australians in the first two days was testament to their discipline and skill as much as to the shortcomings in Australian planning and execution. Despite their exhaustion, hunger and dwindling numbers, the *Stanley Detachment* remained a formidable force. Their ferocious defence over the first two days at Eora Creek was a mere taste of what was still to follow.

Chapter 16

THE BATTLE OF EORA CREEK CONTINUES

The first two days of the Battle of Eora Creek were characterised by mobility. From that point on, movement became difficult and the battle evolved into one of attrition. This change occurred for two reasons. First, the Japanese defensive positions were well sited and strongly constructed. For the Australians, the unsettling reality was that capturing the positions would take time — a commodity that was in short supply. Second, from the moment the battle began, Major General Horii rushed forward every spare soldier he could find between the beachheads and Eora Creek to man the *Stanley Detachment's* final line. Every day the battle continued, the task of clearing Eora Creek became more difficult as the Japanese drip-fed reinforcements into the fighting.

The morning of 24 October began bleakly for the Australians. Sporadic Japanese gunfire and grenades had kept them awake throughout the night. Dawn brought no comfort as the arrival of daylight coincided with the opening barrages from the Japanese heavy weapons. Lieutenant Dennis Williams recalled the strain of being targeted by the Japanese artillery:

> I had to stay at one stage, on the ... [Bald Spur] above Eora Creek and the gun was firing … every time he fired it, he fired it down the track and it hit somebody ... And I had to be there, I was doing a job checking movements of troops ... And that was a cold business, having to stand there, and be shot at, and not being able to do anything about it. I couldn't charge anybody, couldn't shoot the rag, couldn't raise any kind of adrenaline going, only stand there and wait ... that was the biggest probably test of ordinary personal courage that I ever had to undergo. And I don't want to undergo it again …

Lieutenant Colonel Cullen moved forward from his battalion headquarters near the second bridgehead to inspect Captain Catterns' position beneath the lower Japanese defensive zone. Catterns was in a vulnerable position, with the Japanese mortaring his men from their perch above. It was a terrifying ordeal. Some rounds would explode high in the trees, sending a spattering of metal and organic shrapnel in every direction. Other rounds would slice through the canopy and land close to the Australians who could only pray that the bombs would miss their slit trenches and not detonate.

Cullen realised that any decisive attack would have to come from the west. He petitioned Lloyd for a minimum of two companies to attack around his left flank. Lloyd agreed and ordered Lieutenant Colonel Stevenson to augment the 2/1st Battalion and help it hold the ground it had fought so hard to win.

At 10.00 am Stevenson and his C Company, commanded by Captain Ian Fulton, braved the second bridge crossing. They rendezvoused with Cullen and Lysaght, and agreed that the 2/3rd Battalion would attempt to scale Eora Ridge to attack the Japanese from above. Essentially, this was the same plan that Cullen and Stevenson had pushed Lloyd to adopt two days earlier. Had this plan been executed from the outset, the men would have had a much easier time gaining the elevation they needed to reach the attack start point. Implementing this plan on 24 October once the 2/3rd Battalion had crossed the bridges destroyed the element of surprise. Now the men of the 2/3rd Battalion would be in contact with the Japanese every step of their climb up Eora Ridge.

The 2/3rd set off and struggled up the steep slope against steady Japanese resistance. The men were soon joined by Captain Gall's company which had been waiting on Eora Ridge since the aborted attempt to secure the bridgeheads two days before. With the onset of dusk at 5.00 pm the battalion dug in. Stevenson suspected something was awry with Lysaght's B Company at the centre of his dispositions. Sergeant Denis Hickson was sent to contact the company but disappeared. Stevenson's concern heightened when Private Edgar Nean reported that, in attempting to resupply B Company with ammunition, he and Warrant Officer Class 1 Gordon Duff had encountered five Japanese soldiers who had fired on them, killing Duff. A patrol was sent to investigate and discovered that the signal wire to Lysaght had been slashed. A Japanese force had slotted in between two of Stevenson's companies. Stevenson ordered Fulton to evict the Japanese and seal the gap between the companies, a task he accomplished before the 2/3rd bivouacked for the night.

Throughout the day, as Stevenson's battalion began climbing Eora Ridge, elements of the 2/1st Battalion which had been isolated in pockets on the same ridge passed in the opposite direction and filtered back to Cullen's battalion headquarters. These were remnants of Captain Sanderson and Captain Barclay's companies which had been decimated the day before. As the survivors straggled in, Cullen organised them into a composite company and appointed Lieutenant Colin Prior to its command.

Also returning was Lieutenant John Frew and 12 Platoon which had been patrolling on Eora Ridge. Frew's arrival completed Catterns' B Company, and he was immediately ordered to plug a hole that had developed in the 2/1st Battalion's perimeter. However, Frew's own role in the battle was short-lived. Having moved his platoon into position, Frew was crawling up the incline, attempting to line up a shot, when he was hit twice by a sniper. The two shots narrowly missed his head, wounding him in both feet. Frew's only satisfaction was returning the favour by despatching the culprit with his rifle before being evacuated from the battlefield.

In the afternoon, Lloyd himself crossed Eora Creek to inspect the area and gain greater clarity of the 2/1st Battalion's position. In conference with Cullen, Catterns and Lieutenant Edmund Body (whose platoon was closest to the Kokoda Trail), Lloyd commented: 'I can't see any Japs, what's holding you up?' Body cautioned him, 'Sir, the Japs are only around that corner, and if you get past that fellow in the weapon pit there, you'll get killed.' Cullen finishes the story: '[Lloyd did not heed the warning] So he walked up, I was behind him, Catterns was behind me, and Body behind Catterns, and so he stepped out one foot, rat, tat, tat, tat, tat, tat, tat. So he jumped back … knocked me down, I knocked Catterns down, and Catterns knocked Body down, and the four of us finished up in the bottom of this bloody steep track together, so we all stood up, and I looked at the Brigadier, and he looked at me and said, "I see what you mean."' Before returning to the bald spur, Lloyd expressed concern over the flanks and ordered Cullen to bolster them with additional manpower.

The Australian side of Eora Creek was a hive of activity. The 2/2nd had shifted forward east of the bald spur to occupy the ground vacated by the 2/3rd Battalion. In turn, the 2/31st Battalion — transferred temporarily from the 25th Brigade to Lloyd's command — had arrived at Eora Creek and moved into the 2/2nd's former position south of and behind the spur. Lloyd considered sending two companies from the 2/31st to Eora Ridge and called Allen to request permission. To Lloyd's disappointment, the request was denied. In a sign that the time it would take to secure Eora Creek was still being grossly underestimated, Allen told Lloyd that the 2/31st was Eather's only fresh unit and he wanted the battalion held forward but not committed, so that it could push on towards Alola as soon as the opposition at Eora Creek was overcome. Lloyd needed an alternative, and instead directed the 2/2nd to provide a patrol to support the attack on Eora Ridge. Captains Bruce Brock and Jack Blamey were selected for the role and led 100 soldiers from their battalion to carry out Lloyd's orders.

As heavy rain tumbled, the day ended at Eora Creek without any appreciable change to the Japanese or Australian position.

A group of diggers rest from an active patrol during the Battle of Eora Creek. This photograph was taken by the patrol leader Captain Bruce Brock who, incredibly, managed to carry a camera with him throughout the campaign (AWMP02038.144).

In spite of the extremely cold and wet night, the morning of 25 October dawned bright and clear and the veil of gloom that hung over Eora Creek temporarily lifted. However it raised only false hopes. Just after 9.30 am, two Allied aircraft took advantage of the break in cloud cover and attempted to lend close air support. Their cannons blasted along the Kokoda Trail north of the creek crossings. The appearance of the aircraft warmed the hearts of the Australians but the attack proved pointless. The aircraft attacked too far forward of the battlefield and missed the Japanese defensive positions. In all but one instance throughout the campaign, close air support to the ground troops was inadequate, if provided at all. Lloyd was aggrieved that no further air attacks took place throughout the day despite the favourable weather conditions.

This was not the only setback. During the night, the 2/1st Machine Gun Platoon had constructed a firing pit on the bald spur to provide fire support to its mates on the opposite side of Eora Creek. The platoon worked all night to site its Vickers, but the crew's efforts came to naught. The Japanese mountain guns, which were a constant menace, opened up at daybreak. The very first shell was aimed at the spur and blew apart a tree which toppled onto the Vickers and bent the barrel. The men who had laboured to carry the weapon across two-thirds of the Kokoda Trail could only curse that it never fired a shot. The 2/1st Mortar Platoon was also harassed by the Japanese artillery. Located on the southern side of the bald spur and out of the Japanese line of sight, the mortar crew presumed they were in a safe position. They were wrong. A direct hit from the mountain gun quickly ended their cameo.

To make matters worse, supplies were now running dangerously short. With no dropping ground forward of Myola, the supply line was overstretched. Carrying forward one item meant that something else had to be left behind, so a delicate balancing act was required to ensure critical materiel reached the forward areas where it was most needed. Allen issued a general order for all units to conserve their ammunition because every available carrier was already carrying supplies forward and ammunition at the front was scarce.

On the 2/1st front at the lower Japanese defensive zone, Lieutenant Andrew Murray returned to the battalion having completed a stint on Lloyd's brigade headquarters staff. As he approached Cullen and Catterns, he overheard them devising a means to penetrate the Japanese defence. Cullen wondered whether the troops could crawl forward during the night to dislodge the enemy with grenades then follow up with a bayonet attack. Catterns was emphatically opposed to the plan and told Cullen it was suicide for any man to crawl forward because the Japanese were highly alert and prone to discharge their machine-guns at the slightest sound. This was the second occasion during the Battle of Eora Creek when Catterns felt compelled to protest against the hazardous plans of a superior officer. The first had occurred during Lloyd's visit to the front line the day before, when he had encouraged Catterns to be vigorous with his attacks by alluding to his own Great War exploit of charging from trench to trench during the Battle of Pozieres. Catterns was unconvinced, certain that the same tactics would not work in the current circumstances.

Despite Lloyd and Cullen's preference for movement, Catterns' company was completely immobilised and the 2/1st was trapped in a battle of attrition. The best Catterns could do was to tie down as many enemy as possible while Stevenson manoeuvred the 2/3rd into a commanding position for his attack. Catterns did this by telling his men to constantly shift their position to keep the Japanese on edge and create the impression that an attack was impending. He also sought to convince the Japanese that a larger force was facing them than in reality.

While Catterns was thus engaged, Stevenson was still fighting hard on Eora Ridge to gain higher ground. The Japanese were fighting tenaciously, contesting each metre of ground. Every time a Japanese post was encountered, the Australians would spray it with Bren and Tommy gun fire while other troops would charge forward from another direction with grenades to destroy it. While effective, this method was slow and the Japanese were quick to re-establish their posts when given the opportunity. A sense of despair was spreading through the ranks. Sergeant Griffith Spragg recalled, 'We were feeling pretty miserable and it was wet as hell … and the Japs had the upper hand, they were sniping and cutting people up, cutting people off and people were disappearing.'

Bren gunner Private Fred Williams described the frustration of not being able to rescue mates who were shot:

> You only fired bursts … and only hoped that what come back didn't get you. It was real confusion. It was wounded being carried back and you could hear them crying and screaming and everything like that. And if somebody was badly wounded … you couldn't go to them because that's what they do. Try and shoot them in the stomach so that they're painful and then as fellows went to get to them, shoot them. And you end up losing a lot. So the idea is why waste three lives for one. So you only had to either wait till dark or something like that to get them out.

Stevenson was convinced that the Japanese had a regiment defending Eora Ridge. He needed more men, and asked Lloyd to return his D Company. Lloyd agreed, and the company — which had been patrolling the eastern side of Eora Creek since the first day of the battle — returned to Stevenson to complete his battalion as it dug in for the night. The battalion had lost four men killed and a further 12 wounded throughout the day.

The sole comfort for the troops in contact with the Japanese was the arrival of rations. These were transported during darkness when the mountain guns were dormant. Getting supplies to the two battalions that had crossed Eora Creek was an exhausting task. While the headquarters companies worked non-stop to move the supplies forward, the food reaching the men in the front line was barely enough to sustain them. Private Neville Blundell recalled, 'our ration was a tin of bully beef a day plus army biscuits. We were virtually on a starvation diet. A third of a tin of bully beef … that's a meal. [We looked forward to it though,] it tasted like manna from heaven.'

HUNGER

There was very little variety in the food supplied to the Australian soldiers in the front line on the Kokoda Trail. The two main staples were bully beef and biscuits. Even then, the difficulty of supply prevented sufficient quantities reaching Maroubra Force, which meant the troops often felt hungry. Although their diets were occasionally supplemented by locally grown foods such as taro and sweet potato, even these diminished throughout the campaign as both sides raided native gardens.

The *Nankai Shitai*'s problem with hunger was worse, particularly as the campaign dragged on. With their supply lines disrupted and the shipments of supplies to Papua few and far between, the Japanese soldiers saw their ration of rice decrease as the months passed. Many died of starvation, while those who survived lost weight which made them susceptible to sickness and disease. In a few documented cases, the dire lack of food caused some Japanese to resort to cannibalism.

Corporal Gilbert (Stewart) Simmons of the 2/25th Battalion could clearly remember the hunger pangs during the campaign:

> I get very, very upset to see any food wasted. I really do ... [my wife would cook lunch for our boys for school], and they'd say, "We like this, we like this." And I said, "Well, it's all good food, there's none of this liking or anything." And my wife still doesn't believe me because I remember we had been somewhere [on the Kokoda Trail] and we were almost knee deep in mud. But there in the mud there was crumbs of biscuits, the box must have broken open and out bounced all these crumbs about as big as the top of your thumb. And we knelt in that mud and picked up every crumb and ate it. You were hungry when you did that.

Soldiers of the 2/31st Battalion cook their frugal meal of bully beef and biscuits on the Kokoda Trail near Menari (AWM027047).

Night brought some relief, but the jungle was uncomfortable and a difficult place to sleep. According to Lieutenant Dennis Williams:

> You lay down in the mud and slept. Each of us carried half a blanket which was always sodden … If you tried to dig a trench for example, it very rapidly filled with water. So if it was necessary for fighting purposes, you were lying in water, and you didn't dig a trench or anything to sleep in, you only lay down on the ground as you were.

By 26 October the general situation had not changed substantially — certainly not enough to placate the discontent of the senior Allied commanders. MacArthur, Blamey and Herring continued to demand more from the Australians. The battle had entered its fifth day and a breakthrough looked remote. The trio's impatience for forward progress was borne by Allen, who in turn impressed on Lloyd the importance of gaining traction against the defenders.

The *Nankai Shitai* was also in poor shape. The troops were holding on, but as their casualties grew, their ability to mount counter-attacks diminished. Horii demanded Eora Creek be held until at least 28 October, which would allow time for the preparation of a new defensive location closer to Kokoda. Relief arrived for the *Stanley Detachment* in the form of Major Koiwai's *2/41st Battalion*. Koiwai had implored Horii to leave his men at Giruwa so they could recover from the sickness that had thinned their ranks. Horii was unswayed. The *Stanley Detachment* needed urgent reinforcement and no man could be spared, particularly since the *144th Regiment* had carried the bulk of the Japanese fighting in the campaign to this point. Horii himself did his best to rally the troops. He walked to Eora Creek and drank sake with them which temporarily raised their spirits.

The Japanese artillery continued to frustrate the efforts of the Australians to bring their own ranged weapons into the fight. The 2/1st's 3-inch mortar was ready for use again after previous attempts to employ it had been thwarted. It began firing on the lower Japanese defensive position at 7.30 am. Retribution was swift: 15 minutes later the Japanese mountain gun retaliated and obliterated the mortar crew. In the blast, Lieutenant Ion Reardon was severely wounded when a piece of shrapnel tore open his rib cage. Despite the continuing danger, Sergeant Edwin Madigan ran to Reardon's aid and carried him to safety. He then rushed to find a replacement weapon and crew to carry on the task. Private Bernard Moore of the 2/2nd Battalion who was also on the bald spur recalled, 'we called it "jittery ridge", every time you moved, they'd lob a mortar or a mountain gun onto you. They were directly opposite us, and they could see everything we were doing, and we could see what they were doing too, but you couldn't do much about it, cause we didn't have any artillery in them days.'

The ongoing lack of artillery support had blighted Australian defensive and offensive operations throughout the campaign. The value of using such weapons had been proven time and again by the Japanese whose three types of field pieces had provided superior firepower to anything the Australians could bring to bear. The only saving grace was that the individual arms of the Australians were superior to those carried by the Japanese:

the Lee Enfield service rifle was a superior weapon to the Japanese Arisaka Type 38, and the Tommy gun was unmatched in jungle warfare as the Japanese were not equipped with small sub machine-guns.

On the other side of Eora Creek, Stevenson told Lloyd that he had to move his men higher up Eora Ridge to find the necessary impetus to drive down on the defenders. Sergeant Spragg recalled the exhaustion caused by the endless climbing: 'It was amazing what the human body can put up with, that always impressed me. Only what you took, what you had to stand.' As Stevenson slogged westward, his battalion pulled away from the 2/1st, creating a breach in the Australian lines. The fortuitous return of Captain Simpson's D Company from a long-range reconnaissance patrol enabled Cullen to fill this gap. Earlier, on 22 October, Lloyd had given Simpson personal orders to bypass Eora Creek and head directly to Alola. Simpson's patrol had struggled through the jungle to reach a vantage point above the village. From here his men had shocked a group of Japanese soldiers in a camp area, lashing them with grenades and Tommy gun fire before fading back into the jungle. The venture cost Simpson two men killed, but he was certain that at least three times as many Japanese had been killed and more wounded.

On the return leg to Eora Creek, Simpson had come across clusters of the 2/1st Battalion, more survivors of Captains Sanderson and Barclay's companies from the bitter fighting of 23 October. These men had joined Simpson and the group reached Brigade Headquarters during the night of 25/26 October. While Lloyd heaped praise on Simpson, the value of the patrol is questionable — through no fault of Simpson's. On its own, D Company was not strong enough to make any lasting impression on the Japanese stronghold at Alola. And with insufficient rations to last more than a few days, the company was not equipped to remain beyond Eora Creek to continue to harass the Japanese lines of communication. After a night's rest, Simpson and the other assortment of 2/1st personnel recrossed Eora Creek and returned to Cullen's command (thus allowing him to plug the hole created by Stevenson's westward movement). For the first time since the battle began, Cullen had almost his entire force available in the one location.

There was little else to cheer the men. Even small routine actions sapped their energy and were extremely dangerous. Exercising bodily functions was fraught with danger. Moving out of fighting pits was a certain way to draw gunfire, such was the proximity and alertness of the Japanese troops. Soldiers were forced to ignore their modesty and relieve themselves in whatever vessel they could find before disposing of the waste as best they could. Cooking fires were banned because they signalled the Australians' position, so the troops lived on cold bully beef. Lloyd stressed to Allen that further rations of biscuits were needed because the monotony of the bully beef diet was draining the troops' strength. In response to increasing physical ailments, Lloyd acted on the advice of the CO of the 2/4th Field Ambulance, Lieutenant Colonel Arthur Hobson, who suggested that a rest area be established behind the bald spur for troops to recuperate following long-range patrols. However, this did little to help the bulk of the troops who were in close contact with the Japanese and could not be withdrawn.

That afternoon the canyon was engulfed in a tremendous deluge. Lieutenant Dennis Williams observed: 'Of course in New Guinea, they only have two seasons, they have a wet season and they have a dry season. And in the dry season it rains every day, and in the wet season, it rains all day.' The avalanche of rain caused the water level in Eora Creek to rise sharply. Its powerful current swept away the log bridge, slamming it into rocks further downstream where it partially submerged. The effort of supplying and evacuating casualties now became a gargantuan affair. With teamwork the Australians combined to carry out what Cullen called a 'rotten job'. Waist deep in the icy water of Eora Creek, the men braced themselves against the wreckage of the bridge. Standing in a line with their arms raised above their heads, they passed supplies in one direction, and then hoisted stretchers back in the opposite direction. The whole time they worked in darkness as the Japanese dropped shells on them hoping to score a lucky hit. The work was terrifying and required enormous fortitude and physical strength. Chief among the willing workers was Padre Charles Cunningham, who was made a Member of the British Empire for exceptional meritorious service for this action. With the rain showing no signs of abating, another gruelling day drew to a close.

****

As the Australian advance became bogged down at Eora Creek, the pressure on Allen and Maroubra Force boiled over. Blamey had arguably already decided to replace Allen. He told a journalist that he would have sacked 'the old bastard' but for the fact that it would take six days for a replacement to reach him. A letter written by Major General Vasey to his wife on 22 October corroborates this. In the letter, Vasey recalls that Blamey told him he regretted not having replaced Allen after his initial delay in pushing to Myola.

On 26 October Blamey signalled Allen and told him his previous correspondence had not disproven any of MacArthur's criticisms. Blamey continued:

> … progress [since 21 October] has been negligible against an enemy much fewer in number. Although delay has continued over several days, attacks continue [to be made] with small forces. Your difficulties are very great but enemy has similar. In view of your superior strength, energy and force on the part of all commanders should overcome the enemy speedily. In spite of your superior strength enemy appears able to delay advance at will. Essential that forward commanders should control situation and NOT allow situation control them.

For the first time, several of Blamey's criticisms of Allen were accurate. At Eora Creek, particularly during the first few days when the consequences of the defeat at Templeton's Crossing were still being felt by the Japanese and Horii was busy rushing reinforcements forward, the Australians *had* significantly outnumbered the Japanese. It was not however, a numerical superiority of the magnitude envisaged by MacArthur who, at a conference with several high-ranking Australian officers in Brisbane on 27 October, revealed his conviction that the Japanese had only one battalion in the Owen Stanleys. Second, the assertion that the Australian attacking manoeuvres were being conducted by small forces was fair, and they continued in that vein until Major Hutchison led a coordinated three-company attack on 27 October.

Allen responded to Blamey's signal on the same day he received it, and his attempts to mollify his critical commander were obvious:

> One. Every effort is being made to overcome opposition as quickly as possible. Present delay has and is causing me considerable concern in view of its probable effect upon your general plan. Jap however is most tenacious and fighting extremely well. His positions are excellent, well dug in and difficult to detect. I feel it will be necessary to dig him out of present positions since his actions to date indicate that a threat to his rear will not necessarily force him to retire. I have already arranged for 2/31 Bn to assist 16 Bde 27 Oct but it must be realised it would take 36 hours to get into position. Owing to precipitous slopes movement in this particular area is extremely difficult and a mile [1.6 kilometres] may take up to a day to traverse. I had hoped that 16 Bde would have been able to clear enemy position today. Two. As I feel that a wrong impression may have been created by our sitreps I must stress that throughout the advance a brigade has always been employed against the enemy but up to the present this has been the maximum owing supply situation. Three. Jap tactical position at present is extremely strong and together with the terrain is the most formidable up to date. No accurate estimate can be given of Jap strength except that commander 2/3 Bn reports that at least one battalion opposes him alone. Four. You may rest assured that I and my brigade commanders are doing everything possible to speed the advance.

By the time Allen sent this response, Blamey had already decided to remove him, having divulged his plan to Herring the previous evening. While Blamey forwarded Allen's message to MacArthur, he edited the original signal removing the first, second and final sentences. This was a highly manipulative act. It distorted Allen's signal and made him appear oblivious to GHQ's wishes and offering nothing but excuses. This made it easier to condemn him. In forwarding the edited signal to MacArthur, Blamey concluded by informing the Commander-in-Chief that the decision to replace Allen had been made, a decision MacArthur supported.

Allen was notified by Blamey: 'Consider that you have had sufficiently prolonged tour of duty in forward area. General Vasey will arrive Myola by air morning 28 October. On arrival you will hand over command to him and return to Port Moresby for tour of duty in this area.'

Allen was aggrieved at the lack of understanding of his predicament. Nonetheless, he responded: 'It is regretted that it has been found necessary to relieve me at this juncture especially since the situation is improving daily and I feel that the worst is now behind us. I must add that I feel as fit as I did when I left the Base Area and I would have preferred to have remained here until my troops had also been relieved.'

Allen's own mention of his physical health is interesting as, following his removal, it was this reason that Blamey seized on and used as one of the primary justifications for his decision. He later told Army Minister Forde that tropical warfare sapped the strength of personnel and caused operational fatigue, and that this was the major reason he had been forced to replace Allen. It is true that tropical warfare causes fatigue — as all warfare tires commanders and troops alike — however there is no evidence and no first-hand accounts to indicate that Allen's physical health had affected his performance. On the contrary, Lloyd had commented in the 16th Brigade War Diary that Allen looked 'fit and confident'. If Allen's physical exhaustion was as Blamey suggested, it was likely that a contributing cause was the excessive pressure exerted on him from his superiors. As Colonel Frank Kingsley Norris recalled: 'We fought two wars in the days before Kokoda [was recaptured], one against the Japanese, and another against Corps HQ in Moresby, which was completely unable to understand the conditions in which we lived and fought, and the appalling shortages of everything from food to ammunition ...' When informed of his removal, Allen commented simply, 'Well, that's that, then.'

* * * *

As these events were unfolding, at Eora Creek on the morning of 27 October there was much activity. Lloyd was still dissatisfied with the level of close air support being received. He again requested that the Air Force pound the enemy on the Kokoda Trail north of Eora Creek. He stressed the point that the singular nature of air attacks to date had been ineffectual and that only continuous attacks could effectively harass the enemy.

Lieutenant Colonel Cullen, seeking to exert greater pressure on the enemy in front of his left flank, moved his battalion headquarters higher up the ridgeline behind his C and D companies. No sooner had he moved to the new location than he received an urgent phone call. The caller was Catterns, who informed him that the enemy had withdrawn from their positions in front of his company. Cullen ordered Catterns to push forward behind some probing patrols while he descended the ridge to follow close behind.

Catterns had advanced just 450 metres before strong resistance sent his company to ground once again. The Japanese had merely given ground to tighten their perimeter. In ceding the ground, the Japanese had left behind a wealth of supplies including small arms. They also left the body of another Australian who had been cannibalised, with portions of his thighs and buttocks removed, the wounds described as neat and butcher-like. The Japanese now occupied an even stronger position on a steeper part of the ridge. This position would need to be destroyed before the general advance could continue.

At Brigade Headquarters, Lloyd was delighted with Cullen's news of the Japanese withdrawal from the lower defensive position. He moved the 2/2nd forward, while a platoon from the 2/25th under the command of Lieutenant Kenneth Jefferson was released from the 25th Brigade to assist the 2/3rd on Eora Ridge. Lloyd wanted more than a platoon from the 25th Brigade to provide extra clout for the looming attack, but Eather was nursing his men, conscious of the central role his brigade would play in the anticipated battles ahead. When he agreed to lend Lloyd engineers from the 2/6th Field Company, he did so on the proviso that they would not be used in a role that could result in casualties. This was not practical as the engineers were needed to fix the bridge over Eora Creek that had been washed away the day before. With the Japanese shelling the general area, Lloyd could give no such promise, but the engineers were released anyway owing to the critical importance of re-establishing the crossing. The engineers set to work and had the bridge repaired by 29 October.

Shortages at the front continued to impair Lloyd's ability to crush the opposition, and he noted that biscuits, tobacco and signal wire in particular were in short supply. The dearth of signal wire was especially troublesome as Lloyd needed to communicate with his front-line troops and the wireless sets were of no use because they had become waterlogged and were malfunctioning.

Australian Signalman James Pashley of the 16th Brigade at work on the Kokoda Trail (AWMP02038.146).

On the bald spur, the irrepressible Sergeant Madigan was still doing all he could to help his colleagues on the opposite side of Eora Creek. A mortar crew successfully dropped more than a dozen bombs on the Japanese and rejoiced at their apparent success. However, the euphoria was short-lived. Tragically, the next round, another that had been air-dropped at Myola, prematurely exploded in the mortar tube splitting it open and killing all three crew members. Madigan, who had watched in horror, was blown off his feet, suffering severe concussion that caused blood to run from his ears. The series of deaths caused by the defective mortar bombs infuriated Lloyd, and he ordered that no ordinance be fired unless it had been carried forward along the length of the Kokoda Trail. As safe mortar rounds were now in extremely short supply, the gulf in attacking firepower between the Japanese and Australians widened once again.

High up on Eora Ridge, Lieutenant Colonel Stevenson finally succumbed to the ear wound that had afflicted him throughout the battle. The wound was not only painful, but was causing severe headaches. Deciding he could no longer offer the leadership required by his battalion, he called Major Hutchison and instructed him to take command. He then made his way back to Brigade Headquarters where Lloyd noted his sickly condition and agreed that Hutchison was more than capable of spearheading the 2/3rd.

Major Ian Hutchison (left), speaking with Generals Blamey and MacArthur at Owers' Corner on 3 October as the 16th Brigade commenced its advance along the Kokoda Trail. Following the wounding of the 2/3rd Battalion's CO at the Battle of Eora Creek, Hutchison found himself elevated to battalion commander at a pivotal moment (AWM013422).

Hutchison took command of the 2/3rd at the pivotal moment. After days of toiling to reach the top of Eora Ridge, he told Lloyd by telephone that his men would be in position to attack by 9.30 am. Hutchison energised the troops with a positive attitude that seemed to have been lacking in Stevenson over the past few days. With Brock and Blamey's 2/2nd patrol of 100 soldiers attached to his battalion, he had a sizeable force ready to roll down the ridgeline. His force was arranged in three columns. On the right he placed Brock and Blamey's men. The centre was allotted to Lieutenant Luke McGuinn, OC D Company, who had a force of company strength comprising two of his own platoons and one from B Company. The left flank — where the heaviest resistance was expected — was given to C and A companies under Fulton, with Headquarters Company and Battalion Headquarters following.

Hutchison's key instruction to his company commanders was simple: they were to eradicate any Japanese posts that stood in their way. Brock did not share Hutchison's confidence. He told Hutchison that, based on reports he had received, he feared his column would be hopelessly outnumbered. Hutchison told him that each column would provide mutual support and, to that end, each column would advance 900 metres before halting and making contact with the other.

The moment to advance had arrived. Hutchison gave the order and the three columns were away, moving down and along the spine of the ridge as it curled back towards Eora Creek. Half an hour before noon, it was Brock and Blamey's men who first struck opposition, having advanced 275 metres. The Japanese defence was stout and the column struggled to make further ground. Private Fred Williams in Brock's column recalled:

> I'm standing next to [Sergeant Ron Cadell] and he kept coughing. I'm saying to him, "Don't make a noise, don't make a noise" … We come round this big tree, he went round that side, I went round this side and there was a bang and he got it. And as soon as he got shot, I sort of half turned and as I turned, woof, straight past me. There was two of them there. One on one side of the tree, one on the other side of the tree. So I dropped straight down and every time I went to move … bang'… I could have got up and started shooting like mad but you're only going to get shot straight away because he could see me and I couldn't see him. [Later] I went to get help for Ron … But it wouldn't have made any difference. He was shot in the stomach, he was going to die ...

> The next day, because I knew where Ron Cadell was, I was told to go back to bury him … And when I say buried, all you do is put the tin hat over their face, took their wallet and part of their identity. And they were to go back … I [also] took his compass. It was no good to him anymore. And we left them there and the padre and the intelligence section fellow were supposed to mark the graves.

To the left, McGuinn's central column also met fierce resistance. Five casualties were suffered as the Australians crashed into a defensive position that was stronger than anticipated. McGuinn considered his force too small to break through and requested help. As the left column's progress had been easier (it was able to advance 730 metres), Hutchison ordered Fulton to divert two platoons towards McGuinn. Fulton complied, but because dusk was falling, the men dug in ready to resume the offensive the next day. The offensive would have to be continued by the 2/3rd alone as Brock had rounded up his men and returned to Brigade Headquarters after losing contact with Hutchison and the other columns which had advanced further down Eora Ridge.

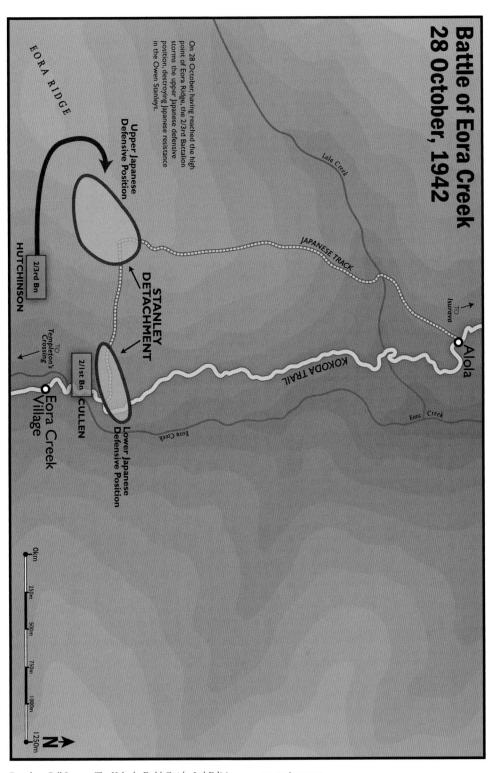

Battle of Eora Creek
28 October, 1942

On 28 October, having reached the high point of Eora Ridge, the 2/3rd Battalion storms the upper Japanese defensive position, destroying Japanese resistance in the Owen Stanleys.

EORA RIDGE

Upper Japanese Defensive Position

2/3rd Bn

HUTCHINSON

STANLEY DETACHMENT

TO Templeton's Crossing

2/1st Bn

CULLEN

Eora Creek Village

Lower Japanese Defensive Position

Lala Creek

JAPANESE TRACK

TO Isurava

Alola

KOKODA TRAIL

Eora Creek

Eora Creek

0km 250m 500m 750m 1000m 1250m

N

Based on Bill James, *The Kokoda Field Guide*, 3rd Edition, accompanying map.

The close-quarter combat was nerve-wracking and exhausting, taking a physical and mental toll on both sides. Staff Sergeant Imanishi Sadashige from the *144th Regiment* recalled: 'We were under a barrage and it was like bullet rain. But we were not allowed to withdraw and were told to hold our position until the designated date. Because it was an order, I thought we would have to hold the position until we all died.'

If there was one day during the entire Kokoda campaign on which the Australians were able to settle scores with the Japanese, it was 28 October. Hutchison's 2/3rd was now almost in a position to unleash carnage on the upper Japanese defensive position.

The attack from the previous day was not immediately followed up because two factors held Hutchison back. First, he was unaware of what had happened to Brock's column and was trying to establish contact. Second, the troops were in need of water and had to wait an hour and a half while supplies were carried up to them. With Brock back at Brigade Headquarters, Lloyd realised that the 2/3rd Battalion would need support. He quickly ordered B Company from the 2/2nd to rush to Hutchison as a replacement. At around the same time, Lieutenant Jefferson's platoon of the 2/25th rendezvoused with Hutchison, having been sent forward a day earlier. When Jefferson learned of Hutchison's impending attack, he pulled his patrol back and returned to the 2/25 Battalion which was pushing north along Eora Ridge from Templeton's Crossing in his wake. This raises the question of why Jefferson's platoon had been ordered to go forward to Hutchison if it was not going to support the 2/3rd's attack. The 2/3rd was in clear need of support with Brock's column back at Brigade Headquarters.

With Hutchison preparing his men for the final thrust on Eora Ridge, the ordeal of the 2/1st Battalion — grappling with the Japanese in the canyon below — was almost at an end. Nevertheless, during the day, Cullen lost another five men near the Kokoda Trail. These men were hit by projectiles that were literally 'bowled' at them down the cliffs from above. Catterns recalled, 'They drop[ped] stones, they drop[ped] grenades, they dropped empty tin cans where they'd eaten rice or something, all went down this [hill].'

With the 2/2nd reinforcements unable to reach Hutchison in time, he divided his attacking force into two columns under the command of Captain Fulton. Fulton was given simple instructions: 'destroy the enemy'. Fulton's C Company would attack on the right with McGuinn's D Company on the left. The two columns would advance in unison and punish any enemy caught between the pincers. Two platoons probed forward to confirm the flanks. The leading scouts were shot, as was their misfortune throughout the campaign. However their role was crucial and allowed the Australians to identify the breadth of the Japanese position.

At 5.00 pm the battle began. It opened with a storm of fire from every available weapon: machine-guns, small arms, grenades. The Australians used whatever cover they could find, dashing from tree to tree and dropping every enemy that stood in their path. The thick jungle opened up as bullets tore leaves and branches from the trees. The diminutive Corporal Lester Pett was ruthless. He single-handedly wiped out four enemy machine-gun posts — a deed for which he was awarded the Military Medal. The Japanese tried to resist, fighting desperately to hold back the tide, however the Australians drove forward purposely, maintaining relentless pressure.

As the outlying posts were overrun, the Australians soon barged their way into the core of the Japanese forest fort. This was the turning point after six days of grinding attritional warfare. Without the shielding of their outposts, the Japanese were routed, flayed by the Australians as they fled in terror. Their panicked cries echoed across Eora Creek before silence signalled that the battle had been won only an hour and a half after it had begun. Lloyd summarised the final moments of the battle succinctly: 'Tenacious though the Japanese are, the vigour and ferocity of this attack was too much for them, and they broke and fled.'

One of the reasons for the Japanese collapse lay in the fact the Hutchison had caught the *3/144th Battalion* at the worst possible moment. Horii had earlier ordered the *Stanley Detachment* to 'Repel the frontal attacks of the enemy and withdraw during the evening of 28 October.' Lieutenant Colonel Tsukamoto was in the process of executing these orders and withdrawing the *Stanley Detachment* from Eora Creek when the 2/3rd Battalion's attack rolled through.

Earlier that morning the Japanese mountain guns and artillery had been withdrawn, followed by the *1/144th* and *2/144th Battalions* which were blocking the Trail and the lower part of the ridgeline opposite Cullen. Higher up on Eora Ridge, Koiwai's *2/41st Battalion* was waiting for the *3/144th* to withdraw from the forest fort so that it could act as a rearguard. Koiwai later recalled:

> The time designated to leave our position was 8 pm. According to previous arrangements, the Kuwada Battalion was to have withdrawn to our position by that time, then proceed to positions on the road held by Lieutenant Colonel Tsukamoto Masao [sic]. Our battalion also undertook preparations for withdrawal, then waited for Kuwada's unit. However, 8 pm passed without any sign of them. We began to think something had befallen them but they finally arrived around 8.30 pm. Lieutenant Colonel Kuwada then said: "Elements of an enemy force penetrated our battalion's position and engaged us in close fighting. We were finally able to repel them and I issued the order to withdraw."

Kuwada's comments are suggestive of the Japanese tendency to downplay the true extent of their military defeats. As Koiwai continued:

> We waited for a further hour, but there was still no sign of the rest of ... [*3/144th*] by 10 pm. The moon was bright and thin beams of light penetrated here and there between the thick growth of the forest. Lieutenant Colonel Kuwada said to me: "We cannot wait any longer for the unit. We have to leave. The company commanders may be somehow able to withdraw." I replied: "No. Our unit is to defend the withdrawal. We must leave friendly forces to the rear of the unit. Let's wait for another hour." ... Kuwada then replied: "But perhaps another company will come out on the road further down. Even if we wait here it will be a waste. Let's leave now."

The 2/3rd's attack had routed the *7th* and *9th companies* of the *3/144th Battalion*. The survivors could not join Kuwada in any form of organised withdrawal. Instead, they were forced to labour through the jungle carrying their casualties in the hope of finding their parent unit in the days ahead. Kuwada's battalion had been shattered by the strength of Hutchison's attack.

As 29 October dawned, the Australians remained uncertain as to whether any further fighting awaited them. But it was soon apparent that the drudgery that had characterised the Battle of Eora Creek was finally past. Australian casualties for the battle were 72 killed and 154 wounded. Most of these were suffered by the 2/1st Battalion on 23 October, the day Cullen's men later referred to as 'Bloody Friday'. For the Japanese, it was the *3/144th* that was most battered, many of their number killed on the final afternoon in the fighting at the forest fort. Hutchison's men found no fewer than 69 Japanese bodies at the scene of their epic encounter, and they suspected there were many more in the area as yet undiscovered. The bodies were searched for intelligence then buried.

With the battle over, Cullen and Hutchison's men enjoyed their first hot meal in over a week and took the opportunity to marvel at the extent and quality of the Japanese entrenchments. The impressive work of the Japanese engineers was particularly visible at the lower defensive position, while the forest fort was far larger than imagined. From this location, empty firing pits for the Japanese mountain guns were identified. The Japanese gunners occupied a lofty position with a commanding view of the Australians on the southern side of Eora Creek. Their ability to predict where the Australians were setting up their own ranged weapons now made sense.

War relics left at the lower Japanese defensive position from the Battle of Eora Creek (N. Anderson, NAA029).

A Japanese bunker at the lower Japanese defensive position (N. Anderson, NAA028).

While the Battle of Eora Creek was a substantial victory for the Australians, it also represented a needless cost in time and casualties. The first two days of the battle were indecisive and shaped the grinding nature of the days that followed. Had Brigadier Lloyd sent a sizeable proportion of his force west from the bald spur to directly scale Eora Ridge, it would surely have paved the way for an easier ascent than that experienced by the 2/3rd Battalion, which instead crossed the bridges and was thus in contact with the enemy the entire time the men were trying to gain altitude.

The Australian attack had to occur on Eora Ridge because patrols that had pushed down the eastern bank of Eora Creek during the battle provided bleak assessments of the possibility of attacking from that direction. Their reports estimated it would take an attacking force a full day to march to a suitable place to cross Eora Creek, by which time the men would be exhausted and would then have to attack uphill. In addition, the creek was much wider downstream, which would make the actual crossing extremely difficult, particularly if it was opposed by the enemy.

The most significant event to occur during the battle was the removal of Major General Allen. However it is doubtful whether the length of the engagement or the mishaps that occurred significantly influenced that decision as Herring and Blamey had already committed to that course of action before the battle began. The disasters of 22 and 23 October only compounded their dissatisfaction with Allen's performance.

The most disappointing aspect from Allen's perspective is that his replacement, Major General Vasey, won plaudits as the Kokoda victor, when he had arrived far too late to have any bearing on the Battle of Eora Creek, let alone the campaign in general. Those most deserving of credit for the victory at Eora Creek were the Australian troops who had endured immense hardship throughout the week of fighting in arguably the most trying circumstances encountered throughout the campaign.

Chapter 17
KOKODA RECAPTURED

There was no fighting in the final days of October, nor in the very early days of November. The *Nankai Shitai* withdrew beyond Kokoda to Oivi, where it planned to block the mountain pass and stage the next step of its Papuan resistance. The hard fighting that the Australians anticipated would be needed to seize Kokoda never eventuated.

On 29 October, when it was apparent that the Japanese had vacated Eora Creek, the Australians recommenced their northwards advance. The 2/1st led the way, followed by the 2/2nd and the 2/31st. The 2/3rd finished clearing the forest fort at Eora Creek then rejoined the remainder of the 16th Brigade further along the Trail.

Alola was retaken on 30 October without opposition. This had an immediate impact on the supply situation, as the Australians now had a site for air drops north of Myola, closer to the front line. Supply drops commenced at Alola on 31 October, the 3rd Battalion tasked with collecting the packages. Initial results were disappointing as many drops missed their mark and cascaded over the mountain lip on which Alola is situated, tumbling down into the depths of the jungle.

At the same time, companies from the 2/1st were pushing forward through Isurava en route to Kokoda, while the 2/2nd had crossed Eora Creek and was travelling along the eastern Abuari ridgeline, closely followed by the 2/3rd. When the 2/31st took the lead on the Kokoda Trail, Lieutenant Colonel Cullen swung over to join the remainder of the 16th Brigade near Abuari.

The other two battalions of the 25th Brigade — the 2/25th and 2/33rd — were finding the journey extremely tough. They were trudging northwards on a rough foot pad, some distance to the west of Eora Creek. Here the altitude exceeded 3000 metres and the terrain was so difficult that moving 500 metres could take as long as two hours. Eventually these two battalions reconnected with the Kokoda Trail north of Eora Creek and followed behind the 2/31st.

A patrol led by Lieutenant Alexander Black of the 2/31st was the first Australian group to enter Kokoda on 2 November. The event was an anticlimax as the village had been abandoned. The moment is best captured by the *Official History*: 'So, quietly, the Australians re-entered Kokoda. Apart from its airfield its significance lay only in its name which would identify in history the evil track which passed across the Papuan mountains from the sea to the sea.' The airfield that had been so eagerly sought had fallen into disrepair and had not been used by the Japanese. Working parties were immediately detailed to clear it and prepare the strip for aircraft landings to allow much-needed supplies, ammunition and comforts to be flown in.

At around 3.30 pm on 3 November, Major General Vasey led a flag-raising ceremony on the site of the old administration building. The Australian flag, a brand new nylon-weave, had been air-dropped by an American fighter pilot earlier that morning specifically for that purpose. The occasion was described by Lieutenant Kienzle as sombre: there was no band, no cheering, just hundreds of weary Australians standing silently to attention in the rain.

A group of Australian soldiers watch as the Australian flag is raised at Kokoda (AWM013572).

Several days later, on 6 November, a further ceremony was held next to the airfield in a show of gratitude to the Papuan natives who had assisted throughout the campaign. Bravery medals were awarded, knives and ramie (a type of plant-based textile used to make rope) were given as gifts, and a feast was organised to reward the natives' loyal and dedicated service. The Papuans had been dubbed the 'Fuzzy Wuzzy Angels' for their bouffant hair and the tenderness with which they treated wounded Australians while bearing them on stretchers along the Trail. The Fuzzy Wuzzy Angels became synonymous with the Kokoda campaign and helped forge an enduring legacy of friendship between the Australians and Papuans.

Within the week, both Australian infantry brigades were again committed to battle, fighting the Japanese at Oivi and Gorari. The recapture of Kokoda had immediately alleviated the problem of supply, with stores flown into Kokoda and transported to the troops at the front. The constancy of supply removed the torment of the Kokoda commanders who had struggled for three and a half months with the pressure of fielding forces in an environment that could not adequately sustain them for any significant period of time. The Kokoda campaign had ended, but the daunting challenge of defeating the Japanese in Papua remained.

CHAFORCE

Following its relief on the Kokoda Trail, the 21st Brigade returned to its base at Koitaki for a brief period of recuperation in late September and early October. Shortly after, the fittest men were selected to form an independent force tasked with harassing the *Nankai Shitai*'s line of communications. The force was initially named Barforce, however this was soon changed to Chaforce when Major Hugh Challen was selected to command the force. Chaforce's three rifle companies were drawn from each the 21st Brigade's three battalions. Challen summarised the objective of Chaforce when he told its members, 'It won't be textbook soldiering ... It will be plain bastardry.'

Chaforce commenced its move from Port Moresby on 11 October. On their way across the Kokoda Trail, the men stopped at the sites of Maroubra Force's earlier battles to bury fallen comrades and to mark the locations of the graves of those who had already been buried. By 18 October, Chaforce had reached the remainder of the 7th Division at Myola. On arrival, the unit's role was modified. Instead of raiding enemy lines, the unit was tasked with general labouring duties at Myola, including the construction of a landing strip and the collection and ferrying of supplies. The change in role occurred because supply problems persisted and the rapid Japanese retreat had reduced the need for Chaforce to operate to the rear of the Japanese lines. The men disliked the menial tasking and yearned for a combat assignment.

Chaforce's namesake Challen was soon recalled to Port Moresby to take command of the 2/14th Battalion. With his departure, the newly promoted Major Frank Sublet took command of the unit. Chaforce continued its work detail in the Myola area until a movement order came through on 1 November. Chaforce was to move to Alola.

As Chaforce pushed through to the location of the earlier Battle of Isurava-Abuari, the unit again searched for the bodies of troops and provided them the dignity of proper burials. The men noted with interest that the Japanese did not appear to have searched the bodies for intelligence, as many personal effects remained.

On 6 November, Chaforce moved into Kokoda and assumed responsibility for protecting and improving the airfield and surrounding infrastructure. The men continued this work for a week before advancing once more following the Australian victory at Oivi-Gorari.

Chaforce's members now hoped at last to be employed in a combat role, but it was not to be. At Wairopi, Chaforce was broken up and its elements distributed — a rifle company each to the battalions of Brigadier Eather's 25th Brigade and the remainder to 7th Division Headquarters.

AUSTRALIAN ATTITUDES TOWARDS JAPANESE TROOPS

While there are numerous recorded examples of goodwill between Australian and enemy troops during the First World War, the Australian and Japanese troops in the Second World War shared a bitter animosity. From the Australian perspective, this existed for three reasons. First, there was a view that the Japanese were deceitful, as illustrated in the surprise attacks on Pearl Harbor, Malaya, Hong Kong and the Philippines that had initiated the Pacific War. Second, reports had filtered back of the atrocities committed by the Japanese during their conquests and of their mistreatment and execution of Allied prisoners. Third, the attitudes of some of the Australians towards the Japanese may have been based on latent racism which was not uncommon at the time.

Sergeant Joseph Dawson of the 39th Battalion expressed one commonly held opinion:

> We didn't take any prisoners ... No doubt there were some, but quite frankly, I didn't have any feeling for them [the Japanese] at all. I would say it was probably the nearest approach to hate I've ever had ... They were great, fine soldiers but they weren't honourable soldiers, put it that way. You only have to look at the way they treated POWs. But that's the way they were taught. The Samurai. Kill or be killed. There was no quarter given, and that's what they got. But I had no great feeling for them, as far as that goes.

Despite the fact that it was frowned on by their superiors, the Australians pocketed souvenirs from dead Japanese soldiers, including their hinomaru gokasei (good luck flags) and, on some occasions, even their gold teeth.

Captain Phil Rhoden, temporary CO of the 2/14th Battalion, summarised his feelings towards the Japanese: 'After the Owen Stanley campaign, bitter, absolutely bitter. We'd take every opportunity to do them damage.'

The Japanese belief in honour and duty and their resultant attitude to the value of life contrasted sharply with Australian perspectives on these issues. The achievement of a military goal was paramount, irrespective of casualties, as long as the duty was undertaken in the name of the Emperor. Capture was unthinkable and surrender was broadly condemned, which to some extent explains the Japanese practice of executing Australians captured during the campaign.

Two soldiers hold a Japanese prisoner taken by the 3rd Battalion near Menari. The Japanese rarely allowed themselves to be taken prisoner. The small number of men captured were usually sick and emaciated (AWM027085).

BOMANA CEMETRY

Nineteen kilometres from Port Moresby at the southern end of the Kokoda Trail is Bomana War Cemetery. It is one of the largest war cemeteries in the Pacific, containing 3824 graves. These are the graves of the 3125 known and 699 unknown Australian and Allied soldiers, sailors and airmen from the fighting in New Guinea. Bomana Cemetery is maintained by the Commonwealth War Graves Commission. Any new Australian or Allied remains found from the Papuan and Bougainville campaigns are also interred in Bomana.

The Australians who perished on the Kokoda Trail rest in Bomana. Cecil Driscoll, a veteran of the 39th Battalion, visited Bomana on Anzac Day in 2012, almost 70 years after fighting on the Kokoda Trail. Attending a dawn service at the cemetery he observed, 'I had thought it was going to be gruesome, but as the dawn came up and the birds started chirping, the light was on the Cenotaph and the gravestones appeared out of the gloom, it was lovely. I thought what a happy place. I didn't feel remorse, I felt pleased that the boys were in such a beautiful place and I could see them waiting for the rain to stop so they could go out and play a game of two up.'

Bomana Cemetery, one of the largest war cemeteries in the Pacific (D. Crosbie, NAA030).

Chapter 18
THE COMMAND CRISIS

The months that encompassed the Kokoda campaign saw the greatest direct threat to Australia's physical borders during the Second World War. While the Japanese defeat at the Battle of Midway delivered an enormous blow to their war effort, they remained a dangerous adversary capable of launching substantial offensive operations. As bitter fighting on Guadalcanal continued and the outcome of that campaign hung in the balance, tensions within the Allied leadership remained high.

The 'command crisis' specifically refers to the sacking of Lieutenant General Rowell. However, the phrase can also be applied to the dismissal of a series of Kokoda commanders throughout the period of the campaign. The consecutive removal of Brigadier Potts, Rowell and Major General Allen caused consternation and bitterness at the time, and remain contentious to this day. Supporters and arguments can be found both for the commanders who were removed and also for those who ultimately made the decision to replace them, primarily Generals MacArthur and Blamey.

The sacking of Potts and Allen was based on their perceived lack of aggressive intent. As historian Garth Pratten observed of the Papuan campaign, COs were expected to act 'without equivocation or mental reservation of any kind' regardless of the dubious nature of the operations they were ordered to conduct. Rowell's sacking was caused by the acrimony that arose in his relationship with Blamey after the latter was ordered to Port Moresby to take personal command of operations in New Guinea.

Regardless of the veracity of the official claims for the sackings, a climate of suspicion and animosity pervaded the ranks of the senior Australian officers. Personal rivalries created a toxic atmosphere of distrust which was detrimental to the Australian war effort. As David Horner notes, 'the arguments between generals and politicians might seem of little consequence. But the opposite is the case. It was errors by men like MacArthur and Blamey which led to the near disaster in New Guinea. As usual, it was the men in the front line who paid the heaviest price.'

ROWELL

Several factors led to the episode that resulted in the sacking of Lieutenant General Rowell. First, there was bad blood between him and General Blamey, a legacy of their earlier service together in the Greek campaign of 1941. On that occasion, an ugly disagreement had occurred during the Australian retreat when Blamey told Rowell to leave the country. Rowell had stubbornly protested that he wished to remain with his men, which prompted Blamey to remind him that this was an order and not a request. Second, General MacArthur was under enormous pressure from Washington in September and October 1942. Without the assurances of rapid military success, MacArthur was convinced that, not only was his position as Commander-in-Chief SWPA under threat, but also his burgeoning political aspirations.

MacArthur's anxiety was fuelled by Lieutenant General George Kenney (US Air Force Chief, SWPA) who returned from a visit to Port Moresby and expressed dire reservations concerning the conduct of operations. He told MacArthur that a defeatist attitude permeated NGF and he doubted Rowell's ability and determination to defeat the Japanese.

Spurred on by this assessment, MacArthur pressured Prime Minister Curtin to send Blamey to Papua to take personal command of operations. Given MacArthur's documented disdain for the abilities of the Australian soldier, it would seem safe to assume that he did not necessarily believe that Blamey's presence in Port Moresby would lead to a sudden reversal of fortunes. Rather, it would appear that he was ensuring there was someone else to take the blame if Port Moresby was conquered.

In considering whether there was a genuine need for Blamey to go to Port Moresby, the crucial factor is the timeline. Kenney conveyed his lack of faith to MacArthur in early September having visited Port Moresby for a single day and without having personally met Rowell. On 17 September, MacArthur urged Curtin by phone to post Blamey to Port Moresby. Curtin agreed and relayed the order to Blamey later that day. Blamey was reluctant to go and procrastinated. He did not leave Australia until 23 September.

Australian Prime Minister John Curtin and General MacArthur (AWM 05213).

Two weeks earlier, the Australian position on the Kokoda Trail had provided a valid cause for concern. Maroubra Force had suffered a disastrous defeat at the Battle of Brigade Hill and the Japanese were advancing. As a result, on 9 September, Army Minister Francis Forde — without MacArthur's intervention — had directed Blamey to visit Port Moresby to assuage the government's concerns. Blamey visited between 12 and 14 September and, on his return to Australia, delivered a robust public declaration of confidence in Rowell. He also briefed the Advisory War Council and assured it in the strongest possible terms that the situation in Papua was in hand.

By 23 September the situation was far more favourable for the Allies. On the Kokoda Trail, the Australians were on Imita Ridge, safe and well supplied. Maroubra Force, now strongly reinforced by two AIF brigades, was confident of future success. In opposition, the Japanese were stationary and it was evident that they did not intend to press their advance. The cause for alarm was thus clearly overstated, and there was little reason for Blamey to return to Port Moresby at the time MacArthur urged Curtin to post him there.

However, as Blamey knew all too well, an order was an order. Whatever his personal conviction, he could not defy a direction from the Prime Minister. Anticipating the problems his move would precipitate, he took the unusual step of writing a letter to Rowell and having it hand-delivered to him by a trusted aide to ensure that its sensitive contents remained undisclosed to all but its intended recipient. He wrote:

> The Powers that be have determined that I shall myself go to New Guinea for a while and operate from there ... I hope you will not be upset at this decision and will not think that it implies any lack of confidence in yourself. I think it arises out of the fact we have very inexperienced politicians who are inclined to panic on every possible occasion, and I think the relationship between us personally is such that we can make this arrangement work without any difficulty.

Blamey expressed reservations about the move to those closest to him. As a contingency, he asked Major General Samuel Burston (Director General Medical Services) to accompany him. Burston, a fair man and friend of Rowell, was regarded by Blamey as a potential mediator.

Blamey's trepidation was justified. When he and his entourage arrived in Port Moresby on 23 September, Rowell was courteous but terse. That evening the two senior officers held a heated discussion. Rowell's major objection was that Blamey's presence was an affront to the efficacy of his command. Rowell also argued that his ability to command NGF would be adversely affected because Blamey was not accompanied by headquarters staff. This meant that the headquarters staff already stationed in Port Moresby would have to serve two masters. Blamey rejected Rowell's suggestion to create a new higher headquarters on the sensible grounds that doing so was not practical at a time when projecting supplies and manpower overseas was very difficult. The two were unable to reconcile their differences.

The discussions continued the following day and into that evening. They were unable to break the impasse. As requested, Burston approached Rowell and tried to persuade him to accept the changed circumstances. He told Rowell to do his best and make the situation work to his advantage, but his entreaties were to no avail. Burston later wrote, 'Syd was bloody-minded', and lamented that he 'could not convince Rowell that Curtin really had sent Blamey to Papua, and that Blamey did not want to take over.'

On 25 September Blamey flew to Milne Bay where he inspected the Allied base and was briefed by the successful Milne Force commander, Major General Clowes. During this trip, Blamey told Clowes to move one of his battalions to Wanigela on the north coast of Papua in line with the overall Allied strategy of attacking Buna along three axes. News of this order reached Rowell before Blamey returned to Port Moresby. Rowell protested that the order should have gone through him as the NGF commander. Blamey responded that the words were a suggestion, not an order. Blamey would surely have known that this would rile Rowell as he himself was to have an identical disagreement with MacArthur in late December over unit movements at Buna. But Rowell too must have known he was treading a fine line, confiding to a friendly officer that he had bluntly told Blamey what he thought of him, and quipped 'Any real man would have sacked me on the spot.'

As a result of Blamey's exchange with Clowes, Rowell wrote a procedural letter which he delivered to Blamey on the morning of 26 September seeking clarification of their respective powers. Blamey suspected that Rowell was being intentionally obstructive, an assessment supported by Rowell's letter and the fact that situation reports Blamey had expressly requested were either delayed or failed to reach him. Later that night Blamey issued a directive in which he reiterated the circumstances of his arrival in Port Moresby and the processes he wanted followed.

The following day Blamey's ire was again raised when his receipt of an important intelligence document was delayed. Blamey's ADC, Lieutenant Colonel Norman Carlyon, having spoken with Rowell and his staff, formed the impression that there was a deliberate policy to isolate Blamey from the headquarters. Rowell later disputed this point, but stated that, had this been the case, it had not occurred at his instigation.

The next morning, 28 September, the guillotine fell. The accumulated discord finally provoked Blamey to action. At 9.00 am Rowell arrived at a pre-planned conference with Blamey and was informed that he had been relieved of command. Blamey told Rowell that he had already sent an adverse report describing the fallout to Curtin and MacArthur. Rowell demanded to see the report. Some of the report's critical assessments included:

> [Rowell has] proved most difficult and recalcitrant, considering himself very unjustly used. I permitted him to state his case with great frankness … he charged me with having failed to safeguard his interests and said he felt he was being made to eat dirt. All my persuasion could not make him see matters realistically … Instead of full information here for me I have had to search out details and feel a definite atmosphere of obstruction … Although I have exercised great patience it is quite obvious that … Rowell has taken my coming here [personally and] … he would be [a] seriously disruptive influence if retained here. Moreover [I] am not satisfied that necessary energy, foresight and drive is being put into certain activities … Rowell is competent but of a temperament that harbours imaginary grievances … In view of circumstances I have relieved him of command and directed him to return to Australia.

Rowell considered the report 'dreadful' and was confident that it would not stand careful scrutiny. He was particularly displeased that several statements he had made during the heat of an argument were quoted in the report.

Rowell was impulsive and, by his own admission, insubordinate. Despite entreaties to make the most of a difficult situation, he had reacted poorly to Blamey's arrival, displaying a combative attitude that bordered on petulance. Regardless of his personal disappointment, he should have maintained respect for the chain of command and realised that, in a conflict of personalities, Blamey's seniority was certain to prevail.

Nevertheless, Blamey went further and, in an attempt to validate his decision, he wrote a second letter to Curtin which contained detrimental inferences concerning Rowell's command performance:

> Apart from his insubordinate attitude, my principal criticism is a lack of appreciation of the need for seeking out energetically the possibilities of developing aggressive action. This, I think, is due mainly to limited experience of command.

Blamey's charge was retrospective and, despite Rowell's relative inexperience as a corps commander, is a misrepresentation of the facts. Rowell had steered NGF through a tumultuous period in which the Japanese were ascendant and the outcome of fighting in Papua remained unclear, particularly during the early stages of the Battle of Milne Bay. He was under-resourced in practically every aspect required to prosecute the war. Despite Blamey's views, Rowell retained the respect and confidence of his subordinate commanders. The Australian forces on the Kokoda Trail had already commenced their counter-attack by the time Rowell was sacked and the plans he had devised with Allen were unfolding. His successor, Lieutenant General Herring, did not substantially alter any of NGF's overall plans after replacing Rowell, suggesting that the strategy already in place was fundamentally sound.

The personality clash between Blamey and Rowell was the substantive reason for Rowell's dismissal. When Herring was appointed to command NGF, MacArthur told him, 'the first duty of a soldier is to get on with the man above him.' In the circumstances in which Rowell found himself in late September 1942, he was incapable of doing this and, as a consequence, lost his command.

POTTS

Brigadier Potts' loss of command of Maroubra Force and subsequent replacement as Commander of the 21st Brigade is undoubtedly the sacking that inspires the most residual anger. While the wisdom of removing Potts from command of Maroubra Force may be open to dispute, there appears little to justify his replacement as Commander of the 21st Brigade.

The difficulties Potts faced when he assumed command of Maroubra Force cannot be overstated. First, he was unable to take his complete brigade forward because Major General Allen wanted the 2/27th available to protect Port Moresby. Second, the supplies that had been promised and which were essential for recapturing Kokoda were non-existent. As a consequence, Potts was forced to modify his plans, initially by holding the AIF battalions in Myola until sufficient supplies had been accumulated to be carried forward. He then had to rush these two battalions to Isurava-Abuari as the Japanese offensive threatened to tear through the Australian defence. At Isurava he was only ever able to commit his troops company by company because they arrived individually as the battle was already raging. When the village could no longer be held, he directed the successful fighting withdrawal as the *Nankai Shitai* relentlessly pursued Maroubra Force to Brigade Hill.

The disastrous defeat at Brigade Hill was the catalyst for Potts' relief. This defeat was particularly troubling to Allen and Rowell as they had believed the injection of the fresh 2/27th would blunt the Japanese advance and avert the need for further withdrawal. Instead, the battle almost destroyed Maroubra Force and the 2/27th was effectively neutralised as a fighting unit only three days after its first contact.

Potts was held responsible for the defeat, and Allen signalled him: 'Porter is going forward as your personal relief. Would like you to return to me when you have handed over ...' Potts relinquished command and, in spite of his fatigue, reached Port Moresby within a day and a half. Here he briefed Allen and described the events following Isurava. He told Allen that Maroubra Force had executed an effective fighting withdrawal which, under the circumstances, was the only option available to him. Allen warned him of the prevailing attitude of higher command, telling him, 'You're going to run into a lot of criticism here, old man.' This understandably put Potts on edge, and he carried a pugnacious attitude into a conference with Rowell the following day. But, on receiving Potts' personal account of the campaign, Rowell's opinion of Potts' leadership softened. He told Potts that his obscure and uninformative situation reports had contributed to the lack of confidence at 7th Division and NGF Headquarters, particularly given the relentless pressure from GHQ for regular updates from the front. For the time being, Potts returned to Koitaki where the 21st Brigade was reassembling having been relieved on the Kokoda Trail by the 25th Brigade.

Blamey and Rowell discussed Potts' future employment during Blamey's first visit to Port Moresby in mid-September, when Blamey sought Rowell's advice. Rowell vouched for Potts, stating, 'I don't see any reason why he shouldn't go back to his brigade. This was his first command, and he was out there on his own. He's had a very trying time. I think that Potts will profit a lot by the experience he's had.' At first Blamey concurred, although a month later he changed his mind at the insistence of Rowell's successor, Lieutenant General Herring.

On 22 October, as the 21st Brigade was preparing to return to action, Potts was notified that he was no longer required in Papua. He was to fly to Darwin to swap commands with Brigadier Ivan Dougherty. Blamey allegedly told Potts that 'failures like the Kokoda Trail ... could not be tolerated — the men had shown that something was lacking ... [and he] blamed the leaders.'

Herring later wrote: '21 Brigade had failed to hold the Japanese. We knew the terrain was most difficult and the Japs very good jungle fighters, but the 21 Brigade was sent to stop them and didn't.' That was the crux of Potts' removal, despite Herring's concession that 'The task set Potts was a most difficult one and it may be that many other Brigadiers would have done no better.'

As news of the dismissal filtered through the ranks of the 21st Brigade, the collective response was shock and anger. Many of the brigade's officers threatened to resign, a gesture that Potts appreciated but disallowed. He issued a farewell message to the men thanking them for their loyalty and commending their service.

The letter that Potts wrote to the members of the 21st Brigade after Blamey removed him from command (21 Brigade War Diary, AWM52 8/2/21 August–October 1942).

The rancour of the 21st Brigade was complete when Herring addressed them on 14 November. In a verbose speech, he concluded by implying that the troops had selfishly put too high a price on their own lives and urged them to free themselves from this constraint. Blamey himself had already infuriated the brigade when he infamously lectured them at Koitaki on 9 November. First addressing the paraded soldiers, Blamey denigrated their performance and stated they were 'licked by an inferior enemy in inferior numbers'. He added that, 'it's not the man with the gun that gets shot; it's the rabbit that's running away', and, 'soldiers must not be afraid to die.' Blamey's address was followed by a private diatribe aimed at the brigade's officers. He told them that they were not worthy of their men and had not shared their hardships and dangers, and then questioned their will to fight.

Brigadier Dougherty — who witnessed the Koitaki address — did not believe that Blamey had been offensive or had meant to belittle the 21st Brigade's service. However, the testimony of Lieutenant Colonel Carlyon, Blamey's ADC, who was also present, is significant, given his loyal service and staunch defence of Blamey throughout the duration of the Pacific War. Carlyon said of the Koitaki address: 'It amazed me that Blamey should deal so insensitively with the men of such a well-proved brigade … I doubt if his words on this occasion did anything but make him more misunderstood.' The repercussions from the Herring and Blamey addresses fuelled an ongoing resentment towards these two commanders and colours their reputation to this day.

The Official Historian, Dudley McCarthy, lamented the fact that Potts had been misjudged by Blamey and Herring who, at the time, did not fully comprehend the circumstances and difficulties with which he had grappled. Potts' exile from active command lasted until the Bougainville campaign of 1945 when he was given command of the 23rd Brigade.

ALLEN

The third senior officer to be removed from command during the Kokoda campaign was Major General Allen. Allen's dismissal was the culmination of several factors, the first and foremost, questions over the quality of his command. MacArthur and Blamey believed that the Australian advance along the Kokoda Trail was too slow. This view was also shared by Herring. Second, once Allen had been sacked, his physical health was retrospectively cited as a significant reason for his removal. Finally Allen, like Rowell, had a strained relationship with Blamey but an even more fractious relationship with Herring. This was largely caused by their different backgrounds and upbringing.

Just as he had following the sackings of Rowell and Potts, Blamey made various statements after the event to strengthen his justification. Potts, for his part, had seen the writing on the wall concerning the fate of his divisional commander, writing to his wife: 'I'm scared for Tubby'. Allen himself had quipped, 'I am more afraid of a stab in the back than I am of the Jap.'

It would be unfair to criticise the trio of MacArthur, Blamey and Herring for their egotistical personalities and propensity to place self-advancement at the top of their priority list without acknowledging that Allen at times shared these traits. For example, Allen earned Blamey's displeasure when he wrote to Blamey following Rowell's relief and Herring's appointment as NGF commander. In his letter, Allen had complained that the job should have gone to him. Blamey never responded to this letter, and later commented that it should not have been written. While Allen was far from a saint — his temperament ranged from ebullient to bellicose — the primary reason for his dismissal was his performance, and so this is the issue that must be examined in depth.

One of the initial difficulties that beset Allen's command of the 7th Division was his dual responsibility for both the defence of Port Moresby and the conduct of the Kokoda campaign. Allen was insufficiently resourced for either of these responsibilities and the burden caused him great anxiety. The situation was rectified on 9 September when responsibility for protecting Port Moresby from a seaward invasion (a threat that in fairness had diminished following the Battle of Milne Bay) was reallocated to NGF. As a consequence, Allen was able to direct all his energies towards the Kokoda campaign and he moved his headquarters forward to Uberi. Nevertheless, as soon as Horii's advance stalled and the Australian counter-advance began — which roughly coincided with the appointment of Herring as GOC NGF — frustrations over Allen's performance began to simmer beneath the surface.

The first major criticism of Allen's performance concerned the Australian advance from Ioribaiwa to Myola. The chief bone of contention was Herring and Blamey's insistence that air-dropping of supplies occur only at Myola, as the Australians pushed tentatively across the Owen Stanleys.

Allen felt that dropping supplies forward of his troops was unhelpful. A military operation that relies on rapid forward movement in order to sustain itself is fraught with danger. It is inflexible and quickly breaks down when forward momentum is stopped by the enemy. This is exactly what happened during the Australian advance in October.

A C-47 conducts a low-level air drop at Myola in October during the Australian advance. The photograph's original caption reads, 'In carrying out their missions, many USAAF airmen tended to drop the supplies from too great a height, causing them to drift off into the surrounding jungle-covered hills from where they were never recovered. By contrast, RAAF airmen always carried out their drops at low level, leading to full recovery of the supplies.' As the aircraft in this photograph belongs to the USAAF, the low altitude from which some of the RAAF airmen must have dropped their supplies can only be imagined (AWMP02424.074).

Allen had criticisms of his own: that higher command did not appreciate the conditions in which the troops were fighting and the difficulties with which they had to contend. His assertion is supported by the comments that appear in dozens of interviews with Kokoda veterans. Allen himself asked that judgement be deferred until a liaison officer or senior officer had inspected the situation firsthand.

The irony is that Potts had requested the same of Allen in September. Potts had wanted Allen to move forward, but Allen — burdened with his dual responsibilities — literally could not spare the time or manpower. He eventually sent Captain Lyon forward to Potts as a liaison officer, but the pace of events overtook his original tasking.

In fairness to Allen, the strategic situation had changed since September and Port Moresby was no longer under direct threat. With Blamey based in Port Moresby, there was an opportunity for a senior officer from NGF to move forward to Allen and Lieutenant Colonel Minogue belatedly made the trek. Minogue attended a commanders' conference at Myola on 23 October in which Allen outlined his overall plan for the recapture of Kokoda. However the rationale for sending a liaison officer forward disappeared because Allen was sacked before Minogue could return to Port Moresby and report his findings to Herring and Blamey.

Allen's dilemma was that, by the time the Battle of Eora Creek commenced, there was already a strong undercurrent of dissatisfaction with his performance. With pressure on MacArthur to produce results, a chain reaction pressed down on Allen and nothing but a swift victory would pacify his critics. Regrettably, Brigadier Lloyd botched the tactical handling of the first two days of the Battle of Eora Creek which destroyed any chance of the Australians quickly overcoming their powerful Japanese opposition. Allen wore the blame for this, which he arguably deserved because he had vouched for the professionalism of his brigade commanders and this ultimately made him responsible.

Vocal and strident defences have been mounted for both sides of the 'Allen sacking' debate. Those in support of Allen posit the insoluble problem of supply. This, they assert, coupled with the fanatical Japanese defence, was the primary factor which impeded the Australian advance. Those in favour of Allen's removal argue that he lacked the aggression and fortitude required to accelerate the Australian movement. Accounts from the period appear to indicate that the conflicting and competing personalities of the Australian commanders played a major role in Allen's dismissal, all given further impetus by MacArthur's isolation and ignorance of the events on the ground. Blamey was initially defensive of Allen's performance and emphasised the challenges of his tasking. However, as the vulnerability of his own position was exposed, he allowed himself to be convinced by both MacArthur and Herring that Allen was moving slowly and required replacement.

The most damning factor in the dismissal of Allen was the misconception of the Australian advance as the pursuit of a fleeing enemy. This characterisation shaped the thinking of MacArthur, Blamey and Herring and, as a consequence, they formed the opinion that Allen was performing badly. Yet on each occasion that Allen's progress was denigrated, the question has to be posed: on which specific prior actions were the senior Allied commanders basing their opinions and comparisons? The Allied forces had not previously encountered prepared and entrenched Japanese defensive positions comparable to those on the Kokoda Trail, so there were no prior examples on which these generals could base their opinions.

If their belief was based on a comparison with the Japanese thrust across the Owen Stanleys, that too was erroneous given the significant difference between the two. The Japanese harassed the Australians every day of their march southwards and the Australians did not have time to construct significant defensive positions of their own. And, critically, no Australian defensive position — with the exception of Imita Ridge (which was never attacked) — was ever supported by artillery. Finally, even had Major General Horii not been ordered to move the majority of the *Nankai Shitai* north of the Owen Stanleys after winning the Battle of Ioribaiwa, it is unlikely that his force could have captured Port Moresby as the Japanese supply system had failed and his men were suffering the effects of starvation. This was a consequence of Horii's lightning advance and further illustrates the problem of comparing the Australian and Japanese advances.

Pressuring Allen to speed the Australian advance by comparing his rate of forward movement to Horii's is simply unfair as Horii's logistics system disintegrated. In contrast, Allen sought to maintain the strength of his force to ensure that it would be capable of pushing past Kokoda to attack the Japanese beachhead bases on the north coast of Papua. This was evident during the Battle of Eora Creek when Allen stopped Lloyd from committing units of the 25th Brigade because he wanted them kept fresh for the battles he assumed he would still have to fight once Eora Creek was captured. Horii's advance was all or nothing, while Allen, if anything, is guilty of forward thinking.

It appears that the senior Allied commanders underestimated both the offensive and defensive capabilities of the Japanese soldier. Because Blamey and Herring believed that the enemy should have been easily overcome, they installed a commander they thought would be more aggressive and could accomplish the task with greater speed. Allen was somewhat vindicated when his successor quickly learnt that Allen's observations on the fighting abilities of the Japanese soldier were not mere excuses. Having replaced Allen, Major General Vasey remarked to Herring, 'The Jap is being more stubborn and tiresome than I thought and I fear a war of attrition is taking place on this front.' Vasey's experience goes some way to restoring Allen's reputation as the commander of the 7th Division during the Kokoda campaign.

Chapter 19
CONCLUSION

The Kokoda campaign has passed into Australian folklore for the savagery of its fighting, the desperate battle to keep the Japanese from Port Moresby, and for the rugged terrain that provided a breathtaking backdrop to the war that raged in 1942. The Trail, too, has consequently become a mythical element of the campaign, now attracting thousands of trekkers each year, eager to walk the ground over which so many bitter battles were fought.

However the fighting was not about the Trail itself, but about what lay at either end. While there are numerous tracks that weave through the Owen Stanley Ranges, the Kokoda Trail's name lives in history because it was the easiest route linking Port Moresby to Buna, one of the rare locations on the northern cost of Papua suitable for the construction of an airfield. And, like the majority of the campaigns of the Pacific War, securing and sustaining airfields was paramount.

The Kokoda campaign was an infantryman's war. The task of stopping the Japanese advance on Port Moresby fell squarely on the shoulders of the infantry. The nature of the terrain and the weather restricted the combat support the Army could receive from the Air Force. It also inhibited the ability of the Army to bolster its infantry with supporting arms and artillery.

The early edicts that prevented the Australians from carrying forward mortars and medium machine-guns to meet the Japanese were rued by the infantrymen on the ground who always felt outgunned by their Japanese counterparts who used their support weapons to great effect throughout the campaign. Later, at the Battle of Eora Creek, when the Australians attempted to use medium machine-guns, the potency of the Japanese mountain guns denied their effective employment.

The Japanese proved the utility of larger calibre armaments in the jungle, their artillery dominating throughout the campaign. The determination of the Japanese to lug their artillery pieces and ammunition over the Owen Stanleys was remarkable, and these weapons certainly proved worth the effort. The use of these heavier guns was instrumental in the series of Japanese victories from July to mid-September. By comparison, the Australians used their artillery only briefly during their occupation of Imita Ridge where it made no discernible difference in the fight to turn the Japanese at their furthest reach.

Only in the weaponry carried by individual soldiers could the Australians claim the advantage. The standard issue Lee Enfield service rifle was superior to the Japanese-issued Arisaka Type 38. The Australian 36M hand grenades were also better than the unreliable and underwhelming Japanese Type 97 equivalent, but the most significant difference lay in the fact that the Japanese did not have sub machine-guns. The American-made Tommy gun provided mobile firepower that the Japanese could not match and proved a superb addition to the close-quarters style of combat endemic to jungle fighting. By the end of the campaign the Australians were also trialling Owen guns which showed early promise.

The most critical factor throughout the campaign was logistics. A simple summation drawn from the experience of both Maroubra Force and the *Nankai Shitai* is that adequately supplying a large army in a hostile environment such as the Kokoda Trail with the technology that was available in 1942 was almost impossible. As General Rowell observed, the catch phrase common in the Second World War, 'too little, too late', was often unfair, because 'all too often the "too little" was all the Allies had available.' There was never a period during the campaign when the Australian officers and soldiers felt that the supplies they were provided were sufficient to meet their needs. Air-dropping operations in the SWPA were in their infancy and the Allied Air Force lacked the confidence to land supplies on sub-standard airstrips. Thus supply was generally provided by manual labour, and the manpower requirements of sustaining an army under these circumstances were immense.

Private Richard Shimmin of the 2/33rd Battalion starts on his daily ration of bully beef straight out of the distinctive gold tin. Bully beef, biscuits and water were the three staples of soldiers during the Kokoda campaign (AWM027062).

The Japanese plans to take Port Moresby relied on speed. Once their tight deadline was compromised, they suddenly found that their supply arrangements were inadequate to continue their advance, even if Horii had not been ordered to postpone the capture of Port Moresby because of the setbacks suffered at Guadalcanal. Any appreciation of the Japanese logistical difficulties in the Kokoda campaign must be viewed within the context of events elsewhere in the region. The *Nankai Shitai*'s advance was given lower priority than the conflict on Guadalcanal and, as the fighting there intensified, it affected the quantity of supplies available to the troops in Papua. Because the Japanese generally eschewed air-drop operations, almost all their supplies were landed at their beachhead bases and carried over the Owen Stanleys to the front line. It was a mammoth enterprise, taking considerable time and heavy in manpower.

A fundamental point in evaluating the Australian advance is that comparisons with the Japanese advance should be made with caution. The Japanese were engaged in close pursuit of an enemy, harassing the retreating force with constant attacks and denying them the opportunity to build defensive positions. By contrast, the Australian advance was opposed by a determined enemy who had time to withdraw to and construct an intricate and formidable series of layered defences. It was the failure of MacArthur, Blamey and Herring to recognise this distinction that led to their critical opinion of Major General Allen and, ultimately, his sacking.

There is no question that, during the first half of the Kokoda campaign, the morale of the Japanese soldiers was far higher than that of the Australians. The individual Japanese soldier was exceptionally disciplined and skilful. A decade-long occupation of large parts of China and a run of swift victories through South-East Asia had bred confidence. The Japanese soldiers were warriors of the Emperor and the divine mandate of their task infused them with purpose and a strong sense of duty. One can only marvel at the durability of the two Japanese regiments that carried the burden of the *Nankai Shitai*'s fighting with practically no replacement nor reinforcement throughout the duration of the campaign.

In comparison, individual Kokoda researchers have analysed and rated the performance of the Australians differently. Osmar White considered the campaign a 'debacle' and refuted the world press' view of Kokoda as a great tactical victory of strategic importance. White commented that 'The Japanese did get within 30 miles [48 kilometres] of Moresby — but in such numbers, with such equipment and with such forlorn hope of support and supply that they might as well have been 300 miles [483 kilometres] of it.' Peter Williams reached a similar conclusion, observing that 'the Australians in the Kokoda campaign did not do as well as has been portrayed. Their retreat was a series of defeats without any counter-balancing advantages, and their subsequent advance was slow.'

On the other side of the ledger, media personalities such as Peter FitzSimons have elevated the Australian performance during the Kokoda campaign to the realms of fantasy fiction. Exaggeration, jingoism and outright concoction render this contribution to the study and understanding of the Kokoda campaign negligible.

A fair assessment of the Australian performance throughout the campaign recognises both the good and the bad. The Australian units initially tasked with confronting the Japanese were militia units. The 39th Battalion performed magnificently and beyond expectation. The 53rd Battalion performed poorly and its adverse reputation from this particular campaign is deserved. However, it was underequipped, inadequately trained and poorly commanded. The death of the 53rd's CO early in its first battle compounded the battalion's problems, and many of the men in its ranks later served with distinction at Sanananda and Bougainville.

The 21st Brigade also performed extremely well. The 2/14th and 2/16th battalions were committed to the Battle of Isurava-Abuari piecemeal. They fought desperately to withstand the relentless Japanese attacks and, when the onslaught could no longer be contained, they fought a delaying battle across the mountains buying time for reinforcements to arrive. Their performance as a whole serves as a brilliant example of a successful fighting withdrawal.

The 25th Brigade was committed to the campaign for longer than any other Australian brigade. Special mention must be made of the 3rd Battalion, another militia unit, that endured the Owen Stanleys for a far more protracted period than any other Australian battalion. After the initial mishap at Ioribaiwa that enabled the Japanese to gain a toehold on the ridgeline, the battalion's performance at Templeton's Crossing was commendable and allowed the 2/2nd to finish the job on 20 October.

The 16th Brigade arrived full of confidence and with the benefit of jungle warfare training in Ceylon. The men performed well during their two Kokoda battles as would be expected of the most experienced AIF brigade.

In terms of significance within the larger narrative of the Pacific War, the Kokoda campaign was less important than Guadalcanal to Australia's sovereignty because Japan deemed it so, and consequently sunk the majority of its resources into that campaign. The Allies' triumph on Guadalcanal drained the Japanese militarily and ensured that the lines of communication between Australia and the United States remained open. This was more important to the joint Australian-US war effort in the long term.

Nevertheless, the Kokoda campaign was significant for Australia for three major reasons. First, it ensured that a physical buffer remained between the Japanese and the Australian mainland. Depriving the Japanese of Port Moresby ensured that the Allies had a substantial forward operating base. It also provided a degree of security to the airfields in northern Australia, as Japanese aircraft would have been able to attack them with impunity had they captured Port Moresby.

Second, it allowed the Army to hone its jungle-fighting skills. Prior to the campaign — with the exception of the ill-fated 8th Division in Malaya and Singapore — the AIF had fought in North Africa, Greece, Crete and Syria, in physical environments vastly different to Papua. The Army was unprepared for, unaccustomed to and inexperienced in jungle warfare. Fighting in the jungle was an intimidating experience. Some troops felt they were combating both the enemy and the environment although, as the Kokoda campaign progressed, the Australians adapted well. Their methods and techniques improved, as did their performance. Tellingly, the lessons learned from the Kokoda campaign were invaluable and were incorporated into the training syllabus at the Land Headquarters Training Centre (Jungle Warfare) established at Canungra at the end of 1942. This was a critical move since Australian Army operations for the remainder of the Second World War, and for the better part of the next half-century, were all based in the jungle.

Finally, the Kokoda campaign helped foster a professional respect between the AIF and militia. Prior to the campaign, there was disharmony and enmity between the two organisations. The AIF derided the militia and openly questioned its worth. The militia's performance during the campaign, namely that of the 39th and 3rd battalions, convinced the regular soldiers of their bravery and value in combat. They learned that the militia was a capable asset that could be relied on and trusted in combat. This shared experienced endured, and the AIF and militia were able to work cooperatively throughout the remainder of the Pacific War.

The Kokoda campaign left an indelible impression on Australia. The spectre of a Japanese invasion may not have been real, but the troops fighting on the ground believed it was. The Australian government did not disabuse them of this belief in the interests of promoting the direct invasion threat to motivate an apathetic country towards total war. The graphic content of filmmaker Damien Parer's documentary *Kokoda Front Line!* certainly helped this cause, as it showed the public the deplorable conditions endured by the troops as the campaign was still in progress. Images of Australian soldiers gritting their teeth and digging in on the front line inflamed the patriotic tenets of the young nation and brought home the proximity of the war.

Thus it is the experience of the soldiers who fought along the Kokoda Trail rather than its overall strategic importance that defines the Kokoda campaign and entrenches it in Australian military history. The limitations and adversity faced by the men of Maroubra Force were severe, and yet they rarely allowed this to affect their morale. They pursued their unenviable task with humour and determination. Their efforts, in the face of tremendous hardship, have inspired countless generations of Australian soldiers ever since.

Australian soldiers rarely lost their sense of humour in spite of the adversity they faced on the Kokoda Trail (AWM013254).

COMMON WEAPONS OF THE KOKODA CAMPAIGN: AUSTRALIAN AND JAPANESE

AUSTRALIAN

25-pounder

Gun, 25-pounder (87.6mm) Q. F. Mk. I
Calibre: 87mm
Weight: approx 1800kg
Projectile: 25 pounds (11.34kg)
Ammunition: high explosive, smoke, armour piercing, and illumination
Max Range: 12,252m
Crew: 6
Muzzle Velocity: 518m/sec

The 25-pounder gun/howitzer replaced two obsolete First World War pieces by combining the best characteristics of each. It came into service with the Australian Army just in time for the Western Desert campaign in 1940. The 25-pounder became the mainstay of the Australian and other British Commonwealth artillery. It was highly effective, had a high rate of fire and was equipped with a useful firing platform that allowed 360° shooting. Over 2000 were produced in Australia by Ruwolt and Holden.

Bren gun

Machine-gun, Bren, Mk. 1

Calibre: 0.303 inches (7.7mm)

Length: 115cm

Weight: 10.12kg

Barrel: 63.5cm long, 6 grooves, right-hand twist

Rate of fire: 500 rpm (cyclic) selective fire (semi or full automatic)

Feed system: 30-round, detachable box magazine

System of operation: gas

Manufacturer: Royal Small Arms Factory, UK, and Australian Government Small Arms Factory, Lithgow, NSW.

Originally a Czech design (ZB vz 27), the Bren gun was adopted by the British Army as the standard infantry section light machine-gun in 1938. Other Commonwealth armies, including the Australian Army, followed suit. Accurate, reliable and robust, the Bren gained the reputation of being among the best light machine-guns ever produced.

Rifle, SMLE 0.303 in, No.1, Mk. 3*

Calibre: 0.303in (7.7mm)

Length: 1.13m

Weight: 4.11kg

Barrel: 64cm long, six grooves, right-hand twist

Feed system: 10-round detachable box magazine

System of operation: bolt action

Manufacturer: various, including the Australian Government Small Arms Factory.

One of the most widely produced weapons of its day, manufactured in some 27 models, the Short Magazine Lee Enfield (SMLE) No. 1, Mk. 3* was particularly significant to the Australian Army, remaining largely unchanged as its main infantry weapon throughout the First and Second World Wars and the Korean conflict. Affectionately known as the 'Smelly' by the troops (after its abbreviation SMLE), it had a smooth and fast bolt action compared to the Arisaka (the standard Japanese Army rifle), and was the only bolt action rifle of the Second World War with a 10-round capacity. Ruggedly constructed and very reliable (even in extreme conditions), it was trusted by the troops. Accurate over extreme small arms distances, selected rifles were fitted with a telescopic sight by Australian forces for use as an effective sniper rifle. The EY version with a discharger cup was used to fire grenades.

Sub machine-gun, Thompson M1928A1

Calibre: 0.45 inches (11.43mm)

Length: 84.45cm

Weight: 4.6kg

Barrel: 26.67cm long, 6 grooves, right-hand twist

Rate of fire: 800 rpm (cyclic)

Feed system: 20-round detachable box magazine or 50-round detachable drum

System of operation: delayed blow back, selective fire

Manufacturer: Colts Patent Firearms Co., Auto-Ordnance Corporation, and Savage Arms Co., USA.

First issued to the US Marines in 1928, the Thompson was the only sub machine-gun in production outside Europe in 1939, and consequently many nations (including Britain and France) placed orders when war was declared. Heavy, complicated and costly to produce, the weapon was modified early in the war, ultimately accepted as the standard sub machine-gun for the US Army as the M1 (and later M1A1). The Thomson was introduced as an Australian section weapon during 1941 and found favour due to its high rate of fire and hitting power. It remained the standard section sub machine-gun until the introduction of the Owen gun in late 1942 (which was trialled in the later stages of the Kokoda campaign).

Vickers

Machine-gun, Vickers, Mk. 1

Calibre: 0.303in (7.7mm)

Length: 1.156m

Weight: 18.14kg

Barrel: 72.4cm long, four-grooves, right-hand twist

Rate of fire: 450 rpm (cyclic)

Feed system: 250-round, cloth belt

System of operation: recoil

Manufacturer: Vickers, Son and Maxim; Royal Ordnance Factories; and Australian Small Arms Factory, Lithgow, from 1929.

The water-cooled Vickers was an evolution of the earlier Maxim machine-gun, and entered service with the British Army in 1912. The Vickers Mk. 1 was the standard British and Australian medium machine-gun throughout the First and Second World Wars, the Korean War and into the 1960s. It was an extremely reliable weapon. Heavy and cumbersome to transport, the Vickers was better suited to static warfare. For this reason, NGF directed the early Australian units that embarked on the Kokoda Trail to leave their Vickers behind. This decision proved costly and was rued by the diggers on the ground who felt there were numerous occasions when the guns would have been useful.

Mortar, 2-inch

Calibre: 2in (51mm)

Weight: 4.8kg (10.7kg with base plate and bipod)

Barrel: 63cm long

Rate of fire: 8 rpm

Feed system: muzzle load – trip (small trigger)

Projectile: HE, smoke and illumination

Range: 500 yards (457m)

The 2-inch mortar was introduced to the British Army in 1938 to provide platoon commanders with their own means to generate a smokescreen. The standard first line allocation of ammunition was nine HE and 27 smoke bombs. When British organisations were adopted by the AIF in 1940, so was the 2-inch mortar. It was fired by a detachment of two men that was part of the headquarters of each infantry platoon. The weapon's effectiveness was much debated, but in several instances in New Guinea the extra weight of fire it provided allowed Australian platoons to dominate the firefight. The Japanese hatred of mortars is mentioned in numerous interviews with Australian Kokoda veterans. They commonly refer to the Japanese 'squealing' when the weapon was used against them.

Mortar, ML, Mk. 1, 3-inch

Calibre: 3in (76.2mm)

Weight: 50.8kg (total with base plate and bipod)

Barrel: 1.3m long

Rate of fire: 10 rpm

Feed system: muzzle load – drop striker

Projectile: HE, smoke and illumination

Range: 250m to 1500m (Mk. 1); 2500m (Mk. 2)

The mortar is generally considered to be the infantry's own artillery. The 3-inch mortar was an evolution of the Stokes mortar used by the British during the First World War, and was a smooth bore weapon that fired a fin-stabilised bomb. Initially limited to a range of around 1500m, improvements in propellants, bomb design and the introduction of a heavier barrel and base plate, increased this to about 2500m. It was cheap to make and reliable, although the mortal danger to the crews caused by damaged ammunition air-dropped at Myola, reduced the Australians' ability to use the weapon in the later stages of the campaign.

JAPANESE

Gun, Type 41, 75 mm Mountain Gun (1908)

Calibre: 75mm

Weight: 544kg

Projectile: HE (5.8kg)

Ammunition: HE and AP

Max Range: 7000m

Muzzle Velocity: 400 m/sec

Rate of fire: 10-12 rpm

A copy of the *Krupp* M.08 mountain gun, the 75mm Type 41 was originally used as a field artillery pack gun. From the late 1930s it was superseded by the Model 94 (1934) 75mm mountain (pack) gun, although large numbers of the Type 41 remained in service as an infantry gun or *Rentai Ho* (regimental artillery). The Type 41 was ideal for the mountainous terrain encountered in Papua. It broke down into 11 units, the heaviest of which weighed 95kg. It was normally transported by six pack horses but, as the *Nankai Shitai* advanced south along the Kokoda Trail, the troops themselves had to manhandle the gun.

Machine-gun, Type 92 Juki

Calibre: 7.7mm (0.303in)

Length: 115.6cm

Weight: 26kg (53.34kg with tripod)

Barrel: 72.1cm

Rate of fire: 450 rpm (max) 200 rpm (planning)

Effective range: 800m

Feed system: Feed tray of 30-rounds

System of operation: Gas operated, fully automatic only

The Type 92 was the standard medium machine-gun for the *IJA* throughout the Second World War. It was a modified Hotchkiss-type weapon with a slow cyclic rate of fire which earned it the nickname 'the Woodpecker'. It seldom overheated, and the life of its barrel was unusually long. It was usually fitted to a heavy tripod, which provided stability for use against ground targets, but could also be quickly converted for anti-aircraft use. It was loaded with 30-round strips. Japanese infantry usually employed their medium machine-guns as far forward as possible during their advance. When they encountered opposition, both light mortars and medium machine-guns were used to 'fix' the enemy, while the infantry moved to quickly outflank the enemy position.

Rifle, Arisaka Type 38 (1905)

Calibre: 6.5mm

Length: 1275mm

Weight: 4.12kg

Barrel: 800mm

Feed system: five-round fixed box magazine

System of operation: bolt action

The Arisaka Type 38 was a medium velocity, small bore rifle inspired by the German Mauser, but of a rather clumsy design. Comparatively light for its length and of sturdy construction, it had only a slight recoil and muzzle flash due to its small calibre and bullet. Produced in several variants, including a long rifle and a shorter cavalry carbine, it was the most common rifle in service with the *IJA* during the Kokoda campaign. The Type 38 was eventually replaced by the Model 99 (1939) 7.7mm rifle, which was basically the same rifle, but slightly shorter and of larger calibre.

BIBLIOGRAPHY

ARCHIVAL SOURCES

AWM 52 Australian Military Forces Formation and Unit Diaries, 1939–1945

(war diaries of 8th Military District/New Guinea Force; Aust 7 Div HQ; 16 Brigade, 21 Brigade, 25 Brigade, 30 Brigade; 3rd Battalion, 39th Battalion, 53rd Battalion, 2/1st Bn, 2/2nd Bn, 2/3rd Bn, 2/14th Bn, 2/16th Bn, 2/25th Bn, 2/27th Bn, 2/31st Bn, 2/33rd Bn)

AWM 67 Official History, 1939–1945 War: Records of Gavin Long, General Editor.

AWM 54, 923/1/6, 'Notes on Recently expressed concepts of tactics' HQ 30 Aust Inf Bde, 11 October 1942.

OFFICIAL HISTORIES

McCarthy, Dudley, *Official History of Australia in the War of 1939–1945*, Vol. V, *South-West Pacific area - First Year: Kokoda to Wau*, Australian War Memorial, Canberra, 1959.

Milner, Samuel, *Victory in Papua*, *United States Army in World War II*, Center of Military History, US Army, Washington DC, 1957.

Walker, Allan S., *Official History of Australia in the War of 1939–1945*, Series 5 (Medical), Vol. I, *Clinical Problems of War*, Australian War Memorial, Canberra, 1952.

——, *Official History of Australia in the War of 1939–1945*, Series 5 (Medical), Vol. III, *The Island Campaigns*, Australian War Memorial, Canberra, 1957.

BOOKS

Austin, Victor, *To Kokoda and Beyond: the story of the 39th Battalion 1941-1943*, Melbourne University Press, 1988.

Baker, Clive, *Walking the Kokoda Trail*, Australian Military History Publications, Sydney, 1994.

Barter, M.A., *Far Above Battle: The experience and Memory of Australian Soldiers in War 1939-1945*, Allen & Unwin, Sydney, 1994.

Braga, Stuart, *Kokoda Commander*, Oxford University Press, Melbourne, 2004.

Brune, Peter, *Those Ragged Bloody Heroes: from the Kokoda Trail to Gona Beach 1942*, Allen & Unwin, Sydney, 1992.

Budden, Frank M., *That Mob: The Story of the 55/53rd Australian Infantry Battalion, A.I.F.*, self-published, Sydney, 1973.

——, *The Chocos: the Story of the Militia Infantry Battalions in the South West Pacific Area 1941-1945*, self-published, Sydney, 1987.

Burns, J., The Brown and Blue Diamond at War: the Story of the 2/27th Battalion A.I.F., 2/27th Battalion Ex-servicemen's Association, Adelaide, 1960.

Carlyon, Norman, *I Remember Blamey*, Sun Books, Melbourne, 1981.

Clift, Ken, *War Dance: the Story of the 2/3 Aust Inf. Bn 16 Brigade 6 Division*, P.M. Fowler and 2/3rd Battalion Association, Sydney, 1980.

Collie, Craig, *The Path of Infinite Sorrow: the Japanese on the Kokoda Track*, Allen & Unwin, Sydney, 2009.

Crooks, William, *The Footsoldiers: The Story of the 2/33rd Battalion, A.I.F in the War of 1939-1945*, Printcraft Press, Sydney, 1971.

Dornan, Peter, *The Silent Men: Syria to Kokoda and on to Gona*, Allen & Unwin, Sydney, 1999.

Draydon, Allan W., *Men of courage: A history of 2/25 Australian Infantry Battalion 1940-1945*, 2/25 Australian Infantry Battalion Association, Brisbane, 2000.

Eather, Steve, *Desert Sands, Jungle Lands: a Biography of Major General Ken Eather*, Allen & Unwin, Sydney, 2003.

Edgar, Bill, *Warrior of Kokoda: a Biography of Brigadier Arnold Potts*, Allen & Unwin, Sydney, 2006.

Freeman, Brian, *The Lost Battlefield of Kokoda*, Macmillan, Sydney, 2012.

Givney, E.C. (ed.), *The First at War: The Story of the 2/1st Australian Infantry Battalion, 1939-1945, The City of Sydney Regiment*, The Association of the First Infantry Battalions, Sydney, 1987.

Grey, Jeffrey, *A Military History of Australia*, Cambridge University Press, Melbourne, 1990.

Ham, Paul, *Kokoda*, HarperCollins, Sydney, 2004.

Happell, Charles, *The Bone Man of Kokoda: The extraordinary story of Kokichi Nishimura and the Kokoda Track*, Pan Macmillan, Sydney, 2008.

Hetherington, John, *Blamey: The Biography of Field-Marshal Sir Thomas Blamey*, F.W. Cheshire, Melbourne, 1954.

Horner, D.M., *Blamey: the Commander-in-Chief*, Allen & Unwin, Sydney, 1998.

——, *Crisis of Command*, Australian National University Press, Canberra, 1978.

——, *The Battles that shaped Australia: The Australian's anniversary essays*, Allen & Unwin, Sydney, 1994.

——, *Blamey: the Commander-in-Chief*, Allen & Unwin, Sydney, 1998.

Howie-Willis, Ian, *A Medical Emergency: Major-General 'Ginger' Burston and the Army Medical Service in World War II*, Big Sky Publishing, Newport, 2012.

James, Bill, *Field Guide to the Kokoda Track: an Historical Guide to the Lost Battlefields*, Kokoda Press, Sydney, 2008.

Japanese Army Operations in the South Pacific Area: New Britain and Papua Campaigns 1942-1943, Steve Bullard (trans), Australian War Memorial, Canberra, 2007.

Johnson, Carl, *Mud over Blood: Stories from the 39th Infantry Battalion 1941-43, Kokoda to Gona*, History House, Melbourne, 2006.

Kenzie, Robyn, *The Architect of Kokoda*, Hachette Australia, Sydney, 2011.

Kennedy, Colin (compiler), *Port Moresby to Gona Beach, 3rd Australian Infantry Battalion 1942*, self-published, Canberra, 1992.

Keogh, E. G., *South West Pacific 1941-45*, Grayflower Productions, Melbourne, 1965.

Kuring, Ian, *Redcoats to Cams: A History of Australian Infantry, 1788-2001*, Australian Military History Publications, Sydney, 2004.

Laffin, John, *Forever forward: The History of the 2/31st Australian Infantry Battalion, 2nd AIF 1940-45*, 2/31st Australian Infantry Battalion Association (New South Wales Branch), 1994.

McAulay, Lex, *Blood and Iron: The Battle for Kokoda 1942*, Arrow, Sydney, 1992.

Paull, Raymond, *Retreat from Kokoda*, Heinemann, Melbourne, 1958.

Pratten, Garth, *Australian Battalion Commanders in the Second World War*, Cambridge University Press, Melbourne, 2009.

Rowell, Sydney, *Full Circle*, Melbourne University Press, 1974.

Sayers, Stuart, *Ned Herring: A Life of Sir Edmund Herring*, Hyland House Publishing, Melbourne, 1980.

Stone, Andrew J., *A Walk in their Footsteps: a Kokoda Trail Experience: A Modern Soldier's Personal Story*, Australian Military History Publications, Sydney, 1997.

Sublet, Frank, *Kokoda to the sea: a history of the 1942 campaign in Papua*, Slouch Hat Publications, McCrae, Victoria, 2000.

Tyquin, Michael, *Little By Little: a Centenary History of the Royal Australian Army Medical Corps*, Australian Military History Publications, Loftus, 2003.

Uren, Malcolm, *A Thousand Men at War: A History of the 2/16th Australian Infantry Battalion, AIF*, Australian Military History Publications, Sydney, 2009.

White, Osmar, *Green Armour*, Penguin Australia, Sydney (1945), 1992.

Wick, Stan, *Purple over green: The History of the 2/2nd Australian Infantry Battalion, 1939-1945*, Printcraft Press, Sydney, 1978.

Williams, Peter, *The Kokoda Campaign: Myth and Reality*, Cambridge University Press, Melbourne, 2012.

THESES

Fraser, Bryce Michael, The combat effectiveness of Australian and American infantry battalions in Papua in 1942-193, PhD thesis, University of Wollongong, 2013.

Sholl, John, Points Noted and Lessons Learnt: The Nature and Determinants of Australian Army Tactical Changes, 1941-1943, BA (Hons), ADFA, 1991.

Threlfall, Adrian, The Development of Australian Army Jungle Warfare Doctrine and Training, 1941-1945, PhD thesis, Victoria University, 2008.

JOURNAL ARTICLES

Bradley, Philip, 'The Kokoda Trail', *After the Battle,* No. 137, 2007.

Buckley, John P., 'Kokoda and Guadalcanal', *Australian Defence Force Journal: Journal of the Australian Profession of Arms*, September/October 1988.

——, 'Early land battles in New Guinea', *Australian Defence Force Journal,* September/October 1988.

Bullard, Steve, 'Kokoda: A Japanese tragedy', *Wartime*, No. 20, 2002.

——, 'The Kokoda myth', *Wartime*, No. 29, January 2005.

Horner, David, 'Kokoda Commanders', *Wartime*, No. 18, 2002.

——, 'Kokoda heroes', *Wartime*, No. 20, 2002.

James, Karl, 'The greyhounds of Kokoda', *Wartime*, No. 48, 2009.

——, 'Kokoda "Track" or "Trail"?', *Wartime*, No. 48, 2009.

Lane, Daniel and David McNicoll, 'A century of war [and] Back to Kokoda', *The Bulletin with Newsweek*, Vol. 114, No. 5817, 28 April 1992.

Macdermott, J.H., 'Damien Parer 1 August 1912 - 17 September 1944, a biography', *Sabretache: journal and proceedings of the Military Historical Society of Australia*, Vol. XXXV, No. 3, July/September 1994.

McDonald, Neil, 'Telling the Kokoda story', *Quadrant*, Vol. XLIX, No. 10, October 2005.

Murray, Brian, 'A footnote to history', *Sabretache,* Vol. 37, No. 2, April/June 1996.

Nelson, Hank, 'Kokoda, then and now', *Wartime*, No. 48, 2009.

——, 'Kokoda: pushing the popular image', *The Journal of Pacific History*, Vol. 45, No. 1, June 2010.

O'Connor, Michael, 'Kokoda - the lessons remain valid', *Australian Defence Force Journal,* January/February 1993.

Pilger, Alison, 'Courage, endurance and initiative: medical evacuation from the Kokoda track, August-October 1942', *War & Society*, Vol. 11, No. 1, May 1993.

Tracey, Rowan, 'Conflict in command during the Kokoda campaign of 1942: did General Blamey deserve the blame?', *Journal of the Royal United Services Institute of New South Wales*, Issue 61, No. 2, June 2010.

Vulum, Sam, 'Kokoda Trail: PNG's biggest attraction', *Pacific Islands Monthly*, August 1999.

FILMS

Australian Commonwealth Film Unit for the Australian War Memorial, *War in Pacific*, Canberra, 1968.

Army Doctrine Centre, Headquarters Training Command, *Kokoda: the bloody track*, Georges Heights, Sydney, 1992.

Featherstone, Don, *Kokoda*, Palace Films, Madman Entertainment [distributor], *Australia*, 2007.

Masters, Chris, *The Men who Saved Australia*, ABC, Sydney, 1995.

Parer, Damien, the World War II films, Silver Trak Audio & Video, Australia, 2000.

Phillips, John, *Kokoda: the Stairway to Hell*, Payless Entertainment, Australia, 2006.

WEBSITES

http://www.awm.gov.au

http://www.naa.gov.au

http://www.aaac.100megsfree5.com/ww2kokodaremembered.htm

http://www.australiansatwarfilmarchive.gov.au/aawfa/

http://www./kokoda.commemoration.gov.au/

http://www.environment.gov.au/resource/track-historical-desktop-study-kokoda-track

http://www.cwgc.org

INDEX